D0088462

Girl A

Girl A

MY STORY

EBURY
PRESS

1 3 5 7 9 10 8 6 4 2

First published in 2013 by Ebury Press, an imprint of Ebury Publishing
A Random House Group company

Copyright © Girl A and Nigel Bunyan 2013

Girl A and Nigel Bunyan have asserted their rights to be identified
as the author of this Work in accordance with the Copyright,
Designs and Patents Act 1988

All rights reserved. No part of this publication may be reproduced,
stored in a retrieval system, or transmitted in any form or by any means,
electronic, mechanical, photocopying, recording or otherwise,
without the prior permission of the copyright owner

The Random House Group Limited Reg. No. 954009

Addresses for companies within the Random House Group can be found at
www.randomhouse.co.uk

A CIP catalogue record for this book is available from the British Library

The Random House Group Limited supports the Forest Stewardship
Council® (FSC®), the leading international forest-certification organisation.
Our books carrying the FSC label are printed on FSC®-certified paper.
FSC is the only forest-certification scheme supported by the leading
environmental organisations, including Greenpeace. Our paper procurement
policy can be found at www.randomhouse.co.uk/environment

Typeset by seagulls.net

Printed and bound by CPI Group (UK) Ltd, Croydon, CR0 4YY

ISBN 9780091951344

To buy books by your favourite authors and register for offers visit
www.randomhouse.co.uk

I dedicate this book to any other survivors of abuse.
Together we can make a difference.

This book is a work of non-fiction based on the life, experiences and recollections of the author. The names of people, places, dates, sequences or the details of events may have been changed to try to protect the privacy of others.

Contents

Prologue

It was the image of the clock on the wall that I tried to hold on to that day and, after all this time, it's a memory I still cling to.

It was a child's clock, the sort that a thousand girls might find as they unwrap presents on their birthday or on Christmas Day. The face itself was pink, but it had white letters, and in the middle was an angel with beautiful, outstretched wings and a smile so radiant you could imagine it healing even the most broken of hearts. The second hand was white, too: I could hear every tick, every imagined heartbeat as it arced its way around the angel.

In this room, of all rooms, it seemed out of place. Set high on the wall, it looked down on a single mattress which that day, and probably for many days before, was covered with a grubby blue sheet. The mattress, edged with dust, rested on bare floorboards littered with bubble wrap and a scattering of empty, abandoned cardboard boxes.

There was a central light flex and an over-bright, old-style bulb. But no one had bothered to cover it with a shade. The single windowpane bore a jagged diagonal crack, with no curtains to cover it. Instead, the afternoon light streamed in.

I'd seen the clock briefly as I came in, a blur on the wall, but now I kept trying to focus on it. My head tilted in desperation towards the wall, trying with all my might to take in the sight of the beautiful angel, hoping she might reach down and somehow carry me away to safety.

But there would be no rescue that summer's day, nor for many, many more. Instead, tears streaked my face and my lungs were filled involuntarily by the smell of cheap soap as the unbearable weight of him bore down on me. I tried to scream, but his hand was pressed over my mouth, stifling the sound.

All I could do was turn towards the angel and watch the second hand, barely distinguishable, making its way, *tick*, *tick*, *tick*, past her fading smile.

* * *

My own smile was torn from me that day, discarded along with my innocence on that grubby mattress. I was only a child and had just been raped by the leader of a paedophile gang who preyed on vulnerable, fragile girls like me. Uniquely in Britain, they were all Asian, and almost to a man Pakistani, and their victims were found to be exclusively white girls.

The race of their victims would become a national debate but to me it was irrelevant. These men were nothing more than paedophiles and what they did, whether it was to a white girl, an Asian girl, or to a girl of any other race, was at heart just *wrong*, whatever the circumstances around it.

For seven months these men 'trafficked' me – moved me around from place to place, from sick pervert to sick pervert – across the north of England, not caring about the pain and the suffering I felt, intent on selling me to other men who found a sick pleasure in defiling children in seedy flats and houses.

By the time it was all over, I felt dead inside. But for some it was only the beginning of the story, and it was all anybody wanted to talk about. My parents, Social Services, the newspapers, the courts, *Newsnight* ...

All I wanted to do was hide away from the world, but I still had a role to play. I had to be 'Girl A' – the key witness in the trial that finally saw my abusers locked up. Girl A – the girl in the newspaper stories who had been through the most hideous experience imaginable. When I read those stories, I felt like I was reading about somebody else, another girl who was subjected to the depths of human depravity. But it wasn't. It was about me. I am Girl A.

I can't tell you my real name: I don't want anybody to know who I really am. Slowly, I'm beginning to realise that what happened to me wasn't my fault, that I was taken advantage of by a group of vile, twisted men. And, on top of that, I am becoming aware that I was let down by some of the very people who should have been there to help me: the people who either didn't realise or didn't care that I desperately needed to be rescued, or else turned a blind eye to it because to have acknowledged what was going on was, to them, unthinkable.

Because how could they admit, even to themselves, that teenage girls on their own doorstep were being preyed on in such a way? Trafficking was something that happened in other countries far, far away, wasn't it? And, anyway, if a few girls liked me slipped through society's safety net, did it really matter?

I'm not perfect. I'm a long way from being perfect. Deep within me, I still feel a strong sense of shame for some of the things I did, and for my weakness in falling prey to my abusers. Even now I sometimes find it too painful, too raw, too shaming, to speak about it all. But I will try to tell you how it came to be, in the best way I can. Because if I can stop another girl ending up like me, I might learn to accept myself once again. Maybe.

People tell me my feelings about it all will fade, and I have to believe that they will. I *do* believe that they will, because the bottom line is that this should not have happened. I was a child. I was young and vulnerable. I was a victim.

For now, at least, my real name is one of the few secrets that have not been stripped bare. That's mine to keep. You can call me Hannah, if you like.

So this is it, this is the story of Girl A. It's a story that should never have happened but did, and one that will happen again if the right changes to our society aren't made. This is my story.

Chapter One
Innocent Days

My early childhood was as close to idyllic as I can imagine.

I was born in Manchester in the early nineties, the first in what would become a brood of five happy children, and spent the first four years of my life at my grandparents' home on the outskirts of the city.

Mum and Dad had met on a blind date in Manchester a few years earlier. By the time I was ready to start primary school, they had saved up enough money to afford a home of their own. They had also decided to move away from Manchester, and settled on the west Lancashire coast, where Dad set up a new business.

The new house was within yards of the sea, so from being small I remember being taken to the beach with my two younger sisters, Lizzie and Sophie and, a little later, the twins, Matthew and Stephen. In the summer we'd paddle and build sandcastles; in the winter we'd just enjoy walking our two German Shepherds out past the dunes and onto the flat, windswept sands.

Both dogs are a bit old and worn at the edges now, but back then they would strain on their leads to drag me headlong towards the beckoning waves.

The seaside it may have been, but I actually hated swimming, so I'd never venture far into the water. I was much happier playing on my bike, racing down the massive hill from the sea wall. It was dangerous, but it didn't stop me – even when I went over the handlebars and ended up bruised and crying on the grass. I saw it as a game of dare that I couldn't resist!

I was a little daredevil, but there was a softer side to me, too.

Since I was little, I've wanted to be a nurse and when I was four, I was given one of those white nurse's outfits by Father Christmas. At home, me and Lizzie, who was just a year younger than I was, would spend hours playing nurse and patient.

'Breathe in,' I'd say very seriously, wielding my pretend stethoscope at my poor victim.

We'd wrap tissue around our arms and legs as casts and try to make them set with water. We'd end up looking like little mummies, and the carpet would look a bit of a mess too. But it was the most fun I could remember. Mum's always said I had a caring side.

I didn't particularly notice at the time, but in those early years by the seaside we always seemed to be pretty well off. Dad's business was doing well. I was also busy building up something myself; in my case, a huge collection of Barbie dolls. All high gloss and perfect. I'd sit them in their pink convertible so they could sweep their way around our bungalow.

There was enough money for ballet lessons, and for me to spend a fortune on every bit of S Club 7 memorabilia that money could buy. Lizzie and I would watch the S Club 7 films and dance endlessly to their music. There was a lot of Britney, too.

For holidays we'd go to places like Butlin's at Clacton, Center Parcs in Sherwood Forest, or else to campsites around the country. The family could guarantee that if there was ever a karaoke night, I'd be at the front of the queue, taking my well-rehearsed S Club 7 moves to the stage. I never could sing, but it didn't stop me trying.

At school, though, I was a lot quieter – a bit like I am now – but I did well in all my lessons. Maths was the best, and by the time I left for secondary school I was getting level fives – the best you could do – in every subject. It was only me and a lad in my class that managed that in our SATS, and Mum and Dad were so proud they took me to the local shops and gave me £20 to spend. Some of it went on having my ears pierced, the rest on earrings and bracelets in Claire's. Everyone loved Claire's then, even though it was dead expensive. I think Dad thought there were probably better things I could have spent the money on, but he knew it was my treat and my choice.

'Very nice,' he said, smiling proudly as I showed off my new sparkly ears.

I was always a bit of a Daddy's girl. Lizzie and I could always wrap him around our fingers. Mum would say no to something, and as soon as her back was turned we'd just go to Dad and get round him. Some of my favourite times with him were when we'd head off camping in nearby nature spots. We'd usually go for just a night or two, with our tent, a camp stove and marshmallows for us to toast at night. Mum would come too, if it was a summer holiday, but otherwise she'd tend to stay at home with the little ones so it would just be me, Dad and Lizzie.

Dad's always been a bit of a practical joker, and he'd sometimes send the two of us off into the fields and riverbanks for duck eggs. We never actually found any – at least, not until the day he bought some secretly from a farm and dotted them around so we could have the pleasure of finding them. Years later, he told us he was still chuckling as he cooked them that morning. They tasted fab!

At night, we'd sit there looking up at the stars, the flames from the fire casting shadows across our faces. Sometimes Dad would tell us ghost stories that had us clinging to him once we were back inside the tent. Other times, we'd snuggle up to him while he told us stories from when he was a lad and the escapades he'd get up to, but there'd always be some kind of moral that he'd leave us with.

'You don't get anywhere in this life without hard work,' he'd say, as we nestled into his side. 'Just make sure you always do the best you can, so that you're proud of yourself.'

In those days, Dad was the best teacher you could hope for: in some ways, better than the ones at the rather posh high school I went to. I'll never forget heading off into Blackpool with my mates after school in the first couple of terms there, to go shopping or to the Pleasure Beach, where we could scream our heads off on the scariest rides.

We'd have the time of our lives and it would become a regular event.

But then, one day, things began to change. When I went to ask Mum and Dad for the money to go out, Mum would look anxious.

'I'm sorry, love,' she would sigh. 'I can't give you any today, maybe next week.'

Over the next few weeks, I'd find myself greeted with the same response, and gradually I found myself going out less and less with my mates. I never understood why. I probably thought it was Mum and Dad being spoilsports. But soon all became clear.

* * *

They say that all good things come to an end and, in our case, at least financially, that's what happened. We may never have been middle class, but we'd been comfortable. However, by the time I was well into my first year at high school, sales in Dad's business began to slow down and his cash flow did the same.

He had to sell up, along with our home and, in the months that followed, we moved into a council house when I was just thirteen. It, too, was on the coast, but with no work, Mum and Dad decided it was time to head towards Manchester.

They chose Heywood because it was close enough to Dad's roots to be a good location and yet cheap enough for us to be able to afford. People call it Monkey Town for some reason. One of my mates said it was because the chairs in some of the local pubs used to have holes in, big enough for a tail to go through. To me, it seems to fit. Heywood may have given us *Coronation Street*'s Julie Goodyear, but it's full of folk who can't stop chattering about other people's business. That's the bit I hate about it.

There used to be coal mines around the town, and nearly thirty cotton mills, but they're all gone now – well, none of them have anything to do with cotton, any more, at least. Most of them were torn down to make way for the red-brick terraces and council houses that stretch away towards Ashworth Valley and the Pennines. The only thing that's kept the town going, as far as I can see, is the distribution park there, with all its warehouses and long-haul lorries. We're close to the M66 and the M62, and Bury's just down the road, for some half-decent shops.

Not that it's grim, but a poet once said the back-to-backs all the way from Heywood to Rochdale looked like they'd worked in the local factories themselves, let alone the people who lived in them.

Rochdale itself was big in the days of smoke and cotton, but not any more. There's a fancy town hall, but what you really notice looking down from the surrounding hills are the Seven Sisters – seven huge tower blocks that rise up towards the distant wind turbines on Scout Moor. They loom over the skyline in a really sinister way.

I'll never forget the day we left the bright lights of Blackpool behind us (and all of my friends and lovely home) and drove up to this weird new horizon. I had a really strange feeling in my tummy. A strange sense of foreboding.

Chapter Two
Culture Shock

Starting at a new school is always hard, but starting towards the end of a school year when you've just turned thirteen is even harder – everyone has already made their friends for the year and newcomers feel excluded.

It was due to timings and paperwork that it took a while for me to get a place at school: for three months, I just kicked my heels either at home or else on the estate that was now my home.

Lizzie had started at her new primary school, and after a few weeks her new friends came calling at the house. One of them, Maddy, had a sister called Elouise, who was the same age as me.

I guess that's what threw us together. Elouise wasn't the brightest kid in the area, but we got on together and would hang about at each other's houses, mostly watching TV and having sleepovers.

When I heard I'd be going to her school I felt a real sense of relief. At least I'd know someone there and, who knew, I might even end up in her class.

Despite the delay in getting a school place, it was all a bit of a rush in the end: I'd gone to a meeting at the school on the Friday and started that next Monday. Over that weekend, Mum and Dad rushed me to Asda in Rochdale so we could buy skirts, shirts and a pair of dolly shoes. I was meant to have a jumper, too, but we'd not gone to a proper school uniform place so I had to do without.

Elouise called for me that March morning, and the two of us set off. I felt nervous as a kitten as we went through the top gates of the school. She was smiling, while I tried to ignore the shouts and catcalls as the two of us headed towards Reception.

The staff weren't very welcoming. I'd barely given them my name before they were telling me I'd have to leave if my attendance was no good. I was shocked. Elouise squeezed my hand and headed off to class, while I was taken to the learning mentors so they could decide which class I should be in.

I spent the first morning sitting next to a girl called Courtney. She seemed nice enough, but I hated the class as a whole – the pupils were just so completely wild it made me feel uncomfortable.

Looking around in the first break, I felt a glimmer of hope. In my old school everyone had had brand-new bags and named shoes, and if you didn't have them you'd be picked on. Mum and Dad had got me all the new stuff – the bag, the shoes, the blazer – because they hadn't wanted me to be bullied. I knew they'd struggled to do it, because money was tight and getting tighter. Here, people didn't even take bags and they were mostly wearing trainers. So it looked like one less thing to worry about.

Also, people at this school seemed to smoke everywhere – on the corridors, the playground, and they actually had a smoking area for the kids – not so much because the teachers were being lax and irresponsible, but because they knew the kids would do it anyway. We'd never have got away with that in my old school! They'd have expelled you.

I didn't smoke, but I liked the fact you could because it felt less strict. I guess you could say it was rougher here, but in a way I was relieved by that. It wasn't as snobby; I felt maybe I could belong after all.

That first lunchtime, Courtney pushed her chair back from the desk and started whispering: 'Quick!' she breathed. 'Let's get to the dinner queue before the good stuff goes.'

School dinners were really nice here, and the chicken tikka sandwiches were the best. Everyone seemed to want them. You had to run to the front of the queue to get the chicken tikka!

But I was still worried about the class I'd been put in, and once I'd found Elouise, I asked her whether they might let me change. 'It's worth a try,' she said. She came with me to see the mentor I'd met in the morning, and actually she was fine about it. And so I ended up in Elouise's class, sitting next to her.

This second class was so much better than the first, and by mid afternoon I'd begun to feel a little less nervous. It certainly helped to have Elouise close by. Overall, though, the people at this new school were all tougher than I was used to, and in those first few weeks I discovered that the place had more of a reputation for fighting than for the kids it turned out. It made me realise I'd struggle there unless I found a way to fit in.

It wasn't the sort of place to go in for a lot of school trips – they cost money after all, and this school struggled to find the budget for everyday schooling. So, for us, a trip was a walk up to the shop at the top of school, and that was just so we could buy cigarettes. Yes, it didn't take me long to join in on the smoking. I guess it was the most obvious thing I could do to fit in.

It was a team effort to get your hands on some cigarettes. People used to put bits of their money together, out of their dinner money, so they could buy a pack of ten Richmond. Usually, it was four of us clubbing together: me, Elouise, Courtney and another chubby girl in my class called Hayley.

We'd have to ask someone to buy the cigarettes for us, but that wasn't a problem – there'd always be someone willing to do it. Why would they care?

I didn't smoke properly, and it was only now and again, when I had money. We'd have half a cigarette before school and half at break, in school or out of school – it didn't really matter; school wasn't bothered. The first time I tried, I coughed and spluttered until I was blue in the face, while the other kids howled with laughter. But after a while I found a way of not inhaling properly and, finally, I started to look like the rest of the crowd: leaning back against the wall in our school uniforms, blowing smoke through our nostrils or out the sides of our mouths.

After this, it seemed the next stage of my extra-curricular education would be in drinking; the lessons I was learning at this school were certainly life-changing, but not in the right way exactly.

I started drinking when I was thirteen. You could get cheap white cider and stuff on the estate. You'd buy it and put it in Lucozade bottles from home, then wander around the estate with your mates. The girls I was with – Elouise, Courtney and Hayley – had all grown up around Heywood and, for them, smoking and drinking were rites of passage – just things they'd started doing when they got to a certain age. The normal rules of suburbia didn't seem to apply around my way. In this new world, even twelve-year-olds had weed in their pockets, and I got used to seeing used syringes, cans, bottles and discarded condoms in the play areas. It was all a bit of a shock at first, but gradually I got used to it.

So, there I was, a young teenager, trying to fit in with a whole new world. For the first time ever, my confidence took a real knocking and I did whatever I could to fit in. Where I'd once excelled at maths and been given £20 to spend in Claire's as a reward, the only new skills I was picking up now were the best ways to get hold of fags and booze without my parents or the school or the police finding out. And the reward for my efforts? Acceptance from the other kids. It was becoming a formative year to say the least.

Our initial gang of four extended to six with the addition of Shauna, another of my school friends who was a few weeks younger than me and Milly, one of Elouise's old friends. Together we'd head into the town centre at weekends, or else to each other's houses for sleepovers.

My place was the same house Mum and Dad are still in: a better-than-most council terrace with leather sofas, pet rats, a wide-screen TV in the lounge and never enough bedrooms upstairs. It was a bus ride to the town centre and its landscape of long-abandoned mills, dingy barbers' shops, two taxi ranks near Morrison's, and the tatty kebab shops and pizza places.

We'd not stay over at my house very much, to be honest. Mum and Dad didn't seem to approve of my new friends, so it always felt a bit frosty when they'd turn up. Mum and Dad seemed to think they were a cut above everyone else on the estate, and they thought my new-found friends were beneath me. As far as I could see, though, I was no different – and neither were my parents. It was just that they'd been used to something different where we'd lived before. Me, I just knew I had to adapt, to try to fit in.

We had our wildest times at Hayley's place. We'd be open-mouthed as she'd tell us how she'd first had sex with a lad when she was twelve. For all that she appeared slow, she was pretty quick at getting lads into bed or wherever. Night after night, sometimes as we lay in her room in the darkness, she'd give us blow-by-blow accounts of her lurid encounters. With another girl you might have thought she was making it up: not Hayley.

My life at home began to change, my attitude not helped as teenage hormones began to flood my still boyish frame: as well as the physical effects that took place, a lot of emotional ones did, too. I started to rebel and kick back against Mum and Dad. They'd always been quite strict when I was a kid, but it hadn't seemed to matter then. They'd probably tell you there's always been a rebellious streak in me and now, living in a tough town on the edge of the Pennines, that streak was coming to the fore.

Mum and Dad, especially Dad, had found their drop in social status a catastrophe that they struggled to cope with. They struggled with me, too, and, as the family's money ran out, and they headed into debt, every little row suddenly seemed to go to a whole new level. A simple, 'Can you help with the washing up, please?' would turn into a full-scale war of shouting, stomping and screaming. And I wouldn't be the only one screaming.

'What is wrong with you?' Mum would screech after me, as I shook the whole house with one of my epic door slams. 'You're grounded!'

Maybe like a lot of parents, they were fine dealing with their kids when they were little, but couldn't make the switch to dealing with those same kids when they hit adolescence. Especially when they hit it as hard as I did.

Gradually, Mum and Dad began to get wind of my antics outside the house. As it dawned on them that I was, after all, 'mixing with the wrong crowd', the arguments would get even worse and it would be the front door I'd be slamming as I tried to escape them. Home felt like the last place I wanted to be when I could be hanging out, having a laugh with my new friends. They probably were the wrong crowd, but to me they were cool and I wanted to be with them, wanted to be like them, and just to fit in. The shyness of childhood was still very much with me, but somehow

I'd managed to make these friends and I was going to do everything I could to keep them.

At school, my mates and I would be the first to head off to the top gate to have a smoke, and in the evenings and at weekends we'd hang around together. At our old home, I used to go shopping and to the pictures (though by the time we left I didn't really have the money to do that); here, the kids didn't do those things because they were usually broke, too. They'd just go around the estates or to other people's houses and chill. It was a big difference, but it made me feel that bit happier, like I fitted in.

We used to drink together and listen to a lot of rave music. We'd make up CDs on the computer and dance around, mostly at the weekends. When I got home, I'd try to sneak in without my parents noticing. I'd tell Lizzie what went on – she was my sister, after all, and it was good to tell her what a laugh I'd been having. I couldn't have told Mum and Dad. Well, you can't, can you?

It was the Lucozade bottles that got me into trouble, eventually. Mum thought I really liked it, but of course I didn't: it was just good for putting cider in once my sisters had drunk the pop. I'd just turned fourteen the night we got caught by the police. Not really caught, but my dad got a letter about it.

'Hannah!' Dad shouted, one morning. When I got to the kitchen he was clutching a piece of white paper with the letterhead for the local police constabulary at the top. His face was almost purple with rage.

'What the hell is this?' he raged, waving the paper around. My stomach dropped as I realised what it must be. I was in big trouble.

One night, we'd been going through Heywood as usual when a marked car had pulled up and a couple of policemen had got out. They could see we all had bottles, and that most of them said 'Lucozade' on the label. A bit obvious, really. Anyway, they started asking us what was in the bottles and we said, 'Well, like, Lucozade …?' – that sort of thing. A few of us, Courtney, Elouise, Milly and I, had thrown our bottles into the hedge, but not the others. The police sniffed them and smelled the cider, which didn't exactly surprise them.

'Doesn't smell like Lucozade to me,' one said, raising an eyebrow, while another went through the bush and found the rest of the bottles. All the cider went into the gutter. They gave us a lecture and took all our names.

That's why Dad got the letter, and why I was grounded for a week. Plus, I got a caution.

But, often, not even grounding me worked – I would stay home for a few days, but then slip away when I felt like it. Maybe it was around then that my parents began to lose the fight to control me and make me behave the way they wanted me to. Things certainly got worse at home, and I felt I was gradually growing apart from them and, anyway, they had the younger ones to look after.

That, too, was something that rankled. As I got older, it felt as though I was expected to help look after my younger siblings all of the time. Mum and Dad say they were just trying to get me to do my share, but the rebel in me didn't see it that way. The worst it ever got was after the twins were born. While Mum looked after them, it was down to me to get the others up in the morning, make breakfast and wash up the pots from the night before. To the teenage me, it felt so unfair.

I came to resent it more and more as I got older, and it made me want to wind Mum and Dad up more and more, so I could get even with them. They just didn't seem to want me to have my own free time, and they certainly didn't want me going out and getting drunk with my mates. They seemed to just want me to live a life of homework and drudgery around the house. Whenever I went out, they'd say things like, 'Don't forget, you've got to be home by 11 p.m.' And then, 'You'll be in trouble if you aren't.'

Yeah, whatever, I'd think.

The stricter they tried to be, the more rebellious I grew. Was it all part of growing up? Was it my surroundings or their parenting? Or was it all my fault? I guess everyone will have an opinion. But I didn't have time to stop and think at that age: I was too busy doing what I wanted to do. And that was being a teenage girl, without a care in the world. Nobody was going to stop me having fun.

* * *

Courtney was my best mate by now: funny, mad Courtney, who was really bubbly and had a wicked sense of humour. I was a bit crazy myself, but shyer, more reserved, at least in school. In classes Courtney would have us in stitches, flicking bits of rubber at teachers with her ruler, and then putting on a dead-straight face when they'd turn around. She did it time and time again and always got away with it. Well, usually.

I started wagging school when I was still fourteen – only just fourteen, really, in the spring of 2007. Courtney, Hayley and I would sneak away from classes we didn't like – PE and English, usually – and head off to the railway tracks near school. Hayley took us the first time, mostly because she fancied a lad called Wayne and he'd usually be there: him and Ricky, a lad the same age as me who was so rarely at school you could almost imagine he didn't go there. We'd all sit together on the bank, drinking, smoking, chatting, playing music on our phones as the trains rumbled by. In the evenings, the same gang would often head off into the town centre together, walking, talking, sitting on benches while we drank cider, or else generally milling around as teenagers do.

Mum and Dad would get mad at me when I came home drunk. They seemed to accept that I was drinking with mates, but they hated the idea of me getting drunk out of my skull. They said it wasn't safe, that something bad might happen to me. I just laughed it off.

I was having fun.

The first time I stormed off and stayed out overnight without telling my parents was around June that year. There'd been an argument about me coming home drunk, so I had just gone upstairs, climbed out of my window and gone to Shauna's house. Mum and Dad gave me a roasting when I came home the next morning, but it didn't seem to do any good. Their words were like water off a duck's back.

Chapter Three
Daddy

Tasty Bites was an Indian takeaway in the middle of town. It was on the usual circuit my friends and I would take on our walks around the centre: past the Edwin Waugh pub on Market Street, on towards the Balti House, then cut right by Dunne's store and Morrison's, and rejoin Market Street for a second time, near the barber's where Dad used to have his hair cut for £3.50.

I suppose ending up in Tasty Bites was a natural progression for us, not least because if we were hungry, which was most times, we could pop in late and buy something like chips and curry sauce or a £1 pizza sandwich to share.

And there was another reason to go. By now Milly, more forward and older-looking than the rest of us had started going out with a guy from the takeaway. Saj, she told us in a whisper at school one day, was in his thirties. His thirties! When she told us that we were horrified, though it clearly didn't seem to bother her.

I remember turning to Elouise as we headed off to Art and asking, 'How can she do that? I could never go out with anyone that old. And they can't even talk to each other because he doesn't even speak English.'

Saj used to ring Milly while she was still at school, and there were lots of times she'd wag lessons so she could go off with him. The rest of us would giggle about it at the back of the class or in the playground. It did seem weird, but by the time it got to evening we were happy enough to call at Tasty Bites as we made our late-night tours of Heywood's dull, forgotten streets.

I remember as clear as day the first time we met Daddy. It was Milly who introduced us one night, having seen him around the back when she was hooking up with Saj who she was sleeping with. We'd all piled into Tasty Bites – me, Courtney, Elouise, Shauna, Milly and Hayley – and were hanging around by the counter when Milly peeled away and returned a few minutes later with a beaming Asian guy in tow.

'This is Daddy,' she said, all serious, trying to ignore the sniggers from the rest of us as we took in his name. Daddy worked with Saj and was a friend of his. It seemed such a daft nickname for the guy standing in front of us: a cheery old man in his fifties with a faint moustache, wearing blue jeans and a black, round-necked jacket.

To me, Daddy looked a bit like Father Christmas, but Asian: round and jolly, with a face that lit up when he smiled. He shook each of our hands in turn, smiling broadly and saying, 'Pleased to meet you' to each of us. In my case he winked, and placed his left hand on my wrist as we shook hands. Milly obviously liked him, and in those few moments I think the rest of us took to him, too. It just seemed we could instantly trust him. He looked like a friendly, safe man to be around.

He was also really generous. 'Come, come,' he said. 'Let me show Milly's friends upstairs. Would you like doner? A drink? Come upstairs, you can chill.'

So up we trooped, him leading the way, a little breathless, up the narrow staircase. He took us into what seemed to be a spare bedroom – almost bare, with only a double mattress on the floor.

'Sit,' he said. 'Please sit, and I'll bring you food and Pepsi.'

While he was gone, Milly filled us in about him. She had no idea why he was called Daddy, she said, but maybe it was because he was such a lovely guy. Anyway, he lived with his family in Oldham and was the takeaway's delivery driver – he had a little blue car that he'd pile up with orders and deliver around the local council estates.

There was a radio in the room that first night. It was set to an Asian station, but we quickly changed the channel to Capital FM so we could listen to all the chart stuff.

A few minutes later, we were all tucking into doner kebabs, naan bread and a big tub of garlic mayonnaise.

'This is heaven,' swooned Hayley, and we all laughed.

Being upstairs at Tasty Bites felt wonderful: like a brilliant new adventure that we had all to ourselves. Other people just came in, went to the counter, waited for their order and then left again. We, on the other hand, were treated as honoured guests. I think it made all of us feel a little bit special.

It was late September 2007 by then and, at that age, skint, bored and rebellious, upstairs at Tasty Bites became our favourite place to end up on a night out. In a town with no cinema, no ice rink and no hope – and with no money, anyway – this was as glitzy as it could get for fourteen-year-olds like us. We came to look forward to all the free food and drinks: the doners, the chicken tikkas, the Pepsi. It was always Daddy who'd bring it, huffing and puffing up the stairs, laden with takeaway trays and cans of pop.

'Here you are, my lovely girls,' he'd say. 'Food on the house from Tasty Bites!' He would bring the food up to us in those foil packs, like he was delivering to a house. There wouldn't be any cutlery; we just used the naan bread to wrap things up in. It was always either chicken tikka or doner kebab, and it would always come with garlic mayonnaise.

I can't eat that now. Just the smell of it makes me feel sick.

We'd generally end up there a few nights a week, chatting, smoking and drinking for hours before eventually drifting away to go home.

After a while, Daddy started to bring us free cigarettes and free beer, too. Actually, I don't mean beer; I mean alcohol. Around Rochdale we tend to call everything 'beer', even when it's not. To start with, the 'beer' Daddy brought was Lambrini cider, but one night he came up with some glasses and a bottle of vodka, Glen's Vodka. I hadn't had it before because it was too expensive for us to buy.

I hated the taste but I drank it because it was strong. It was easier to drink with cola. Daddy would leave the bottle, a litre one. To start with, we only drank a bit, but the next night we were there he brought more and so we ended up drinking more and more. It felt wicked.

All through the autumn, and on towards Christmas, we'd sit upstairs with the drinks, chatting, chilling, and gradually, inevitably, getting drunk. It felt so *cool*. For weeks we'd go along to Tasty Bites to chill, and these gullible old men, and Daddy in particular, would give us all this free stuff. We loved it.

The first time or two, I have to admit I'd thought it a bit weird that they'd let us chill there, but I quickly got used to it and saw it as normal. If they were daft enough to give us all this free stuff, why turn it down? We thought we were the luckiest kids in town.

* * *

Daddy spoke English fluently because his parents had brought him to Britain as a kid. Sometimes he would sit on the mattress with us and stay for five or ten minutes, chatting with us about normal things like school, and where we lived, and our families. He'd ask about our teachers, our exams, what we wanted to do, that sort of thing. He was always laughing and joking, as if he was trying to act like one of us.

He seemed to like me the most. He'd always speak to me and say, 'You're special' or 'You're beautiful' and things like that. It was nice to hear, even if it made me blush.

Daddy didn't say much about himself, apart from that he had four children he didn't see much of any more. He never drank with us because of being a Muslim, but he thought it was funny when we were all drunk. He'd get a bit touchy-feely then, too: he'd hug us and kiss us on the cheek. Nothing sexual, just friendly, like he was your long-lost uncle.

We all thought we were the clever ones and Daddy was just a harmless old man. We all felt completely happy and in control – the feeling was that we were taking advantage of him, but he seemed to enjoy it, so what was the problem? It was a bit bad sometimes, because we'd get Daddy to bring us more and more stuff. We'd be sitting there and one of us would say to the others, 'Go and ask him to get us some more of that chicken tikka,' or 'How about another doner?' – things like that. Then one of us would lean out of the door and shout down to him: 'Daddy! Daddy!' and up he would come again. He'd even drive us home!

We all lived in roughly the same area, so some nights Daddy would take two, three, four of us home, all squeezed into his little car until we'd got to where he'd drop us off. He never tried anything and I never even thought he would. It just felt cool and grown-up to be going home drunk and in a car.

Mum and Dad, meanwhile, had no idea about the nights I spent upstairs at Tasty Bites. They just thought I was off around town with my mates. It was one of my secrets. The other girls felt the same. Sometimes I'd manage to sneak upstairs and into my room so Mum and Dad wouldn't know I was drunk, and other times I'd try to con them into thinking I was sober, often with a takeaway bag swinging from my hand. If they realised what was happening because I'd swayed too much or slurred my words, they'd start shouting at me, saying, 'Look at the state of you, you're a disgrace.'

They didn't ask where all the free food was coming from: I think they just thought I was saving up dinner money and things. A couple of times I was so drunk I was sick out of the window and Dad had to keep checking on me every hour. In the morning, he would say he was disgusted with me and ask: 'Why do you get so drunk?'

The hungover me just kept as quiet as she could. Sometimes, I'd feel guilty about keeping Mum and Dad up, making them worry. But those feelings would quickly be squashed by my teenage bravado: what right did they have to interfere? Besides, I was having fun.

One night, Elouise and I were at Tasty Bites alone. As soon as Daddy had brought the vodka and gone back downstairs, she said, 'Hey, I know how we can get drunk quicker.'

'How?' I asked, intrigued.

'Well,' she said, 'you take your drink, stand on the mattress and then you do this …'

And with that, she smiled impishly, took a huge swig of vodka, and began jumping manically, her body twisting around and around in a circle as she did so.

'See?' she yelled triumphantly. 'The vodka goes straight to your head!' She looked so funny I couldn't help laugh along with her, but once she'd come to a staggering halt I said, 'But, Elouise, all that's going to do is make you dizzy, and then you'll be sick!'

'Pah,' she said, and took another giant swig, before going through the same performance again.

She looked so pleased with herself that I had to try it, though for me once was quite enough.

Elouise carried on a few more times before eventually collapsing, in a fit of giggles, on the bed. As it turned out, she certainly seemed to get drunk much quicker than me that particular night: towards the end of it, we'd drunk the whole bottle and she was lying flat out on the mattress on her tummy.

She was lying like that when I heard Daddy's heavy footsteps on the stairs. 'How are you both?' he asked, as he appeared at the open doorway.

'I'm fine,' I beamed, 'but Elouise's drunk out of her head!'

'Ah, she looks as though she needs a massage,' he said. 'Is that right, Elouise? Shall Daddy give you a massage?'

Elouise just grunted in reply. I didn't exactly catch the word she used, but it sounded like a drunken, 'Fine.'

A moment later and Daddy was kneeling next to her on the mattress, massaging her back, then her legs, and eventually her bum, kneading first one cheek, then the other, then both together, over her jeans. That's when I really noticed.

'What are you doing?' I squealed.

'I'm just giving her a massage,' he said, beaming up at me. It seemed so weird, but as he carried on I went along with it. Elouise hardly seemed to notice – she was pretty much out of it.

It went on for a while, until Daddy rocked back onto his heels and the massage was over. He was laughing, and I found myself laughing too, even though I was still a bit embarrassed by what I'd just seen.

At that point Elouise, hazy from the vodka, sat herself up, and Daddy moved in from behind. I watched, half in shock, half mesmerised, as he lifted up her top to show off her bra. Hugely embarrassed, I yelled, 'Pull your top down, Elouise!'

Daddy just said, 'She's fine, she's fine.'

'But she's drunk out of her head,' I retorted. 'Leave her alone.'

He pulled away, still smiling, looking across at me and asking, like a naughty schoolboy: 'Why are you being so serious?'

A few moments later he was heading back downstairs, chuckling to himself, and a short time after that I was half carrying Elouise downstairs so we could go home. That night we walked, or rather staggered, back to the estate.

I suppose you could say Tasty Bites, and Daddy, gave me a real capacity for drinking. While other kids my age were just about starting to drink cider at home with their mums and dads, I was knocking back shot after shot of vodka with my mates. It made me feel good; it made me feel loud.

Early in the new year, however, at the start of 2008, Daddy left Tasty Bites and with Milly no longer going out with Saj, our nights there gradually fizzled out. For us, the place just went back to being a plain old takeaway.

Chapter Four
Grounded

At school in Heywood, we used to have a 'Top Five', where you'd write down the top five boys you liked at school. As a kid, I always used to think about what it would be like to get married, settle down and have kids and all that.

My favourite was always Elliot, the boy I sat next to in English. He wasn't exactly the sort of lad my mum and dad would have approved of, but he was nice anyway, so long as he wasn't pretending to be a gangster, like some of the other lads actually were. He was stocky with dark hair. He got expelled eventually, for bringing in a knife to school so he could look hard.

Elliot was the first boy I kissed properly. It was April 2008. I was fifteen and drunk. We'd gone into the town centre that night, the usual gang, and Elliot was the one I was walking next to. Hayley had told him I liked him, and at some point, while the others headed on towards the Three Terriers, I snuck off with him behind another pub, The Heywood.

He wasn't a good kisser, to be honest, but it went on for about five minutes. It really was my first kiss, and I didn't know what to do. I was so embarrassed, but dead happy too, because I'd finally done it.

Elliot was the person I lost my virginity to, as well. By then, most girls of my age in Heywood had lost their virginity, so I was probably something of a late developer. It happened about a week later, not behind a pub as some of the other girls had done but outside, in a field. I'd like to say I could see stars, not all of them in the sky, but it wasn't like that. Actually, it was horrible, because I felt sick with nerves and it really hurt. But, afterwards I felt happy, almost proud. I felt like I'd joined a club I'd not known was there. As the girls gathered around me and quizzed me on what it had been like, that yearning I felt to belong was soothed once again. I was really one of them now.

I was particularly stoked because Elliot was number one on my 'Top Five' list. The girls were amazed: 'We can't believe it,' they screeched, as my cheeks tingled with joy. 'You're so lucky!'

Elliot and I did it once more after that. It was still rubbish, but it didn't hurt as much. I fell out with him soon after, and that was that.

Looking back, I can't believe there was ever a time I was so laid-back about having sex. But, on the other hand, I'm glad I've had that experience. Sex should be a natural thing that people enjoy together. At least I've experienced the rush it can bring, because, these days, I don't know if I'll ever feel that same thrill again.

* * *

My antics fuelled yet more arguments at home. Hayley's exploits with her various boyfriends gave me the material to wind up Mum and Dad. I'd tell them all sorts of stories about me and boys and what we'd get up to – at least, in theory. Most of it was made up, but it got them yelling at me, which to the teenage me felt like a result. One time I told them I'd slept with someone in the back field, another time that I'd caught chlamydia even though I was a virgin at the time. I don't know why, but I just felt this urge to be rebellious. Mum and Dad were constantly nagging – in my eyes, for no good reason – so I thought I'd give them something to really shock them. It seems immature now, but at the time I didn't see it like that.

Wagging off school wasn't helping my grades, either, and eventually, around May 2008, I got put on report, which meant having to go to the teacher at the end of each class and get a mark for my behaviour: A, B, C or D. Mum and Dad would go mental if I didn't get an A or a B.

One particular night they blew up because I'd got a D. It didn't bother me because Courtney was on report too, and so were lots of other kids. In reality, we were nowhere near being the worst kids in our year – there were girls I knew who were getting drunk in the school toilets and being arrested every weekend. But that didn't wash with Dad – not that night. 'Your mates may be scum, but you're not,' he screamed. 'So for God's sake stop behaving like you are! And stop getting so drunk that you don't know what's happening to you. If you're not careful, one of these days you're going to get raped or pregnant!'

'All I'm doing is having a few drinks with my mates,' I yelled back, appalled that he could think things could ever get so serious. A few seconds later, outraged, I was slamming the back door and heading away from the estate. I could hear Mum screaming at me as I legged it round the corner.

This time I went to Hayley's, and we ended up camping out under the stars with her latest boyfriend, Danny. We set up his tent in the same field I'd been to with Elliot, and then carried down some quilts and a few bottles of cider.

We'd been drinking for about half an hour when I passed the bottle to Hayley. 'No, I'd better not, thanks, Hannah,' she said. She looked momentarily flustered, then embarrassed. 'I'm pregnant,' she whispered.

Danny looked a bit shamefaced but then took the bottle, smiled and carried on drinking. Hayley and I discussed the baby and how she felt about it. 'It was a bit of a shock at first,' she confided, 'but I'm getting used to the idea now. And Danny says he's fine with it.'

I guess for some people being pregnant at fifteen might be a bit of a surprise, but you've probably worked out by now that around our way it was not out of the norm. Of course, Hayley freaked out a bit at first, but then she just got on with it. Her boyfriend was standing by her and they actually seemed pretty happy together. A lot of the kids from our school didn't have much hope for their future, and being a mum was probably one of the better options on offer. At least they could find happiness and love there. And the benefits money was better too.

Sitting in our tent, talking and looking up at the stars, there was definitely celebration in the air – it felt like we were free of any worries. It reminded me of my nights with

Dad and Lizzie when we went camping, and it felt like everything was right in the world and your destiny was what you made it. I found myself quickly pushing away thoughts of Dad, knowing him and Mum would probably be worried sick about where I was. And ready to ground me again.

Just to keep them at bay, this one night I had switched off my phone. They'd texted earlier to ask where the hell I was, but I had ignored it. *Let them sweat*, I thought.

To be honest, I felt a bit jealous seeing Hayley lying there in Danny's arms, all happy, as we talked about the gang at school, the teachers we hated and eventually, later on, baby names.

Danny didn't seem that bothered.

'How about Chelsea, Dan? Or Courtney?'

'Yeah, whatever,' he replied, taking another swig of cider from the bottle the two of us were sharing while Hayley drank cola.

Just before we finally settled down to sleep, Hayley and I nipped out of the tent and set off towards the hedge so we could have a wee. In the darkness she whispered conspiratorially, 'Don't let on, but I'm not sure if it's Danny's baby. He'd batter me if he knew.'

In the gathering silence we both reflected on the fact that Hayley getting pregnant had been an accident waiting to happen. She'd got caught out, just like lots of other girls on estates all over Rochdale and beyond. *It won't happen to me*, I thought pensively. Mum and Dad would go ape.

As I drifted off to sleep, I wondered how close I'd come to getting pregnant those times with Elliot.

In the morning we set off home and, when I got back, Mum and Dad, predictable as ever, went mad because they thought I'd been with a boy. 'Where have you been?' they said, despairingly. 'We've been worried sick. It's unacceptable.'

Mum then tried a softer approach. 'Look, Hannah, we're your mum and dad and we care about you. We don't want you to ruin your life. It's never right to sleep with just anyone, and we want you to save yourself for the right lad. That's all.'

I could see the anxiety in both their faces, shadows under their eyes from lack of sleep. Now, that image makes me feel guilty. But at the time, my judgement was so clouded – in my eyes I had been with a boy, yes, but it was my friend's boyfriend. And all we'd done was sit around talking, not even drinking that much. Rather naïvely, I thought if anything, I'd been very well behaved. What was the problem?

Whatever it was, it ended with Dad's party-piece warning, yelled at full volume: 'You mark my words,' he stormed. 'Carry on as you are and you're going to end up in serious trouble. Pregnant or raped, it wouldn't surprise me. And then don't blame us, because you'll have been asking for it!'

I think they grounded me for two weeks that time.

* * *

Things were getting yet worse at home: grounding me seemed to have less and less effect. My parents would tell me I wasn't going out anywhere, and for a couple of days I might stick to that, but at some point I'd either just kick off again or else slip away. There really wasn't any holding me, and I think they came to realise that. Maybe that's when Dad and Mum finally lost the fight to keep me under some sort of control. I managed to go to Tasty Bites all those times without them knowing – sometimes I'd tell them I was going to stay at one mate's house, but then go to someone else's. When I got home Mum and Dad would say: 'You lied to us!' Then I would know that they must have checked up on me, and that made me madder still.

The girl who played with Barbies was growing up – so she thought – and my parents didn't know how to handle her. They'd try to give me extra chores to do, but I'd either just delay and delay doing them, or else flounce off to my room. Either way, they'd eventually just give up and end up doing whatever it was they'd wanted me to do. A typical encounter would go something like this:

'Will you please take the boys to the park, Hannah?' my mum would ask.

'Why?' I'd invariably reply. 'It's you who had them – you go.' I loved my little brothers, of course, and there were lots of times I'd take them to the park, the shops, sometimes to the river, but there were times, too, that I wanted my freedom.

Mum, of course, would get upset and then Dad would come in and yell at me. Part of me felt guilty, but I wasn't letting on about that.

Dad seemed to be the one who took this transformation in his little girl the hardest. When I was a child, his face had always seemed so jovial, so serene and confident. Now it was lined most of the time by worry or anger – or both.

To be fair to myself, I did come in mostly on time. It was just what I did when I was out that caused the problems. At the end of the day, I was just a kid looking for laughs – anything to get away from the drudgery of everyday life in a town going nowhere.

* * *

I found myself chatting to Ricky more and more than in the early days of wagging school and ending up next to the railway tracks. He wasn't in my top five, and I didn't fancy him at all, but he was a laugh and on the nights we wandered around town, I'd often hang back and talk things over with him.

He lived in a big house, he said, with his dad and various other relatives. It was wild and free there – no rules, just lots of beer that his dad, Harry, bought with his benefits money.

This was another example of how everyone was looking for a little way to make their life seem better: a lot of people in the town lived for signing-on day, so they could get hold of a little bit of money to find a way to forget their troubles for a while.

Ricky's dad's place sounded great, such a contrast to my own house with all of Mum and Dad's, 'Do this, do that, tidy up in the kitchen, get the Hoover out and for God's sake stop getting drunk all the time.'

'You should come up,' Ricky said. 'One weekend, maybe, and stay over. There's loads of room and we can party all night.' I couldn't wait.

Harry wasn't the only laid-back adult around that helped us youngsters have fun. Like I said, most of the teachers turned a blind eye to us smoking at school because they knew there'd be a mutiny if they tried to crack down. Some of them would even join us! But there were limits, especially with the head teacher.

One break time he caught a few of us smoking in the playground and told us to put our cigarettes out and go in. I did put mine out, but only after taking one more drag and blowing the smoke in his face. He went mad.

'Go straight to my office,' he ordered, pointing to the entrance, his finger quivering with rage. Inside, he gave me a long lecture about my behaviour, which ended in a three-day exclusion from school.

I had to wait in the 'naughty room' while my dad was sent for.

When Dad got there, he was as angry as only he could be. In the car he started shouting at me. 'Why do you behave like this?' he asked, not waiting for the reply, knowing I'd just sit there in silence. 'Your sister doesn't, the boys don't.'

It was a good point. My siblings had all been through the same thing, but they didn't cause my parents any trouble – even Lizzie, who was closest in age to me. She was always good, while I was the black sheep. Part of me wanted to be like her, but I can't quite explain it: there was just something in me, for some reason, that craved these 'fun times' I had with my mates.

Chapter Five
The Honey Monster

By early summer 2008, we were all meeting up most evenings, drinking cider as we headed into the town centre to walk around and have a laugh. As ever, we were always on the lookout for something new and fun to do, so when an opportunity arose, we leapt at the chance it offered.

Most of the time the police left us alone. Sometimes, though, they'd suss the old Lucozade trick and would pour the cider away in front of us. I didn't get any more cautions, though. Maybe they'd given up on us, I don't know.

By now it had got to the stage where I just couldn't stand being at home, and my family – or my parents at least – couldn't stand me being there.

If I'd been older, or had some money, I'd have moved out. When I moaned to Ricky about it sometimes, he'd say, 'Come up to my place if you like. You'd like it.'

For some reason I'd still not been to his – most times when I was staying away overnight it was at one of the girls' houses – and I was tempted to take Ricky up on his offer. He made his place, or rather Harry's place, seem like the coolest house in the whole of town. It sounded a laugh: a big house, much bigger than ours, with none of the 'boundaries' and 'responsibilities' and tellings-off about 'respect' that were suffocating me at home.

In the end, there was no particular family row that made me leave home. It had just become inevitable. I'd fallen out so many times with Mum and Dad, vanished into thin air so many times, that it just became a natural step – on both sides. So, somewhere towards the end of Year 10 at school, in the June of 2008, I sort of drifted away and up to Harry's place.

* * *

My first time there had been after a night out in town with a group of mates, Ricky included. Courtney was with us, too, and her boyfriend.

You didn't even have to get inside Harry's house to know it was pure bedlam in there – the graffiti on the walls outside told you that. I nearly turned straight round and headed home that night, but since it was gone 1 a.m. and I was drunk, I thought better of it.

Inside, everyone still seemed to be up. It was like Fagin's kitchen, full of people smoking weed and looking as if they could do with a wash. Mum and Dad would have gone ape if our place was ever like that, but this lot didn't seem to notice.

Most of the people there were in their late teens, early twenties. The four of us were younger than all of them. Out on the streets together, we always felt in charge but there, we felt a bit intimidated. Courtney and I looked at each other. She seemed a bit shell-shocked, but then gave one of her nervous giggles and accepted a can of cider.

Together we looked around, taking in this strange new environment. The graffiti I'd seen outside was also here on the inside walls: in the hall and kitchen were lots of badly drawn people with balloon 'thoughts' coming out of their heads, all of them mindless and making no sense.

There were three dogs at Harry's: all of them mongrels, all mad; one of them with its back legs broken. In the kitchen, I nearly tripped over this one as it came shuffling up to me, dragging up dirt and dust from the floor in the process. I could see fleas all over its head and pushed it away with my foot. Ricky said it had had its legs broken when a mate of one of his brothers had decided to throw it out a bedroom window for a laugh. They'd not taken it to a vet, so its legs hadn't healed properly, leaving it crippled and in pain. The RSPCA eventually put it down after they raided the place.

If the dogs were dysfunctional, the humans in the house were as bad – drinking lager and cider, laid out with smoke from their drugs wafting over them. Some were Ricky's relatives, a lot were just the hangers-on that the family seemed to attract.

There had been a few grunts to say hello as we walked in, but only one of them had spoken properly to us. 'Who's this then, Ricky?' said an old guy, sprawled on the only sofa in the room – a brown fake-leather one with rips in the cushions that meant you could see the stuffing inside. He was smoking a roll-up and drinking from a can of Carling.

This, it turned out, was Ricky's dad. Harry. His shirt was untucked and there was days-old stubble on his face, but he had a nice, reassuring sort of smile. He looked a bit like one of those pensioners you see wandering slowly along Blackpool prom. Sitting there among the rest of us, all much younger, he seemed a bit lost and a bit ancient.

We sat on the floor for ages, listening to all the drunken madness of the place and carrying on getting as smashed as they were. Courtney then went upstairs with her boyfriend, giving me a wink as she did so. Then, a while later, I headed off with Ricky, so he could find me somewhere to sleep. Just sleep, that is. There was never anything between us. We were just mates.

Just before we settled down in the same room as Courtney and her boyfriend, Ricky pushed some drawers against the door. 'No lock on it,' he whispered. 'This way, no one else will get in. The rest can sort themselves out.' I fell asleep on a bed with no sheet and no pillow. It was that sort of place.

It felt like I'd only just gone to sleep when there was a banging on the door.

'Let me in, for fuck's sake,' boomed a girl's voice, deep and threatening.

'Go away,' Courtney said, her voice croaky from alcohol and lack of sleep. 'This is our room.'

'No, it's not – it's mine!' shouted the girl on the landing. 'And you'd better open the door now or I'll smash your fucking face in.'

The girl with the booming voice was clearly someone to reckon with physically, because even as Courtney blanched, then dipped beneath her duvet, the door was beginning to open. Ricky clearly knew the intruder, and quickly jumped up to start pulling at the drawers so she could get in. A moment later, the fat face of a girl, red, blotchy and angry, appeared in the doorway.

'Do that again and you're dead,' she shouted, her lumbering frame moving towards the window, reaching down to shift piles of debris and discarded clothes as she went. 'Who's moved my shoes?' she glowered.

I shrank away from her. I had no idea where her shoes were, nor anything else about her, but I wasn't about to say. She had a presence that said, *If you know what's good for you, stay back.*

Luckily for all of us, she found the missing shoes next to the TV and seemed to calm down, before sitting down on Ricky's bed to put them on.

As I say, she was a big girl, wearing leggings that must have been four or even five times bigger than mine, plus a white, oversized T-shirt that had the words 'Fuck You!' picked out in black.

Her eyes held mine. 'Who are you?' she asked, her voice gravelly, her eyes fixing me with the sort of gaze you daren't ignore. I thought she must be at least a year older than me, maybe two.

'Hannah,' I said nervously. 'I go to school with Ricky.'

'Emma,' she said, by way of introduction. 'His cousin.'

She started looking me up and down, disapprovingly. 'Which school do you go to?' she asked.

I told her, and she scoffed. 'Which year?'

'Year Eleven,' I said. 'Well, in September I will be …'

It turned out that although she looked older, there were actually only five months between our birthdays – and we were in the same school year. Not that it seemed to matter to her, because she said she hardly ever went.

'They can't make me,' she said, breaking into a smile I thought she'd never find. 'I just never turn up. And, anyway, it's shit.'

By that time we were all wide awake, so we went downstairs and spoke some more – her, me and Courtney. Straight off, she told us she was the hardest girl in Rochdale, and we didn't doubt it. 'No one fucks with me,' she added, just to make sure we'd got the whole picture.

Still bleary from the drinking, I found myself drawn to Emma as she sprawled on the sofa as if she, not Harry, owned it. Right from the start, she seemed to have a strange power. It wasn't just her size, her physical presence. Even now I find it hard to understand, let alone explain – there was something menacing about her, while at the same time there was something about her that made me look up to her. I knew straight away that I was scared of her, but I also liked the way she seemed to stick up for herself. I found myself thinking, *If she's my friend, no one's ever going to kick off against me*.

I hadn't doubted her authority from the moment she'd spoken that first time in the bedroom, and I wouldn't doubt it for a long time.

We spoke for an hour or more. She told the two of us how she'd beaten girls up at school, and lads, and how she was so hard that she had to have a social worker. She wouldn't take crap from anyone, she said, and I could see that she meant it.

'Milly's at your school isn't she? You know her?'

I nodded.

'Yeah – threw her down the stairs a while back. Thought she was someone.'

Beside me, Courtney, usually so bubbly, seemed to have gone into her shell.

The conversation ended abruptly when Emma's mobile rang. 'Yeah, coming now,' she said into the phone and, a moment later, she was gone, sweeping up her handbag and heading for the front door.

Courtney and I watched her climb into the back of the cab, a red Toyota. I noticed it had a sign on the side that said it was from a company called Streamline. In the months to come I'd see it a lot.

'Wow,' Courtney breathed, once she'd gone.

'Yeah, I know. Scary, eh?'

'You bet,' Courtney replied, still quiet, quieter than I'd ever known her.

In the silence I tried to fathom this strange new person in my life. If you've ever seen the film, *This is England*, you've had a glimpse of Emma. She wasn't psychotic, not like the shaven-headed guy in the film running the gang of skinheads, but she still carried that sense of menace. Like him, it wasn't always so much what she said as how she actually said it. And, like him, she knew she had a reputation that made people scared. You just felt all the time that she was on the verge of kicking off, even if she wasn't.

There's a scene in *This is England* where the hard guy cries – over a girl, I think. But not Emma. Over the next seven months that I got to know her, I never saw any soft side in her. I'd see her get mad plenty of times, but not upset: never upset. At times she'd rant like she had Tourette's, not so bad that she'd scream, but pretty close. I would also come to realise that she had the kind of look your mum and dad give you when you're little to stop you doing something – as a kid you know that look, and when it comes you can't do anything but obey it. In Emma's case, though, it didn't stop you doing something – it made you do something, even if you didn't want to. Added to this, her mood could switch as suddenly as a taxi light coming on, and it made her incredibly unsettling to be around. You just never knew where you were with her.

Maybe it was that that drew me in, and made me look up to her in some weird kind of way. You could be mates with her, yes, but only on her terms – you had to be scared of her, too. I for one called her by her proper name, never her nickname. Braver kids than me called her the name that fitted her best: the Honey Monster, though it was always behind her back.

The next time we saw her, she said she'd been out partying and chilling with some of her Asian mates. A friend of hers, Roxanne, had been with her and they'd had 'a massive good time'. It only added to her allure for me. I was hypnotised by her, dangerously so.

* * *

Once I'd moved into this house of horrors, I actually found myself settling into the madness of what was beginning to feel like a chaotic version of home. I didn't want to go back to Mum and Dad. Although this place was pretty dreary, I loved the freedom – and the sense that, finally, at fifteen, I could be somewhere where I felt less hassled, less put upon. My very own, independent me.

I hadn't actually heard from my parents. Maybe they didn't mind, or else they were giving me the space to be a teenager. *About time*, I thought, though at the back of my mind, for all the people and wonderful chaos around me, I felt a little lonely, a little confused at times.

Emma and I talked again, her telling me of all the places she knew and all the friends she had. She talked about having an Asian boyfriend and lots of Asian friends. She seemed to know so many people.

As I hung around with her more, I realised the sense of menace about her didn't go away. You just knew that she wasn't a girl to cross. Irresistibly, I was drawn evermore to the way she seemed to have so much control; I felt I was beginning to bond with her, like you do with a new best mate.

I ended up staying at Harry's place for longer than I'd anticipated. I suppose I'd effectively run away from home, without actually really realising it. I preferred living as an outcast at Harry's place to being at home – and, anyway, I knew my mum and dad didn't want me with them (or so I thought).

I had no money, but that didn't matter. For all the dirt and the fleas, there was always food and beer to be had, and

Harry always seemed happy to buy more when it ran out. There were no rules at Harry's, and no one seemed to mind what I did.

One time, when Emma wasn't in, a couple of lads started telling me to watch out 'because she slept with Asians'. I thought they just meant she had an Asian boyfriend, so I ignored it. *She can do what she wants*, I thought. It didn't affect me. And what was wrong with dating an Asian guy? Nothing. I knew some Asian people in the area had the reputation of seeing English girls as 'cheap' due to the fact that we went drinking, and wore the clothes we wanted to, but I knew they were a minority. I did worry about attracting attention from these guys, though, as it could get ugly when it happened – I'd seen it, on the streets. So I just thought these lads were small-minded and didn't really know what they were talking about. I chose to stay quiet.

* * *

For all that it was weird and chaotic, I was becoming attached to Harry's place – relishing the freedom it gave me. I'd started to go home every few days, partly to say hello, partly to get bits of washing done or else collect fresh clothes. Even though Mum accepted that I'd effectively left home, she was still happy enough to do my laundry.

I'd been at Harry's a couple of weeks when Emma asked me to go out with her one night. Well, not so much asked: more like told. But I still felt proud: made up, in fact. We had a ball, swaggering around town, chatting about nothing and everything, and drinking cider, as usual, from Lucozade bottles.

We ended up sitting on a wall outside Dunne's store, swinging our legs, drinking, laughing whenever a taxi driver went by and tooted his horn. One driver actually stopped and then wound down his window to speak.

'Hi, Emma,' he said, and then, glancing at me: 'A new friend? Want a lift anywhere?'

'No, thanks,' she replied with a wink. 'We're walking tonight.'

It seemed an odd exchange, but I thought no more about it. I felt good being with Emma, despite her bossing me about. It was like she understood. We'd both somehow ended up living at the same place, after all. Maybe we had more in common than I thought? Kindred spirits, trying to find a little bit of happiness in an otherwise dreary world. At Harry's place and with each other, we had the freedom we craved. Freedom like I'd never known before.

Chapter Six
Tick, Tick, Tick

It was the start of the school summer holidays, and I'd woken late at Harry's place, hung over, with a vague plan to spend the day watching TV and not much else.

Courtney had been staying there for a while, but she'd recently left soon after the night she and Emma had staggered in at around 5 a.m., Courtney stinking from the cider someone had poured over her. 'Someone' being Emma, I'd guessed, although Ricky had said, all mysterious, that it had something to do with some Asian men. That maybe Courtney had slept with some. 'Don't be stupid,' I'd told him. 'Courtney wouldn't do that.' The way he had said 'some' made it sound dangerous, and I knew Courtney would have walked away from a set-up like that.

Courtney had seemed upset, but wouldn't talk about it. I thought it strange because she was usually so up for everything. Not that day, obviously.

Anyway, this particular morning Emma came into my room, or rather the room I was dossing down in at the time, and said, 'Hey, let's go into town. We can go somewhere they'll give us free food and stuff, probably beer. You'll love it.'

It sounded vaguely familiar, so I asked her the name of the place she was thinking of.

'The Balti House,' she said.

I knew by then that Daddy had switched to the Balti House from Tasty Bites, and that he seemed to have a better job there; a more important one. I thought back to all the chicken tikkas and doners, the vodka, the dancing on the mattress at Tasty Bites, and decided it could be really cool. But then ... 'It'll be closed,' I said. 'It's only ever open in the evenings.'

Emma looked pleased at that. 'Maybe to the rest of Heywood, but not to me,' she said, smiling. 'We'll get in.'

I was impressed. 'Sounds good,' I said. 'OK if I ring Courtney?'

'Whatever,' she replied.

I didn't mention Emma when I rang. I just asked Courtney if she fancied going somewhere for some free beer and food. She didn't have to be asked twice.

I was hungry, and increasingly looking for some excitement. I got dressed as quickly as I could, Emma got ready too, and we headed towards town to pick Courtney up at her house.

Oddly, Courtney blushed when she opened the door and saw Emma, and looked really uncomfortable. I gave her a look, as if to say, 'What's up? What's all this about?' but she looked away.

The three of us walked into town, Emma and I laughing and joking, me saying how funny Daddy was, how he'd given us loads of food and things in the old days at Tasty

Bites. I was wearing pretty much what I always wore back then: jeans, a little vest top and my favourite black jacket I'd bought on Bury Market. Velour, I think it was. God, how I loved it!

The steel shutters were down at the front of the Balti House, but Emma shouted up to one of the windows above. This, it seemed, was how she knew it wouldn't be a problem to get into the Balti while it was closed: 'Chef' who, unsurprisingly, was the chef at the restaurant, lived at the place. He leaned out, a big, bearded bloke, and told us to go round the back so he could let us in. It sounded like something he and Emma had done before.

We walked in, three teenage girls, one big, two of us small to medium, through the back door and into Heywood's worst takeaway. You can probably imagine the smell that greeted us as we walked in: stale *ghee*, rendered fat, from the night before, and a sweaty takeaway chef who'd thrown on some clothes and a smile but hadn't showered.

Chef seemed like he was on a high. He beckoned us in, arms extended, hands waving, and sat us down at a table. The three of us found ourselves seated on little white, plastic chairs set around the table. That was white, too, round, and there was no cloth on it, just a few smears of grease. It was set against the kitchen wall, looking back onto the cooking rings, the sink and the clay oven. There was a set of stairs off to one side, heading up to where Chef had come from. The floor of the kitchen was tiled, with bits of food scattered about on it: lettuce, more splodges of grease, a bit of chicken. Everywhere was just a bit minging, really.

Chef was kind of the same. He had put a white apron on over his jeans and T-shirt, but it was stained with food and as greasy as the rest of his kitchen.

I began to feel a bit nervous, like we shouldn't be there.

On the other side of the kitchen wall was the front-of-house. It was the bit I'd known before from coming in to order there. It had a counter where they had the takeaway menus for people to look at to order from, and the glass-fronted display cabinet, where they kept naff cans of drink. There was a portable TV, too, so customers could see what was happening in *Coronation Street*, *EastEnders*, or whatever.

Once Chef had sat us down, he asked whether we'd like something to eat. Emma said yes, and I flashed a smile at her, thinking, *Yeah, this is working. It's just like Tasty Bites.*

Chef, still seeming a bit high – he was singing as he cooked – went over to the fridge, and then to the burners, where he started heating up some chicken tikka. I guessed it had been left over from the night before, but so what, I was starving, and anyway, he went to the fridge and pulled out some garlic mayonnaise to go with it. Happy days. When the food arrived, there was pilau rice, too, and a couple of chapattis.

We were still eating when he opened a drawer, pulled out a DVD and put it into the TV combo they had back there. When the TV in the kitchen came to life, it wasn't showing *Coronation Street*, nothing like it. Instead, the screen filled with the writhing bodies of a porn DVD. It was hardcore, too, with white men having sex with Asian girls.

It made me squirm because I'd never seen anything like it before. I tried to ignore what was on the screen, and I could sense Courtney doing the same. But Emma seemed to love it.

I was feeling more nervous by the second. Worse, Chef, who must have been in his forties, started trying to touch us up, all three of us, laughing as he did so. He was half watching the porn and either half talking to us or trying to touch us – our boobs, our legs, anywhere his oily hands could reach. At one point he said I was pretty, and then, horribly: 'Today is pay day. I'm going to have sex with you all!'

He made it sound like a joke, but I still thought it was horrid. So did Courtney. Emma just burst out laughing and, for all my nerves and shock, I found myself giggling along with her. Part of me thought it was OK because he'd said I was pretty. I knew it was wrong, but I was full of the sense of excitement, too. It felt like living on the edge.

But enough was enough. Courtney and I asked Emma to tell him to stop touching us, but she just replied, 'It's all right, he won't hurt you.' So we sat there, fending him off whenever he approached. We'd had enough practise in school at fending off boys; this didn't feel any different.

After a while, Emma walked over to him and they had a quiet conversation next to the fridge. When she came back, she said they were going to call Daddy and ask him to bring some drinks.

I actually relaxed a bit when I heard that. *I know Daddy*, I thought. *Maybe he'll stop Chef messing around.*

Weirdly, when Emma made the call, she sounded really excited. 'I've got Hannah here,' she breathed into the phone. 'I've got Hannah here! Now!'

It seemed strange. Why should she be so excited to tell him I was there when I'd not seen him for six months? Looking back, it was the excitement in her voice that should have warned me.

I'm guessing now, but I can't help thinking that she'd told him I was staying at her house and that he'd asked for me. They must have come up with the plan together, but I was the last one to know. God, how naïve.

He came in through the back door, all smiles, all happy. Emma seemed equally pleased to see him, smirking like the cat she was. He asked Courtney and me if he could have a hug. When it came to my turn he held me that little bit longer, saying he remembered me and had missed me. I just muttered 'Hi', a little embarrassed.

He'd brought vodka with him and we had a glass each, just the three of us girls and those two men, one in his forties, the other, Daddy, in his fifties, all sitting together at the table.

They weren't drinking because they're Muslims and they don't. Most Muslim people I have met are very strict like that. Emma poured the drinks and went to the fridge for some cola. The vodka, like before, was Glen's: a litre bottle.

'How have you been?' Daddy asked. 'How's your mum? Are you still living at home? How are your holidays? Will you be back to school in September?'

I felt a sense of relief that the conversation was back on track as something a bit more normal; something I could deal with. Plus, Chef had started to behave himself once Daddy arrived. The TV was turned off and he seemed to calm down.

'The holidays are great,' I told him. 'I'm living at Emma's now. It's cool.'

'And which year are you in next term?' he asked.

'Eleven,' I replied. 'With GCSEs in all the things I hate!'

Emma poured me another vodka, then another. I noticed that Courtney wasn't drinking like she'd normally do; in fact, she looked a bit down. I gave her a friendly dig in the ribs, to try to cheer her up. She didn't seem to notice. Daddy was as chatty and jolly as I remembered him from Tasty Bites. I started to relax, then to get tipsy. Emma lifted the bottle and poured again.

The room was beginning to spin when Emma suddenly said she was going upstairs with Chef and, a moment later, they were gone. Then Daddy looked over at me and said he wanted me to go upstairs, too – for a chat, he said. He was laughing as he said it, and still sounding dead happy.

Even through my vodka haze, I wasn't sure. I asked Courtney if she'd come with me, but she didn't seem bothered and, anyway, Daddy didn't want her to. 'No,' he smiled, 'she'll have to stay here because I want to speak to you in private.'

I still thought it was odd, but curiosity and politeness got the better of me – I didn't want him to think I was being funny with him by not going. Plus, I'd spent so much time with Daddy before I didn't think there was anything to worry about. At the back of my mind, too, I was thinking,

Emma's up there and Courtney's here, so I'll be fine. I had a momentary flashback to the time at Tasty Bites with Elouise, but pushed it to the back of my mind.

And so I climbed the staircase. I just went upstairs with him.

There was an empty, disused freezer on the landing, and some Asian-style pictures on the wall. Emma had gone into the room on the left; Daddy put a hand on my hip and guided me to the one on the right.

Daddy, this family man in his fifties, the one I'd always felt I could trust, opened the door for me and told me to go in. Then he walked in behind me and closed the door.

There was nothing in the room apart from a mattress on the floor with blue, crumpled sheets, and a pink clock, high up on the wall to one side.

Daddy told me to sit down on the mattress. As I did so, he stayed on his feet. I tried to feel reassured by that, but as soon as I sank into it and smelt the stale air wafting up from the sheet, I felt suddenly dwarfed by him; felt, too, the stirrings of a fear that will haunt me for ever.

Dimly, I noticed that the next-door room was silent. No conversation. Just silence. Almost like somebody was listening.

Even now Daddy was still looking happy. 'When are you going to let me have sex with you?' he asked merrily, a big cheeky smile on his face. I tried to answer in the same way, laughing. I thought he was joking, that I could handle it. 'I'm not, Daddy,' I giggled.

And that's when he started to talk about all the things he'd given me for free at Tasty Bites: the vodka, the cigarettes, the chicken tikkas, the kebabs ... and how I should repay him.

'It's part of the deal, Hannah,' he said, as he smiled at me. I suddenly realised that he sounded sinister, like someone I didn't know: had never known. And he went on. 'I buy you things, you give me things,' he said. 'I've bought you vodka. Now it's your turn to give something to me.'

My heart froze as I realised what he meant. I knew then, knew without a shred of doubt, that he was more dangerous than anyone I had ever met; I knew that he meant to hurt me.

Instinctively, I just kept saying, 'What do you mean? What do you mean?' I tried to say it with a giggle, trying to fend him off in a jokey way. But the drink had made me slur my words. He could tell I was panicking, but he didn't seem to care. He just kept telling me I had to pay him back, and all the time he was coming closer.

'We're friends,' he was saying, 'and friends do things for each other.'

By now there was an aggression in his voice that I'd never heard before, a nastiness – as if he'd decided there was no further point in playing at being jolly. There were no smiles either. Instead, I could feel an anger building up in him as I carried on saying no.

I didn't know what to do. I knew he wanted to have sex with me, but I didn't want to with him because he was old. Much, much older than me. But nor did I want to say no, because I'd look soft to Emma.

I just kept trying to laugh it off so he'd leave me alone. I didn't think to try to beat him off because he was so big compared to me, and I had no idea what he would do. Would he beat me up? Kill me? And I didn't want to scream as I knew Emma would hear, and might get angry with me. And then, in the midst of the surge of my rising panic and the fear freezing my veins, I suddenly realised what had happened: that Emma had deliberately led me into a trap and I knew, without doubt, that if I resisted the monster looming over me, Emma would batter me, or maybe worse, much worse.

I just had no idea just how sickening a trap it would prove to be.

Daddy was still talking, saying, 'Go on, go on, you've got to pay me back.' I was still sitting up, rigid, but then he reached over and started to push me down.

'Come on, it's not fair,' he was saying. 'I've got you all this stuff, you've got to.' Then he was pulling on my jeans, unbuttoning them, pulling them down, and putting them and my knickers on the floor.

'No, no, no,' I started to repeat, over and over. I started crying, but he just kept pushing my legs open. I couldn't move, I couldn't breathe. All I could do was keep saying 'no'.

And then he forced himself onto me, his beaded, pungent brow close to mine, saying, 'Shh, shh!' I told him it was hurting, and I was sobbing, but it didn't stop him. I remember the tears pouring down my face, but I couldn't scream because my throat had closed up so tight with fear. Instead, I screamed the sort of scream that could find no release but reverberated around my brain. On and on it went, silently, propelling the tears that were running into my mouth and down my neck.

All the time he was saying, 'Don't cry,' and 'You're beautiful,' and 'I love you.' And because I couldn't look at him, wouldn't look at this old man attacking a girl in a sordid box room in Heywood, I stared desperately instead at the clock and the serene, beautiful angel who couldn't protect me, as the second hand carried on ticking around and around.

Chapter Seven
New Girl

Once Daddy had raped me, he sat up on his knees, wiped away a smear of blood – my blood – then buttoned up his trousers and left the room.

I felt a desperate feeling I'd never known before, my body torn and aching from what he'd done to me. Being with Elliot earlier in the summer had felt clumsy and bewildering, but this? This felt totally alien, like someone had reached inside me and torn out my soul. I couldn't move; I just stared at the sheet below me, the tacky, dirty one, now stained with tiny droplets of red. My mind was numb, frozen, unable to comprehend the enormity of having been raped.

I hadn't moved by the time Daddy returned, bringing with him some tissue for me. I stretched out a hand, eyes averted, mascara running down my face, and a moment later was reclaiming my knickers and pulling my jeans up as quickly as I could.

He just said, 'Don't cry,' and then, again, that he loved me. Then he gave me either a £10 or a £20 note. I think it was £10. As he handed it to me he said, 'This is for you because I love you. You're my special girl now.'

I still didn't understand what had just happened. I knew that I'd been raped but I was confused. From the things he was saying, it seemed as though nothing had happened and it was just normal. To this day I don't know why, but I stuffed the note into my pocket.

I felt sick and dirty, loathing him for what he'd done to me, and loathing myself for not fighting him off, for not dying in the attempt. How could he have said all those things to me – 'Don't cry' and 'You're beautiful' – when it was obvious I hated what he was doing the entire time he was raping me?

It was as though he didn't know he'd done anything wrong. I couldn't get my head straight: I knew he'd forced me, but then, after trying to push him off, I'd just lain there – I'd reasoned I would be safer that way. So now, afterwards, I was thinking, *Was it rape or wasn't it? He obviously doesn't think so from the way he is acting.*

Daddy told me we'd go downstairs. Courtney was still sitting at the kitchen table, just as she had been those few minutes earlier. And so were Emma and Chef.

It was obvious that I'd been crying, and I tried to give Courtney an imploring look so she could help me. But, weirdly, my friend of old wouldn't look at me. Daddy, however, wasn't having any of it. He gave me a look like thunder that sent a chill through me.

I looked at Emma but she just started laughing. She knew I'd been raped, but she actually found it funny. She seemed to be gloating. The thought seared through my mind, *What kind of monster is she?* And no sooner than the thought had formed, I felt a new fear building up inside.

Whatever Courtney may have been thinking, she said nothing. I think she knew it was best to keep quiet because of the way the other two were behaving. She looked almost as scared as me. Distantly, at the back of my mind, I wondered why.

We'd been back in the kitchen for about ten minutes when Daddy ordered us into what turned out to be his own car, a silver Honda Accord, so we could go and collect Immy, his 'nephew', who was due to work a shift at the takeaway that night. He was smiling as he said it, but I knew there was a veiled threat in every word he spoke.

Daddy came from Oldham, and that's where Immy lived, too. All three of us girls sat in the back, me wedged in behind Daddy, next to Emma. I was still trying to grapple with what had happened to me upstairs at the Balti House.

Emma had brought the last of the vodka with her and now offered me a swig. I didn't want it, but I drank some anyway, recoiling at the taste but wanting the effect it would bring, hoping it would start to relieve the feelings of sickness and revulsion that were coursing through me.

Then the girl I'd felt was becoming my best mate turned to Courtney and told her how Chef had given her £20 so he could go down on her. 'Sad fucker,' she said.

I couldn't help but imagine the scene: her, sprawled, fat and leery on a bed in the room next to the one in which Daddy had raped me. I realised then that the things I'd heard about Emma were true – that she did go with lots of men, and, worse, that she'd let someone as greasy as Chef slaver all over her just to get £20 from him. The dawning realisation horrified me.

Again I tried to catch Courtney's eye, but each time she'd look away. Feeling terribly alone, I drank some more of the vodka.

As we came into the main Asian district of Oldham, we pulled up at some traffic lights. There were two lanes, and as Daddy looked across at the car next to him he recognised the people inside. There were four of them, all men.

'Shady!' one of them shouted, his arm resting on the open window frame. I'd never heard Daddy called that before, but suddenly it fitted. It suited this new version of the man I'd once trusted. 'Three girls, eh?' the man went on. 'You must be doing all right!'

Daddy laughed, and Emma did too. She was still holding the bottle of Glen's, and held it out towards the guys in the car, whooping like she was at the best party ever.

I could only think, *Is this real?*

The lights were just changing when the chatty guy looked over at me, pale, and so obviously young, sitting in the back seat. 'New girl, eh?' he asked.

'Yeah,' said Daddy. 'I'll give you a ring.'

It was then that I dimly began to realise that my personal hell was only just beginning.

A few minutes later, we were picking Immy up from the fruit stall he worked on in a local market and heading off back to the Balti House. Immy was thin, in his twenties, with a pinched, mean-looking face. He sat in the front, and he and Daddy chatted in a language I had no way of understanding.

I wanted to run away screaming, but it felt as though I had nowhere to run to. And Emma made doubly sure I didn't leave: she turned towards me and whispered, 'So, what will your mum and dad think of their lovely little daughter now? Shagging a Paki, eh? They wouldn't want to hear that, would they?'

For the rest of the journey I felt a relentless, creeping sense of self-loathing. I convinced myself that Mum and Dad wouldn't want to know me. They'd see the fact that I had 'allowed' this to happen as the final straw. I knew – or at least thought I knew – exactly what they'd be like. In my mind's eye, as we sped through that alien town, I could see them saying it: 'You've brought it all on yourself. We told you, we kept telling you – and now this. People will just look at you and think, "Slag." You shouldn't have been there in the first place. They obviously wanted something from you, otherwise they wouldn't have kept giving you free things. What did you expect them to do?'

In the emotional haze that engulfed me after the rape, I couldn't see that I was the victim in all of this, and that for all their misgivings about my behaviour, Mum and Dad would have wanted to help me, to protect me. True, they'd come to despair of me, and it felt to me they were as happy as I was that I'd seemingly left home. But they were still the people who'd given me life; they were still my parents. I wanted to throw open the car door and run to them. But the shame of what had happened to me, and my growing sense of failure, wouldn't let me. Instead, I closed my eyes, suppressing the sickness I felt in my stomach, crushed between the car door and Emma's podgy, immoveable thigh.

I was trapped. I had nowhere to run.

* * *

In the space of a few hours, my whole life had become a surreal nightmare. I wanted to wake up. I wanted to know that it wasn't the conscious me that was in such pain and fear.

I was still confused by the way Daddy and Emma were behaving. It made me wonder whether what had happened to me *was* normal. Everybody seemed to be acting like nothing had happened at all.

Back at the Balti House, Daddy – the new Daddy – told Emma to take me upstairs and to send Courtney home.

'Please don't go,' I begged her, looking pleadingly at Courtney, just as I'd done in the car. 'Please.'

Courtney bit her lip, nervously, looking from me to Emma. In that single, awful moment she looked desolate, but before she could speak, Emma started shouting, telling her to leave.

Courtney seemed terrified of Emma as well, so she took what she must have seen as her only opportunity to bolt, leaving me all alone. Emma turned to me and gave me that look she had.

'You're staying,' she spat.

I wanted to run but I couldn't move. I didn't feel I could argue. By now, all the fight, all the spark, had gone out of me. I was numb, too confused and tired to even think straight.

We sat upstairs for what seemed like hours. At one point, Emma leaned her huge frame towards me and in a low, menacing whisper said: 'You'll do what I tell you from now on, OK? You know what they'll think at home. It won't be rape to them. They'll think you loved it. They'll think you loved being shagged by a guy even older than your dad.' She paused, then said, 'A bit like Courtney the other night. Remember? When she came back with cider all over her?' My mind fought groggily to remember, and I nodded dumbly. 'Stick with me now, though, and you'll be fine. I'll look after you. All you have to do is do what I say. You can carry on living at Harry's; you'll still get to eat and we won't even make you pay rent. I might even give you some money.'

I was too frozen with fear to reply. Instead, I nodded slowly, my eyes lowered to the floor, avoiding the gaze I knew was bearing down on me. Inside, I shivered, and wondered about Courtney and what she, too, may have been through.

The takeaway opened at 5 p.m. and they gave us more food and more vodka. I drank it silently, just praying for this nightmare to end.

At about 11 p.m., Daddy came upstairs and told us to go to his car. 'We're going to a party,' he said. His words reignited my fear. Why didn't they just let me go?

They led me outside and I joined Emma on the back seat. What did they have in store for me now?

* * *

We headed off to a flat that I think was somewhere in Oldham, but in a different area to the one we'd been to before. We pulled up outside a nondescript-looking house, and an Asian man opened the door.

It seemed we were expected because as soon as we arrived, Daddy started pulling me into a bedroom.

I knew what was coming, or at least I thought I did, and I started trying to talk him out of it. 'We did something earlier,' I whispered. 'We don't need to do it again.' I was so frightened I even said, 'We'll do it another day.' Anything to try to keep him away.

But it wasn't just Daddy I had to fend off this time. Emma joined in, persuading me, forcing me to do what he wanted. She said she'd come in with me, and then started pushing me through the doorway as he pulled. I tried to resist, but then she shouted: 'Just get in the fucking bedroom and get it over with!' For a few seconds the three of us were in the room together, but as soon as Daddy told Emma to get out she turned on her heel.

'I thought you were going to stay,' I said.

She shrugged and reached for the door handle. 'Well, sorry, but I'm not,' she said over her shoulder.

With Emma gone, and the door closed, Daddy took off his trousers, sat down on the bed and looked up at me. 'It's time to give Daddy a blow job, Hannah,' he said matter-of-factly, like he was asking for a cigarette or something.

Instinct took over and I reverted to what I'd done previously. 'No,' I giggled, trying to make sure I didn't make him angry. Maybe I could make him feel guilty; he'd remember how well we got on?

But it was no good.

I hated what he made me do then even more than earlier, because it somehow felt more intimate. I was choking and crying but still he didn't seem bothered. He just kept a steel grip on my head. Eventually, he pushed me away and told me to lie down. Through the fear I sobbed. 'But I'm only fifteen,' I whimpered.

He wasn't fazed at all. He just looked me in the eye and said, 'It doesn't matter. Where I come from, I can have sex with girls who are eleven.'

I didn't know if that was true or not. But it horrified me. Instantly, my heart went out to any girl who had to endure what I was going through at such a young age.

I tried to get dressed again, tried to regain some dignity, but Daddy wasn't done. 'No, Mulla is coming in now,' he revealed.

Mulla? Another man? My throat tightened. I couldn't take any more.

'No, please!' I begged. 'I've just done it with you.' Daddy shook his head and stroked my head like I was a sleeping baby. 'Shh,' he breathed. My stomach churned as every inch of me trembled with fear.

Mulla, in his forties, with a black moustache, smiled as he entered the room. He could see that I was crying, that mascara had left smudges on my cheeks, but the smile stayed in place. He just didn't care either. He and Daddy laughed and joked for about thirty seconds, before Daddy walked out. I could tell roughly what it was about because of the smutty looks on their faces and the way they both kept glancing towards me. But the detail passed me by because it was all in their own language – Mirpuri, I discovered later on. Much later.

My jeans were still on the floor because I'd had no time to retrieve them. In Mulla's sick mind it just made it easier. This time, I didn't do anything to resist the attack because I felt it would make no difference: he'd get what he wanted one way or another and it would just prolong my agony. Instead, I bit my lip and turned my face away from his leering smile.

As he raped me I could feel him touching my chest, my still-flat chest.

When he finally allowed me out of the bedroom, Emma looked up, then glanced over to Daddy and asked: 'Right, are you finished now? Are we going?'

'Yeah,' he replied and, within moments, me in a daze, we were heading towards the car. Once inside, Daddy gave Emma £30 and she turned towards me, handing me a £10 note.

'Get yourself some fags,' she said, breezily.

So that was it: Emma had given me to two paedophiles, and now she was handing me money as some sick kind of compensation. In the front of the car, on the way home, the two of them – Emma and Daddy – chatted away as if nothing had happened. I spent the journey wiping away tears with the back of my hand.

Back at Harry's place, she closed the front door and headed off to bed, telling me she'd see me in the morning. I stood in the hallway, still in shock. It was gone one o'clock in the morning and I felt broken and dirty beyond anything I had ever known. I wanted to have a shower, to scrub the filth of those two men away from my body. But my strength, my will, had gone, and instead I just slipped into bed beside the girl I was sharing with.

She was only about eight, and part of me wanted to snuggle up next to her. But I felt too dirty. I just lay there, gripping the very edge of my side of the bed, the duvet up to my shoulders, my body aching, looking at the darkening shadows on the wall.

I knew that life would never be the same again. My spirit had been shattered. Somehow, a girl just a few months older than me had sold me to perverts who wanted to have some depraved version of sex with me. I couldn't understand the motives of either. I couldn't work out how to escape. All I knew was that I felt exhausted and unclean.

A temporary escape finally came to me: sleep. I dreamed I was caught in a spider's web, held in the middle of it by threads, each silky and thin but with a grip like steel. Every time I tried to break free, I was pulled back, slowly, reluctantly, inevitably, by the spider that wanted to consume me.

* * *

Lying in bed the following morning, sore, aching, the images from the night before wouldn't leave me. As I watched a lone flea negotiate its way along the coverless duvet, I realised that, just as in the dream, I was trapped, and there was nowhere for me to hide.

Trying to go home wasn't an option now. Until I'd been raped, first by Daddy, then by Mulla, I'd hated home, I'd wanted to be a rebel, and I'd wanted to be free. But was this freedom? No, it was a trap – a spider's web in which I was the fly. I couldn't go home, I realised, not ever, and least of all now that Emma held this sick secret over me. Oh, I might still be able to pop back to see Mum and Dad and my brothers and sisters, but never again with the freedom of knowing I could actually stay. I could never now fit back into normal family life. I felt I was tainted, that I was an outcast, different. Instead, I would be for ever linked to Harry's place, and to Daddy, by the near-invisible threads being pulled by Emma. Hannah, the free spirit, the teenage rebel, was now a prisoner. Lying there, reluctant to face the day, I suddenly realised that with Emma controlling my life, Harry's house was going to become a hell of its own.

* * *

I had, perhaps, one hope. Over my first couple of weeks there, Harry had become a real father figure to me. With my own dad suddenly out of my life, I felt I could get on with him. In the early days he didn't say much, but gradually he'd include me in conversation and I came to feel part of the household. I thought it was really cool that he bought vodka and cider for us, and let us come in and go out whenever we wanted.

There were times, usually in the day, when he'd have long chats with me and maybe Emma. By then, Courtney had stopped coming by. It didn't feel like she was my friend any more; we'd drifted apart. Instead, at least at weekends, there was another of Emma's friends, Roxanne, who was thirteen. Roxanne had been coming to the house for ages so they all knew her.

Part of me wanted to tell Harry what had happened to me, but I didn't dare because of Emma. She warned me the morning after those first rapes not to say anything. It would be our secret, she said, and, anyway, Harry was never going to believe me if I said I'd been raped.

So for all that I'd speak to Harry, and try to take comfort just from him being there, I didn't dare confide in him.

Chapter Eight
Emma's Lying

Daddy had moved quickly in taking me to Mulla, and now Emma did likewise. Within a couple of days, my rapist's little blue car pulled up outside Harry's just before 7 p.m. and she led me out to it. Afraid, I did as I was told and squeezed into the back, while she sat next to Daddy in the front.

He dropped us off outside the Balti House, telling us to go round the back while he collected some curries from the kitchen and delivered them.

We were sitting on the stairs when he returned ten minutes later. Smiling benignly, as if the last few days had never happened, he held out another bottle of vodka, some cola and a couple of glasses.

'Here,' he said. 'Don't look so sad, Hannah. This will cheer you up.'

It didn't, of course. It couldn't. But sitting there, one step below Emma, I put the glass she'd poured for me to my lips and sipped. I'd never liked the taste. Now I liked it even less.

He brought us some food, too. Immy had been working front of house when we'd arrived, but the takeaway was quiet enough for him to join us, and for a few minutes

Daddy and he were talking to each other. I'm guessing now that they were deciding what to do with us. All the time, I was nervously sipping the vodka, Emma refilling my glass every time.

It was a litre bottle and we'd had about half each by the time Immy came up to us. He started trying to hold me, his hands roaming around my top and leggings. Everything was getting a bit hazy when Daddy came up onto the staircase to join us.

Once again, he started to talk about the treats he'd given us, meaning the vodka, and that I should give Immy a treat in return. He kept saying it was his birthday present. He said we'd just go upstairs and chill for a bit.

I should have tried to push my way past them and headed to the front of the takeaway and out of the door past the customers I guessed would be there, ordering or collecting their takeaways, oblivious to the sort of place this was. But I didn't. I just did what Daddy told me. I was too frightened.

Emma and I went upstairs and into a different room from the one when Daddy had first violated me. There was a mattress on the floor in this room, covered with an orange quilt; a table and two chairs; and a window with scruffy beige curtains that were hanging from nails.

The two men joined us. Daddy continued to press the whole thing about the vodka and how it meant Immy deserved a treat. While he was talking, his nephew was touching me and trying to persuade me. I said I wanted to go, and reminded them that I was only fifteen. But it didn't matter to them: Daddy just kept saying that in his country they could have sex with girls as young as eleven. 'You've got to do it now,' said Daddy. 'It's too late; you're already upstairs. I gave you a treat, now you've got to give him a treat.' And Immy wanted his treat.

Daddy and Emma left, closing the door behind them as Immy moved in on me.

He told me to get onto the bed and take my leggings off, and when I said no he started to take them off me himself. He was much stronger than me: I kept trying to shut my legs, but he forced them open again. Eventually, I realised I had no option, that there was no escape. Even if I'd pushed him away and managed to get out of the bedroom, there was still Daddy downstairs, and Emma.

He was still forcing my legs open and pushing down on me, saying, 'Come on, please, you've got to do it now.'

In the end, I just lay there and let him do what he wanted. I realised dimly that the more I fought back, the longer it would take. The whole time, I just stared at the wall, trying to block it all out. When he'd finished, he just put his trousers back on and went downstairs, leaving me, in pain and in tears, on the bed. He'd worn no protection.

I was putting my clothes back on when Emma walked in.

'Come on,' she said brusquely, 'we can go now. I'll go and get some money for you.'

A few moments later she returned, handing me a £20 note. 'I got it off Daddy,' said my recruiter. 'For giving Immy his treat.'

As if that was going to make everything all right.

* * *

The whirlwind continued. Just one night later, Emma walked me into Market Street, supposedly just to have a drink. We were sitting on the steps of Dunne's store, a few yards from Morrison's, when Daddy drove into the car park and pulled up beside us.

At the time I had no idea how he knew we were there, but I know now: it would have been from a text from Emma, or a phone call.

'Get in,' he said.

'No,' I said, rediscovering the belligerent tone I'd used so often with Mum and Dad. Out of nowhere, I'd decided to stand my ground.

But it was pointless. 'Look, Hannah,' he said, leaning out of the open car window. 'You're my bitch now, and if you cross me someone might just kill you. So get in.'

In a moment, Emma had grabbed hold of me, her nails digging into my wrist, telling me it was for my own good and that I had to go with him.

'Listen to your friend,' said Daddy. She wasn't my friend, she was his! And so, finally, I climbed into the back of a car that normally bore trays of the Balti House's gloop-like curries.

I asked Daddy where he was taking me, and he said, 'We're just going for a drive.'

Emma asked him if he'd be heading back to the Morrison's car park. Yes, came the reply. 'Hannah, I'll wait for you,' she said.

Daddy drove for about five minutes: out past the Morrison's petrol pumps, up the Bamford Road for a while and then onto a side street. His headlights picked out a couple of buildings and a set of gates. The gates were open and he drove through, then parked on a little slope next to a garage.

There was nothing there beside an empty car park. Nothing beside Daddy and me. This time I was more frightened than ever, because it was the first time I'd ever been alone with him. At the back of my mind was the thought that if he wanted to kill me, here, now, he could do so and no one would be able to stop him.

He switched off the engine and got out, his shoes scrunching on the stone chippings beside the car, and climbed into the back seat with me. I was in the furthest corner of the back seat, as far away from him as I could get.

I was asking him if he was going to take me home. Yes, he said, but then came the inevitable: 'Are you going to have sex with me?'

I told him I didn't want to – that I wanted it all to stop. I wanted to go home. But he just glowered at me and said, 'You're going to have to, my special girl. Because if you don't, then maybe you'll be killed or your sisters raped. And if you try to go home, maybe one day your house will be burned down.'

With that, he shuffled towards me so he could begin making his sick moves on me.

His breath was as stale as the smell of *ghee* from the takeaway that had seeped into the car's upholstery. He took his jeans down and ordered me to use my mouth on him so he could get hard. I thought I was going to throw up because it tasted horrible. He grabbed hold of my hair so he could move my head up and down. Then he broke off and told me to lie down. I lay there, still, beneath him, and he knelt up and lifted my legs towards him. I begged him to take me home but it was no good. He just kept carrying on.

Partway through, he complained that he had too little room to do what he wanted and he ordered me to sit on top of him. I didn't want to. I'd never done that before, and I felt a further wave of embarrassment coursing through me.

As it happened, I felt more disgusted with myself than ever before, because doing it like that made me feel that I was the instigator, the one in control, the one who wanted the movement I detested so much. I tried to block out the thought, and the pain, as he laboured beneath me. But I couldn't.

Afterwards, he wiped himself, threw the tissue away and drove me back to the Morrison's car park where Emma – fat, violent Emma – was waiting for me, smirking.

The whole sordid episode had taken no more than twenty minutes. As I got out of the car, dishevelled and in tears, she asked where he'd taken me.

When I described it, she nodded. 'Yeah, I know it,' she said. 'Been there loads of times.'

* * *

I had a bath as soon as we got back to Harry's that night. The water was only tepid, but I was desperate to scrub away every trace of Daddy.

The next morning, I ran another bath. I was about to climb in when Emma called out, realised where I was, and walked into the bathroom. She hadn't bothered knocking, and there was no lock on the door to stop her, so in she came, lowered the loo seat cover and sat down.

She looked me up and down, a frown coming to her face. I was embarrassed because she was looking at my breasts, or rather the tiny bumps that still hadn't developed. Then she looked lower.

'You need to shave,' she said. 'Shave it all off. It'll make you look younger.'

She looked around for a razor and handed it to me, then some gel. While I was drying myself she checked it to make sure I'd got every hair.

'Make sure you do it every couple of days,' she said, and then she was gone. The whole episode, and the thoughts it brought into my mind, made me feel weird and scared at the same time.

* * *

I think that was the day she took my phone. Without it, I was even more helpless and even more dependent on her. There seemed to be no respite. Two days later, Daddy called for us and said we were going into Rochdale. He set off in that direction, but then Emma told him we'd have to go via Mum and Dad's house because I needed fresh knickers. 'She's not changed them since yesterday,' she said. 'She's run out.'

I went crimson – I had just kicked all my dirty clothes under the bed, not wanting to have to deal with them, or touch them, as they reminded me of what I had been through.

In the front, Daddy laughed and said: 'You'll need some clean knickers for tonight.'

He parked just down the street from my parents' house, and Emma and I walked up the pathway to the front door. It felt like the longest walk of my life as I struggled with my emotions. Dare I say anything to Mum and Dad? Should I try to stay? Or was my fate sealed? In the end, fear got the better of me.

'Just come for some make-up,' I said, still frightened, but probably just sounding like an everyday morose teenager to my family.

'Are you stopping?' asked Mum.

'No, we're off out again,' I replied, wishing for all the world that she and Dad would insist I stayed.

I desperately wanted a hug. I desperately wanted to escape.

Instead, I climbed the stairs with leaden feet and went into my bedroom, looking briefly out of one of the tiny slit windows that looked out onto the estate. Emma came with me, and waited while I changed into clean knickers. Two minutes later we were saying goodbye, and another couple of minutes after that we were back in Daddy's car and heading towards Rochdale.

At a set of traffic lights I leaned across to Emma, who was in the back seat with me, and asked where exactly we were going.

'We're going to Lateef's,' she said. 'At least, that's what he says he's called.'

Fearing what was coming, I told her I didn't want to. I pleaded with her not to make me. 'You've got to,' she said, her voice level. 'And, anyway, it'll be me he'll be having sex with – not you.'

We drove for about twenty minutes, with me getting ever more nervous. Had Emma really meant it about it just being her? Could I ever believe her now, after she'd handed me over to men who had raped me?

We pulled up outside a grey, characterless block of flats. There was a man, tall, about forty, wearing traditional kurta clothes, waiting outside. Instead of inviting us in, he spoke quickly to Daddy and then climbed into the front passenger seat. Daddy then drove to a rank of shops around the corner. The man, presumably Lateef, got out and returned a few minutes later with a bottle of vodka. As usual, it was a litre of Glen's.

Back at the flats, Lateef led us upstairs. He had a big moustache and the thickset build of a boxer. I felt intimidated by him, even though he didn't speak beyond telling us his name or, more likely, nickname.

I knew what was coming and felt petrified. Emma was just giggling.

The flat had a buzzer that was answered by a thin, wrinkled old man with thin grey hair and a moustache. He looked about sixty and was pulling up his trousers, traditional Asian ones called *shalwar*, as he answered the door.

There was a white girl with him who looked around seventeen. She was tall and skinny with bleach-blonde hair that she wore up. I'm guessing they'd come out of the bedroom – she was kissing him as we walked into the living room. It looked perverted to see such a young girl kissing someone as old as him.

The old man offered us some weed. Emma took a joint, but I didn't want one. I'd tried it once, but it had scared me. The two of us sat together while the men spoke to each other in their own language. The other girl barely spoke to anyone. I think she was high on weed. I never did get to know her name.

I reasoned that the vodka would help numb the pain of this latest encounter, and, as usual, I wasn't wrong.

We'd been drinking for nearly an hour when Daddy stood up and told me to go to the bedroom with him. 'I need to speak to you,' he said.

He knew he was going to rape me, and I knew too. I just hoped the vodka would make it easier to bear. Once in the room, he told me what I knew he would: that I had to have sex with him again, and if I didn't, he'd leave me there, miles from home and probably much, much worse.

'But Emma said you'd leave me alone,' I said, more in desperation than anything else. He just smirked. 'Emma's lying,' he chuckled. 'You have to do it.'

Then he started pulling my leggings down. I was crying, saying, 'Just leave me alone, I don't want to do it any more.' He said I had to, and he raised his hand. I thought I had no choice.

There was a mattress on the floor again, which reminded me of the box room in which he'd first attacked me. But this time I had more to endure, because while I awaited my inevitable fate he took off every shred of his own clothing.

His nakedness made it even worse than before because it meant I could feel his skin on my skin. He was incredibly hairy, not just on his chest, but on his stomach, his legs, everywhere.

I felt him breathing on me. He was saying, 'Do it like you mean it,' and 'You're supposed to be my bitch.' He told me to touch him. I tried to block it all out but I couldn't. I felt so dirty.

Like the last time, he'd worn nothing – no condom – and I was worried in case he'd made me pregnant. I shouted for Emma and we went into the bathroom together. She told me just to have a wee and I'd be fine. That would stop me getting pregnant. She didn't care, and Daddy didn't care.

She then took me out of the bathroom and into the kitchen where Lateef was standing. The look on his face told me he was expecting to have sex with me as well. Daddy was there by now, and he started to tell me to go back into the bedroom with Lateef.

'No,' I said, 'I can't. I don't want to.'

The tears welled up and began running down my cheeks, but I knew they weren't going to save me. Lateef grabbed hold of me and started pulling me by the arm. 'Come on,' he was saying, 'come on.'

He was a big man and I was no match for him. In the room he took his own clothes off, pushed me onto the mattress and started to pull at my leggings.

I was trying to shuffle my legs to fend him off, but he was all over me. I couldn't stand it any more and so I kicked him, aiming at his groin but only managing to catch the top of his leg. He reacted by hitting me hard across the face.

I screamed and, astonishingly, Emma came to my rescue, though I still don't know why. She stood there in the doorway and yelled at him to get off me. Lateef was standing there naked and angry, but not quite sure if he fancied taking Emma on.

I used the moment to hitch up my leggings and run for the door. We ran out of the bedroom and away from the flat, waiting for the sound of him, or Daddy, or both of them, to come chasing after us.

Neither of us knew where we were, but we headed towards a main road, running part of the way but then slowing to a walk when we thought we'd got away and that they'd not bothered giving chase. But then, out of the darkness, we spotted Daddy's car, driving on side lights and heading towards us out of the gloom. I didn't bother running. The fight had gone out of me and, once more, I felt defeated.

Emma and I both climbed into the back seat, Daddy shouting at us as we did. He was livid. Livid with both of us for running; livid with me for not having sex with Lateef.

'He's a fucking gangster, you don't mess with him,' he said, glowering at us in the rear-view mirror as he pulled away. 'How dare you! Do you know what he could do to you? Or to me?'

For once even Daddy looked scared, and as his eyes refocused on the road ahead I allowed myself a brief smile.

He dropped us off at Harry's house. As we were about to get out, he leaned into the back and gave each of us a £10 note. 'Don't tell anyone what happened tonight,' he said.

* * *

For all his apparent fear that night, Daddy was still happy to carry on raping me over the next few nights. Five, six times, they all merged into one, always punctuated by the smell of his sweat and the soap he used to keep it in check.

Just into August, less than a week after the time with Lateef, he picked us up from Harry's place at about 6 p.m. and drove us, again in his Accord, to a house in the Coppice area of Oldham.

By now I was terrified of Daddy and too scared of reprisals to fall out with Emma. I felt well and truly trapped, mentally and physically. The place we went to belonged to a guy called Pino, who worked at Tasty Bites. I'd not been in Tasty Bites for ages, but I'd seen him outside so I knew he worked there.

He was tall and skinny, with long, swept-back black hair, aged about thirty. There was another man there, again Asian, tall and big, in his late twenties or so.

I knew they'd want sex because they always did. Wherever Daddy took us, I'd know that that was what was going to happen. That night, while we were driving over, Emma had actually been saying how much she was looking forward to it. How she was going to sleep with them. How much she really wanted it. Stuff like that. She loved it; I hated it. But it had somehow become my life.

Daddy had driven away as soon as he'd dropped us off. The house was in a big block in a scruffy part of town. It had an overgrown garden.

Pino let us in. There was vodka for us as usual, and we sat there talking to each other while the two men chatted in their own language. They were obviously deciding what was going to happen next.

After a while, Pino told me to go upstairs. He said it as though it was a request, but I knew what was on his mind. I was used to it by then, and just tried to block it out because I knew it was going to happen anyway.

Emma started to come with us but he said he didn't want her, and sent her back downstairs.

The walls of the main bedroom had been painted a garish red. You could tell there had been patterned wallpaper underneath that had just been painted over. There was a double bed, along with a sofa, a big mirror, a wardrobe and a stereo.

I was on the bed and Pino was telling me how pretty I was and that I should relax. He was trying to kiss me, pulling at my top and trying to pull my leggings down. It felt horrible. My head was spinning and he just kept on touching me.

I started to cry. I was saying, 'I don't want to do it. I've got a boyfriend.' I didn't, but I thought it might persuade him to leave me alone. It didn't, though; it just made him angry. He kept shouting at me, saying I knew why I was there and that I should bloody well get undressed and do it. Then he was on the phone to Daddy, shouting at him too, complaining about me. I could hear Daddy trying to smooth things out with him, but he wasn't having it.

One of them slammed the phone down; I think it was Pino. He turned towards me, pulling at my clothes again. Something inside me snapped. I couldn't stand it and screamed at him to get off me. Then I was shouting for Emma. A few moments later, there was a banging on the door and we heard someone shouting, 'Police!'

The fight suddenly went out of Pino, and a look of panic came over his face. He told us to hide and so Emma and I ran into the other bedroom. When we came out and crept downstairs a few minutes later, neither of the men was there and the kitchen window was wide open. The police had gone too.

I was glad the police had turned up, but scared as well. I thought of the trouble it might bring: the questions, the shame, the recriminations from Daddy and Emma if I dared say anything. And, of course, if the police got involved they'd get in touch with Mum and Dad. And they couldn't know.

They must never get to know what I'd got myself into.

We were still worried we'd get done by the police so we climbed out of the same window. Once we were outside, we needed to climb over a fence, and the man next door moved his wheelie bin so we could clamber up and away. I've wondered since whether it was him who'd heard all the shouting and called the police.

I didn't have a phone, of course, and Emma's was out of credit, so we walked to a local community centre where she asked to use the phone so she could call Daddy.

When he drove up he went mad at me. He kept screaming at me for supposedly betraying him by not letting Pino sleep with me. I'd defied him and I was going to pay for it.

'I'll have to pay him back,' he shouted. 'Am I really going to have to stay with you every time to make sure you do what you're supposed to do?'

When he dropped us back at Emma's he said he'd see me again soon. He said it with such menace that as I went inside, I knew I was as trapped and as helpless as ever. I felt like I couldn't breathe. I'd tried to stand up for myself, but nothing had changed.

* * *

In just a few days I'd fallen into a depraved world I'd never known existed. Now, with my wish for rebellion crushed, I was reduced to thinking that the only way to survive was to just give in and try to close my mind to the horror of what they were doing to me.

At fifteen, and still a kid despite my pretence at being grown-up and worldly, I really couldn't escape. Daddy and his friends knew exactly where I lived, and kept making it clear that they knew. He'd already threatened me with all sorts of violence: to kill me, to rape my sisters, to burn down our family home. I convinced myself they could do all of those things because of what they'd already done. If they could rape a sobbing teenager without a pang of conscience, murder was only a small step away.

I couldn't believe that all this had happened to me in just a few weeks.

To Mum and Dad it must have just seemed like I was off on an act of teenage rebellion, using the start of the summer holidays to stay at a friend's house in defiance of them. They thought it best to back off and leave me to it. They had no idea of the misery I was going through each and every day I spent away from them.

Maybe they were reassured when I kept popping back, even if it was mostly only to have my washing done. Mum must have thought it a sign that her eldest hadn't completely abandoned the family, that there were still ties between us.

Emma, though, usually came with me, not wanting me to go there alone. She'd always be careful to come across as my big buddy, chatting with my parents as if everything was fine and normal. On the days she didn't come, she'd warn me not to say anything.

I wanted to tell Mum and Dad the truth, that I was a prisoner. They could see that I was dirty and dishevelled, angry, and they came to hate the increasingly foul language I'd come out with whenever I saw them, but they didn't know *why*. They had no idea. When I got mad at them, they didn't know to look behind the shouting to wonder what was making me that way.

Those times at home should have been brief moments of respite, but they weren't. Rather than trusting my parents to help me, I was taking everything out on them, so much so that by the time I'd leave they were, unsurprisingly, sick of the sight of me.

Usually, we'd just bicker, with me screaming such vile abuse they'd come close to throwing me out of the door.

Most times, though, I'd storm out and head, like a lemming over a cliff, back to the house that had once promised freedom, but was now just a staging post for degradation and violence.

I was desperate to tell them what was happening to me.

What held me back was my fear of what the gang might do to them if they found out I'd told them. And, if I'm honest, part of me blamed Mum and Dad for not realising there was something terribly, terribly wrong in their daughter's life. I couldn't understand why they couldn't see the hold Emma had over me. They didn't seem to suspect anything. Now, I realise that she'd managed to pull the wool over their eyes too. She could convince anyone of anything.

Chapter Nine
Nowhere to Turn

It was around this time that I realised that the Glen's Vodka Daddy gave me was becoming my only friend. I'd drink it either neat or with cola. I came to hate the taste so much that I'd want to be sick even before it was poured, but I knew that if I drank it, drank it quickly, things wouldn't be so bad. I wouldn't be so scared, not quite so hurt.

The vodka meant I could at least forget. Even when it was happening, if I was drunk it felt somehow as if it wasn't real, that I wasn't actually being raped, that the body being violated was someone else's, and that I, Hannah, wasn't actually there.

Before falling prey to Daddy I'd drink with my friends to get happily drunk. It was fun with them. Now, each shot of vodka became its own anaesthetic. And the quicker I could drink each shot, the sooner I could embrace its numbing effect.

But, deep within me, in the hours and days after the time with Pino, I started to feel stronger. A new rebellion was building.

* * *

The day of my escape from Daddy, 6 August 2008, began like so many before it: waking up late at Harry's house, realising that the nightmare still had hold of me, and in the evening being taken by Emma to the Balti House.

Daddy wasn't there that night, and I felt a sense of relief as Emma and I sat on the stairs – hidden from the view of any customers who might be calling in – drinking straight out of the bottle. Emma had produced yet another bottle of cash-and-carry vodka, but it was me that drank the most. She just sipped it as she always did, ruthless, anxious to stay sober while her latest victim drank to forget. She must have reasoned that it was easier that way: less trouble. I couldn't understand that about her, because in my mind the vodka made the horror of each night that much easier to bear – I still couldn't bring myself to believe that she actually enjoyed all this, as she'd told Courtney in the car.

Although Daddy wasn't there, Chef was, and he loved to touch. He couldn't really speak much English: just the odd word or phrase to get by on. When it came to sex, he used the words: 'jiggy jiggy' was a favourite, so was 'puddy'.

Now, he came out of the kitchen and stood over me. His hands started roaming, just as he liked them to, heading south towards my 'puddy'.

He was saying, 'Do you want sex?' He wouldn't stop, and he wouldn't stop trying to reach into my pants. I said I'd ring my dad, and when he still didn't stop I punched him in the face.

I hit him so hard he reeled back on his heels.

A second later, I heard the crack as his hand slapped the side of my face. Then he slapped me a second time. He was going mad, standing right in front of me and calling me a slag.

It was chaos. My cheek was stinging as Emma began dragging me away from the stairs and out into the empty restaurant, heading towards the front door. Then Immy raced out and caught us up. He was angry, but I was angrier still.

Looking around for anything I could get my hands on, I grabbed a big jar of mayonnaise and threw it at Chef, catching him in the throat. Then I started kicking and punching the glass front to the counter. In the end, I hit it so hard I put my fist through it. I've still got the scars.

I could hear Chef screaming at Immy to call the police, but the man who'd taken me as a 'treat' barely a fortnight earlier seemed suddenly anxious. 'No, no,' he shouted. 'We'll call Daddy.'

Just the name was enough to propel me out of the door. I ran into the night, with Emma behind. We ran across the road and then slowed to walking pace, victim and recruiter, using the Morrison's car park as a cut-through. I know I was bleary from the vodka, but it felt like only moments later that a blue police van screeched around the corner and pulled up beside us.

Immy, it turned out, had been talked out of ringing Daddy and had instead dialled 999. It was something he'd come to regret, but not then, not in the summer of 2008.

Two police officers, one a man, the other a woman, both glaring at the drunken teenager in front of them, took only moments to arrest me but left Emma to slope off. They had to half lift me into the back of the van before slamming the door shut.

As the van headed out of town towards Rochdale, I looked dully at the two bobbies through the mesh bars, wondering what would happen to me next.

They parked at the back of the station and led me inside, first to the front desk, then to a cell, having taken all my belongings – my rings, bag and laces. 'We can't interview you until you've sobered up,' I was told.

Quite suddenly I felt safe. Yes, I was scared, because I'd never been in a police station before, let alone a cell, but I felt a sense of relief that, finally, I was somewhere that was completely out of Daddy's and Emma's reach: a place of refuge they couldn't deny me because, miraculously, I was there already. I wasn't at Emma's, I wasn't at the Balti House, and I wasn't at a flat being abused by Daddy and his friends. I was behind the safe, welcoming gates of a police station.

I slept, or tried to sleep, beneath the blanket they gave me. It was around 1 a.m. that the cell door opened and I was taken to an interview room.

But then the old fear came back to me: I was scared – not so much of what might happen to me here at the station, but scared of everything else: of what my dad would say about it all, of what my mum would say, and, most of all, of what Daddy would do to me if he ever got to me again.

It was at that point, somewhere between the cell door clanging shut behind me and the tape recorder going on, that I decided I really had to get help. If I didn't, I'd be trapped in this world for ever.

I had to tell them what had been happening to me. It felt that this was my only chance. No matter how painful, how embarrassing, I had to do what Mum and Dad had always told me: to tell the truth, so things could be right again. If I didn't, what would the gang do to me once I'd left the station? I'd be right back to doing what they wanted me to do.

The realisation was like a bright light going on in my mind. I was in a police station, after all. They'd look after me, and my family would, too, once they knew the truth.

But, first of all, there was my dad to cope with. He'd arrived at the station with a friend, bleary-eyed and mad at the news that his daughter had been arrested for criminal damage and thrown into a cell. He glared at me as he came into the interview room, then shook his head and sat on the chair beside me. It was obvious that he wanted to be anywhere else than there.

I remember how warm the room was, and how bare – just a table, some chairs, and the tape recorder on the table. I could feel the heat building up on my brow, the first trickle of perspiration on my palms.

The officer conducting the interview was about thirty and was clearly expecting a routine procedure, ending with a charge and a referral to court. He wasn't aggressive, just methodical and probably a little bored, carefully reading out the statements of both Chef and Immy. They were lies, of course, the gist of what they were saying being that I'd walked into the takeaway and randomly smashed the counter.

I think he expected me to say something like, 'Yes, that's what I did. And I'm sorry.'

But this wasn't going to be the easy shift for him that night.

'No,' I said. 'That's wrong.'

So he asked me why that was wrong, and why I'd done it.

I think I paused for a few seconds, wondering how on earth I could say it. There were no tears because suddenly I could see that I was about to be set free. But I remember looking down at the table, not wanting to look at the uniformed officer in front of me and even more desperate to avoid the expectant gaze of my father beside me.

'Because they raped me,' I said.

Across the table from me the officer looked astonished, alarmed even; as if he had no idea how he should react. He then collected himself, refocused and said sternly, 'You do know that's a serious accusation you're making, don't you?'

My dad has told me since that he went into shock, and I guess the policeman had a similar reaction, with his mind still on the criminal damage. I started to go through what had been happening to me – the rapes, the car journeys, the threats – but every time I paused, the officer tried to bring the conversation back to the Balti House counter. As if the counter mattered!

It angered me that he didn't seem to believe me, presumably thinking I was making it up to avoid the embarrassment of going to court. I didn't go into all the detail, though I did name Daddy and I did say he'd forced me to sleep with other people as well. I thought that would be enough to convince them.

Moments later, the officer stood to usher out the father of the strange, wild teenager in front of him so he could speak to him in private. Dad, whose gaze had shifted towards the ceiling, looked suddenly old as he pushed back his chair and went with him.

I could hear only muffled voices as they talked about me in the corridor outside. When they returned, the officer said he would pass on my allegations of rape and trafficking – it was the first time I'd heard that word – to a different team of officers so they could investigate. But he still charged me.

I learned later that the officer had told Dad he believed me, saying he'd heard of similar complaints from other girls in the past. All of them connected to Tasty Bites and the Balti House.

What neither Dad nor I knew then was that the latest of these complaints had been made no more than twenty-four hours earlier.

We were a few paces away from the station when Dad turned to me and said: 'You do know that what you're saying is incredibly serious?'

'Yes, Dad, I know,' I mumbled.

And then, as much to himself as to me, he continued, 'Why didn't you tell us, if it's true?'

* * *

It was an uncomfortable journey home. I was tired and hung over. Dad was in a space somewhere between disbelief and a kind of mourning for the innocent daughter he'd once known. Through the fog, I was trying to think about what would happen with the police, my parents and, most of all, with Daddy and Emma. I was glad that I'd spoken up, but beneath that was the thought I dreaded most: *what if nothing comes of it? And what will Daddy do to me, or worse, to my family, then?*

Mum was in tears, utterly distraught, as I went to bed in the half-light of dawn.

I should have felt safe back in my own room, with my brothers and sisters around me, but actually I didn't. I spent most of the rest of that night wondering whether any of the gang – Daddy, Immy, Chef, Mulla and others – would turn up at my home.

At the same time, Mum and Dad were coming to terms with the knowledge that I'd been raped, but they still had no idea how often and how violently. Nor did they know of Emma's role in the abuse. In their minds, it was just Daddy who had done those things to me.

The next day, the police came around lunchtime, asking what evidence I had to back up my account. I looked blankly at them for a moment, but then thought about the knickers I had stuffed under my bed at Harry's house.

I'd not been back home with my washing, so I realised that some of them must still have had Daddy's DNA on, and maybe even Immy's. I said I thought there were three pairs there. The police said they'd go round and collect them, but I went instead, because I didn't want the embarrassment – or the possible conflict with Emma their presence would create.

That afternoon, I went back to Harry's, frightened, wondering whether anyone had latched on to me being a 'grass'. Upstairs, I scrabbled under the bed and found three pairs of knickers: a pink thong, a blue pair and a green and pink pair.

Emma was in the hallway as I came downstairs, but she didn't guess what I'd been doing. Fortunately, I'd stuffed the knickers into my jacket pocket. She insisted on coming home with me, but she had no idea about the evidence I was carrying in my pocket.

When we arrived, I gave Mum the rest of my washing in the kitchen and, upstairs, mortified, I handed her the knickers, scrunched up in my hands so she wouldn't see the stains.

Later, she put them into Tesco bags and put them on top of a kitchen unit for safe keeping. They'd be there for a week before the police finally called at Harry's house for them – only to discover they were with Mum.

The day after I'd gone to the police they arrested Daddy. He admitted having sex with Emma but said he'd thought she was sixteen. He completely denied having sex with me. What did the police do? They let him go, saying they'd be in touch. I didn't know it then, but it would be another two months before they arrested Immy.

* * *

Once I had got home with the knickers, I had wanted to stay, I really did. But I was terrified in case any of Daddy's mates tried to come after me in revenge for having told on him. I also had Emma digging her nails into me as we sat on the sofa, talking to my parents.

She rang for a taxi, all casual, and told me to get my things. I was frightened to go, and frightened not to in case something happened to my family. In the end, like a zombie, I packed a few things and we set off back to Harry's house – the last place in the world I should be.

Mum and Dad made no move to stop me, resigned to this latest departure because they thought I'd only been raped by Daddy and Immy and would now be safe.

This didn't stop me being angry with them, however, because even though they didn't know the full story, and obviously it wasn't their fault, I wanted them to say, 'You're not going anywhere, you're staying here.'

They never did. To be fair to them, though, they didn't know the full picture, and they couldn't guess that Daddy may not even have been needed for what was going to happen to me next: Emma.

To my parents, Emma was a supportive friend who was on my side. They even thought she was going to be giving evidence against the men who'd raped me.

It was an ordinary taxi that called for us that afternoon; not one of the ones Emma would so often use when she was off with the gang.

As the cab pulled away, the pair of us in the back, I kept hold of the thought that it would be all right because I'd spoken to the police and they knew what I'd been through. I'd be rescued. They wouldn't let anything happen. And nor would Emma. With the police involved, she wouldn't dare, would she? But we'd barely negotiated the first speed bump away from the estate when the mask dropped and she reverted to the monster they'd made her.

'You bitch,' she snarled. 'Why did you grass on Daddy? It'll do you no good, you know. If you take him to court, I'll give evidence for him. Not you: him. And then how will it look?'

I wanted to scream at the taxi driver to turn around, but he just kept going, lurching over the bumps, out onto the main road, and on, towards the house that had become my dungeon.

* * *

I should have stayed at home, of course, and perhaps someone should have made sure I did: my parents, the police, myself. But I didn't.

At that stage, all the people who could have rescued me still thought it was just Daddy and Immy who'd attacked me. They had no idea how deep I'd been taken in by the gang; how they'd infiltrated my mind, body and soul. Mum and Dad thought Emma could be a help to me after being raped. She was a mate, after all. Or, so they thought.

That's why they did nothing to stop me when I said I had to go back to Harry's house – the last place on earth I should have been going to – and why they even waved me off in the taxi Emma had rung for.

I didn't want to go, but Emma still had a hold over me. Looking back, she must have been relieved to have me back. She'd have realised by then that she couldn't use Daddy as the link to the men she liked to 'chill' with. So, while she looked around for someone else to act as her link, she wanted to make sure she kept her talons in me.

Which is why, within twenty-four hours of first saying I'd been raped, and the same day I'd gone to retrieve the knickers that proved it, I was walking into Heywood with two other girls, one younger, one older, the latter of the trio for all the world looking like a honey monster.

* * *

It was a Thursday evening, and Emma, Roxanne and I were heading for the drop-in clinic on Taylor Street. It's the place where they help girls like I was: the ones having under-age sex – whether willingly or not – the ones who might be risking STIs and pregnancy.

Girls like these would call in at Taylor Street for advice, a bit of affection sometimes and, mostly, condoms. Certainly in Emma's case, and Roxanne's.

Emma had effectively been abandoned by her family, and Roxanne too. She spent so much time at Harry's because her mum didn't give a damn about her. I suppose we were all, in our own way, looking for love; all of us listless and directionless. All of us, for whatever reason, were scraping along near the bottom of society. And, all of us were targets for men with no consciences.

Even now, I find it really hard to sit here and write down the full truth, the absolute, cross-your-heart truth, even though it's there in a dark corner of my mind, and probably always will be. But Jane knew, or at least, she came to know: Jane at Crisis Intervention. She was based at Taylor Street and, after every one of my visits, would jot down a page or two of notes and then write up a report.

She'd been long enough in the job and was good enough to spot the signs. She'd tried in the past to help lots of other kids like me. She'd also tried to tell some of the people who had the power to intervene. Like Social Services. And the police. She made notes on my case and would be making notes for all the coming months in which I was in the grip of the gang; passing on the information to the powers-that-be if she thought it could help other people to help me: discreetly, of course, and on a completely confidential basis.

Unlike me, she had no need either to cover things up or disguise things, or make things look not quite as bad as they were. What she wrote down was the truth as she saw it every time I turned up: a thin, waif-like girl with a troubled life, who, she suspected from very early on, was being abused by the most evil of men. Of course, Emma would never allow me to let on what was really going on, building up a smokescreen of us having fun with our boyfriends. But even so Jane was suspicious. She *cared*. And right from the start she tried her hardest to help me.

This is her very first report on the young girl the media would come to know as 'Girl A':

**Crisis Intervention Team Report,
August 7th, 2008**
Hannah came into Taylor St clinic with friends Emma and Roxanne. Hannah is going out with Jake who is nineteen. Hannah wanted to talk about contraception and asked to go on the pill. Advice given and Hannah went to see the nurse.

You could be forgiven for thinking that that report might have applied to any one of a thousand under-age girls in Britain.

But appearances can be deceptive.

Jake was my other secret. He was one of Emma's friends, and lived in Harry's house too. In the middle of all the degrading sex I was having with the gang, I'd started to sleep with him, too.

Ricky now had a girlfriend, so didn't want me in his room. And I'd found out that Emma was now sleeping with Harry in his double bed, and I didn't want anything to do with that.

I had known Jake would come on to me at some point, but when it happened, it didn't really seem to matter. The way I had seen it, my life was filled with abuse, and one more man using me wasn't going to change anything. He wasn't actually my boyfriend, as I'd told Jane, but at least he was more my age. And it gave me another smokescreen to hide behind at Crisis Intervention.

Emma would take me to Taylor Street most weeks. The teenage part was always open between 5 p.m. and 7 p.m. on Thursdays. She'd been a regular for years, having pregnancy tests, being checked for STIs and eventually walking back into the night with a smug smile and a bag full of condoms. She wanted her new recruit, her new meal ticket, to be looked after in the same way. She was taking care of her goods.

That first time I joined her, just after talking to the police, I didn't know where to look. There was a front desk, and the receptionist gave each of us a form with little boxes so we could tick the things we wanted. The form was then given to the relevant sexual health worker. In Emma's case it was Jane, and when it was her turn, we both went in.

It was another chance to escape, another chance to get help. But I'd already gone to the police, and it seemed pointless to involve this woman as well. Plus, I had Emma with me, so I knew I had to stay silent.

Emma set off the same way she would do on every other occasion: talking nineteen-to-the-dozen, making up lies about her boyfriends, my boyfriends, everything. She'd describe the men we knew, but give them different names. She couldn't stop herself showing off. She never let on about what was actually going on, but talk about the sex she'd have with them like it was the best ever. 'I love shagging Pakis,' she said that first time. 'They've got bigger dicks.'

Looking back, Jane must have seen a few girls like Emma in her time. She'd heard it all, I suppose, and wasn't easily shocked. All she could do was to listen to all the girls she saw, to reach out to them, to try to 'save' as many of them as she could.

Chapter Ten
A New Master

The local police do their video interviews in a specialist police suite in Manchester.

I did my first one there within twenty-four hours of my arrest at the Balti House, but they had to abandon it. They'd run out of time, they said; the room was needed for someone else.

My rescheduled video interview was held on 15 August. Thankfully, Emma was asleep as I crept away from Harry's house and back home, so Dad could get me to the station by 10 a.m.

We drove into the city in silence, but as we walked in towards the interview suite Dad took my hand and squeezed it. I responded with the faintest of smiles.

I certainly didn't look like a girl who was being abused, but then, I suppose I wouldn't. I'd gone along in the same sort of clothes any other local teenager might have worn at that time: a light grey tracksuit and black T-shirt, my hair pulled to one side, my favourite, huge, heart-shaped earrings swinging every time I moved my head.

The interview was carried out by a detective constable from the local CID called John with a colleague, Tim, in the monitoring room checking the recording equipment that would capture my words of evidence. My dad was in the waiting room.

As I say, it was a specialist unit. The room itself was bare but for two cream sofas and a round table. John sat on one of the sofas; I was on the other. One camera recorded the whole of the room, the other just me.

I started fidgeting pretty much straight away. I was nervous – understandably, I reckon, given what I'd told them, and what I thought they'd be thinking about me.

John asked about Daddy, and then moved on to Immy. How had I become his 'treat', he wondered.

I went through the story once, and the detective, pen in hand, a pad resting on his knee, went through it for a second time. Slowly.

'Why go upstairs?' he asked.

'Daddy kept telling me he'd given me a treat, so I'd got to give his nephew a treat. He said, "We'll just go upstairs and chill for a bit."'

'Why not just leave?'

'I don't know.'

I was looking down, desperate to avoid the camera and its inquisitive gaze. 'We could have walked out of the front, but the customers and everything were there.'

'Was there anything to stop you walking out the front or the back?'

'Daddy said we couldn't leave. There was nothing apart from that.'

I told him about the room where Immy attacked me: the window with its tatty, dirty curtains that were held on by nails, the orange quilt on the mattress. It also made me think about the children's clock with the little angel on it, in the other room.

At first there had been four of us in the room, I said: Daddy, me, Immy and Emma. Then it was just me and Daddy's nephew.

John asked me what each of the men was wearing, but I couldn't remember. 'I don't know,' I said.

'What was going through your mind?'

'That I'm going to have to do it.' I told him how he'd bent over me and pulled down both my leggings and my knickers. How I could see his erection and hear him saying, 'Come on, please, you've got to do it now.'

'How did you feel?'

I was suddenly aware that my right hand was pressed against my face, resting against my cheek. *How did I feel?* 'A bit scared, I just lay there with my legs open. He put it in with his hand.'

'Was he wearing a condom?'

I shook my head. 'No.' It had hurt, I said, and at the last moment he'd withdrawn and ejaculated over the grubby sheet I was lying on. I told him about him leaving and about Emma coming back with some money.

Then John asked me about the time – less than a fortnight earlier – when Daddy had met Emma and me outside the Balti House and he'd taken us to a flat in Rochdale.

I told him that Daddy had taken me into a room and ordered me to have sex with him. I'd protested, I said, telling Daddy that Emma had said it would be her he had sex with that night.

Feeling the same shudder go through me as it had those two awful weeks ago, I recalled Daddy's answer: 'Emma's lying,' he'd said. 'You have to do it.'

I told the police officer I'd not wanted to go to the Balti House that night. The expression on his face gave nothing away. 'Why did you go, then?' he asked.

'Emma wanted to,' I said.

'Didn't you think you were putting yourself in a compromising position, bearing in mind what'd happened previously?'

I knew the answer, of course I knew the answer, but I didn't want to say it. But I did.

'Yeah,' I said. And then added: 'Emma was telling me to go, so I just did.'

'Why didn't you say "No" to her?'

'I don't know.'

As I said it, I realised I had unconsciously slipped my hands into the sleeves of my tracksuit, as if I wanted to hide, hide all of me, from these questions.

Then I was recalling how Daddy said I had to have sex with him again, and that I felt I had no choice but to go into the bedroom with him. There was a mattress on the floor, I said, and I was trying to finish the vodka they'd given me when Daddy had come up behind me.

I'd moved away from him at first, but eventually pulled my leggings down so he could get it over with.

I was so embarrassed at admitting to that that my stomach was twisting into knots. But I tried to keep going.

'He had to play with himself to get an erection,' I said. 'I told him to get off me, and I was crying. But he was just ignoring me. I felt dirty, and I was worried because he didn't wear a johnny. Afterwards, I went into the bathroom to wipe myself with a tissue and put my knickers back on.'

'Had he come inside you before?' the detective asked.

'I don't know.'

When we moved on to the time Daddy raped me in his car, John had to ask me to take my hand away from my mouth. Instead, I locked my arms in my lap. By the time we'd gone through my rapist's entire repertoire of abuse, I realised I was running my fingernails back and forth across my mouth, as if I wanted to block the words that were coming from it.

I told John how afterwards, Daddy had driven me back to Emma, who'd waited for me in Morrison's car park, and she had asked where he'd taken me. I also told him that she'd said she'd been there too.

John asked how long the whole business had taken, from start to finish.

'Twenty minutes,' I said.

We were getting towards the end of the interview and I was telling him how Emma liked all the free food and the beer. And how she liked having sex with all these men.

'How come you'd gone with her?' he asked.

I was still too frightened of Emma to tell this policeman everything. 'I don't know,' I said. 'If I don't go with her, she'll fall out with me.'

Perhaps the strain of the interview had taken its toll on him as well as me, but as he asked his next question, about an address we'd been taken to, he suppressed a yawn. I heard it, and it must be on the tape.

John went on to ask what happened at this address, a place I didn't know but which was about a twenty-minute drive from the Balti House.

'What did you think was going to happen?' asked the detective.

'I don't know. I had an idea they were going to want sex.'

'What made you think that?'

'Because they always did. Everywhere he takes us.'

Then John asked whether anything had happened in the eight days since I'd first made my allegations to the police.

So I told him how the day before I'd overheard Emma taking a call from Daddy, who was asking where I was, and then, knowing I was in the background, screaming: 'She's a bitch! Tell that Hannah she's a bitch! I know people in Oldham. They're going to get her!'

As I spoke, the fear I'd felt at hearing his voice again came back to me, seeping through the walls of the police station and into the interview room.

But there was something I didn't tell him; something I was holding back, which I'll explain later. Yes, Daddy had rung Emma, and he had screamed abuse at me down the phone. But what I couldn't tell the detective sitting

patiently in front of me now was that at the time of the call,
Emma and I were in someone else's car; the car of a man
even more sinister than Daddy, and someone – even in the
few hours I'd spent with him – I was even more frightened
of betraying.

Worried that John might guess that I was holding back
on him, I kept my head down and began playing with
my nails. He took it as a sign I had nothing else to say,
and a moment later was asking if I was happy to finish the
interview there.

'Has anyone else given a statement?' I blurted out.

John said something about things being under control,
but I wasn't really taking it in. I wanted to know whether
they'd spoken to Emma by then, but I didn't dare ask.

The interview was over, the recording ended. As I stood
up from the sofa, John glanced up at me and said, 'Look, the
tapes are off now. Did you just do this for a bit of money?
You might as well admit it if you did, because why would
you have kept going back?'

I could hardly believe what he had just said. It made
me feel sick and angry at the same time: as though I had
been violated all over again. Why on earth would I have
sat through all this if it wasn't true? Why, for nearly three
hours, would I have given him the sickening detail of what
Daddy and his gang had done to me?

Through gritted teeth I told him as much. 'Every word
I've told you is the truth,' I said.

'OK, let's leave it there for now.' And with that, he led
me out of the room.

Dad was waiting near the front desk when I emerged. As we left, he told me of a conversation he'd had with one of the investigators. 'This happens all the time,' the officer had told him. 'We get lots of it around here, and it's always Asian men and it's always young white girls. Never Asian girls.'

On the surface everything seemed to be vaguely normal. Mum and Dad at least knew of the rapes by Daddy and Immy and were trying to be supportive; the police were investigating; and Emma hadn't battered me, despite both Daddy and Immy being taken in for questioning.

A couple of days after the police interview, detectives drove me around so I could show them the flats and houses Daddy had taken me to. They told me the knickers had finally gone off to a forensic lab to be tested. Once that had been done, they'd really start making progress. Soon, they said, they'd be able to get a file sent to the Crown Prosecution Service.

'If the DNA matches, it will be proof enough,' said one of the detectives. At that point, they would bring charges and it would go to court. They also told me that in cases involving children, defendants are brought to trial as quickly as possible because everyone in the legal system, from the police and the CPS to the barristers and the judges, all want to save kids the trauma of a long wait for justice.

So in my case – a case of multiple rapes and being passed around, trafficked, by Daddy – it shouldn't take too long. It was easy, simple and it would mean I could get on with my life.

* * *

In the end it was me, rather than my abusers, who appeared in a courtroom first.

I went with my dad to Rochdale Magistrates' Court, where we sat on a hard wooden bench for ten minutes, me half terrified, half angry, hauled up on the charge of criminal damage. At the end of it, the magistrates decided to adjourn the case because of the allegations I'd made.

Meanwhile, Daddy and Immy were still out there. Daddy had been given bail the same day he was arrested. In Immy's case, the police didn't even arrest him until the October. It seemed astonishing that they were still free to roam the streets. And always in the back of my mind was the thought, *What if they come for me?*

Fatally, Mum and Dad were still happy for me to stay at Harry's house with Emma. They thought it was all about the Balti House and nothing remotely to do with her. And she, cunning as ever, made out as if her new best friend had been raped and she'd be there to support her. So, she came to collect me not long afterwards, watched as my parents gave me a hug and off we went – me and Emma – back to the last place in the world I should be.

I don't know to this day how Emma held her nerve about being my ever-caring friend, but somehow she did. I'm sure that most normal people, even criminals, would have laid low to see if the coast was clear, but not Emma. Maybe she had some sixth sense that regardless of Daddy's arrest, she was safe from the police. But, whatever the reason, her phone was crammed with the numbers of the Asian men she'd met in Heywood, Rochdale and far beyond. And she wasn't slow to start ringing some of them.

I knew nothing of this, of course, but what I did know, from the moment I stepped back over the threshold at Harry's place, was that she still wanted to control me. And, as usual, she had a plan.

'Time for a bath,' she announced. 'And make sure you shave. I can't have them seeing you like that.'

Them seeing me? I shrank back in fear. The police involvement had made no difference to her. She was still determined to control me, and I, submissive, broken, couldn't fight back. I know I should have done, but I always felt so incredibly weak when I was with her – and even when I wasn't.

I never, ever had a real heart-to-heart with her, and I always felt she was on the verge of laughing or sneering at me. Her reputation as the hardest girl in the area made even lads tremble and I knew that if she ever battered me, I'd be pulp. I made it a rule right then to try as hard as I could never to show any weakness in front of her. All the time I tried to put on a front to make her think I could take it – and also so that she wouldn't get any pleasure out of whatever was happening to me.

The police interview had been on the Friday. That very weekend, Emma was taking me into Heywood. Depressed, fearful, I clung to the hope that maybe I'd read things the wrong way: that it was all over, and she wouldn't dare do what she'd done with me before.

It was a forlorn hope because we ended up at the front door of Tasty Bites. I had a shock when Emma and I walked in because there was a girl I recognised – Paige, a dizzy blonde from my school. She was two years younger than me, incredibly naïve, and still very much a girl. I shuddered. Could she have been caught up in this as well?

We barely acknowledged each other as the three of us climbed the stairs. I'd been here before, of course, but had Paige? Maybe after I'd stopped going all those months ago? I could barely lift my feet as we made our way upstairs.

So, there we were, back at the place where, a lifetime ago – or so it seemed – I'd had such a great time. Climbing the stairs this time, though, was a totally different experience. Whereas in my old life I'd have almost skipped up the stairs, this time, recalling the almost identical staircase of the Balti, and what had happened once I'd got to the top, I could barely lift my feet.

On the landing we could hear the sound of muffled laughter coming from a bedroom. It turned to silence as soon as Emma twisted the door knob and pushed her heavy frame into the room. Following on behind Paige, I was confronted by half a dozen Asian men – all of them old, in their thirties, forties, maybe even fifties, like Daddy.

One of them, a thickset man with tousled black hair and dense eyebrows, broke the silence, leaning across with a bottle of vodka and saying: 'Here, you can have this ... Saj, give them some glasses. The cola's over there.'

The man's voice, low and hard, carried an unmistakable authority and menace. It was Emma, of course, who poured the drinks and handed one each to me and Paige. As she did so, she glanced up at the man with the tousled hair and said: 'This is Tariq'.

Tariq. Emma's new sinister 'boyfriend.' The same man I had been too afraid of telling John about in the police interview.

The men, Tariq included, had been leering at us before, but now, as we sipped the vodka – me scared, Paige scared, Emma her normal, impassive self – some of the men started pointing at us. Mostly they were speaking in their own language, but occasionally I'd catch the odd word in English: like 'fat' when they looked at Emma, and 'young', 'tight' and 'pretty' when they looked at Paige or me. I felt like a piece of meat.

Then one of them asked me if I'd have sex with him, then another. I said no. They were asking Paige too.

'You do sex,' said one, his eyes burning first into mine, then into Paige's. It was an instruction. Another pressed close by. 'Do it, do it, do it,' he said. Others took up the chant. 'Do it, do it, do it!'

That was it for me. It was a small room, scarily so with all these men in it, and as they herded around us I started to panic. I looked around wildly for Emma. For all my new-found intentions never to show weakness in front of her, I clutched at her, begging her to let me leave.

'I've got to go, Emma. You've got to let me go!'

Maybe she did have a lingering concern about the police, because rather than batter me she just shrugged, reached into her purse and handed me a two pound coin. It felt like a miracle.

'Go on, then,' she sneered. 'Get a taxi back to Harry's. But don't do anything stupid. Understand?'

I nodded and headed for the door, brushing away the alien hands that grabbed at me as I fled. I tried to catch Paige's eye so she'd come with me, but by then Emma was already putting a chubby arm around her to head off any possible escape.

One of the men followed me out, trying to grope me as I headed downstairs, but Tariq pulled him away. 'Sorry, master,' said my would-be groper.

I got a taxi outside Morrison's and, in the darkness, me quivering on the back seat, the car headed back to Harry's.

Harry was still up when I got back, watching a late-night show on TV. 'You all right, pet?' he asked as I walked in, mascara down my face, still shaking.

'Fine, thanks, Harry … well, almost. Though I don't want to talk about it.'

'Fine by me,' he said. 'But come over here if you need a hug.' And so I did, falling into his arms, feeling suddenly safe after the trauma and fear of the evening.

'There, there,' he smiled, looking down into my eyes. 'Things are never as bad as they seem. Everything just seems tougher when you're a kid. I'll always be here for you – Harry will always be here.'

It helped, it really did.

* * *

The next morning, I asked Emma what had happened after I'd left, but all she would say, with typical sarcasm, was, 'Poor Hannah, you missed all the fun.'

I saw Paige the next day but didn't get a chance to speak to her. Maybe Emma deliberately kept us apart. To this day I still don't know what happened to her that evening, though I heard later that because she was so young the gang just used her for blow jobs.

The next night, Emma took me for a drive with Tariq.

I mumbled a greeting before climbing into the back of the silver minibus he drove for Eagle Taxis. As we sped away, his two-way radio crackled into life. 'Car 40,' said a remote voice, 'Car 40.'

'Yes, this is Car 40,' said Tariq, and the two of them then carried on a conversation in their first language, so I couldn't understand. That night we just drove around Heywood and Rochdale for half an hour. Emma spent most of the time in the front with him, chatting inanely, while I sat in the back wondering where my life had gone.

At one point he got out briefly to go into a takeaway. While he was gone, Emma turned round in her seat, saying to me, 'He's great, isn't he?'

Yes, brilliant, I thought. *A forty-year-old boyfriend for a girl of fifteen*. Even I, for all that my mind was skewed, guessed that to Tariq, Emma was no more than a meal ticket, a way to make money by providing 'free' young girls for him to sell sexual access to.

At least he never touched me, not that day, not any day. He still frightened me, though, because he looked so moody and so menacing. His nickname – Master – seemed entirely appropriate.

That first drive with Tariq proved to be the first of several that week. Slowly at first, then more so, I began to relax – even when we went back to Tasty Bites.

I felt even better when, with one of her rare smiles, Emma said: 'Now that Daddy's out of the way, it won't ever happen again, OK?'

Did she mean it? I desperately hoped so.

Regardless of my own fate, Emma still wanted what she called shagging – and not just with her 'boyfriend'. Late at night, once the place had closed, I'd be left downstairs while she clambered up the steps with Tariq and a few other men he'd obviously arranged to meet there.

Pino was one of the guys Emma slept with on those nights; Saj another of them. I guess that whatever Emma thought, Tariq, like a true entrepreneur, was just happy to get paid.

One night, towards the end of August, there was a variation to this new routine – the routine my fear had led me to become part of again despite going to the police. We stopped off briefly at Tasty Bites with Tariq, but then he drove us to a scruffy, depressing flat just off the Whitworth Road in Rochdale.

I've forgotten the address, but I could take you there. We'd always go round the back and up the stairs to get in.

It belonged to Saj, but he was renting it out to his cousin, a guy called Aarif. He had designer stubble and his hair was always cut in a short-back-and-sides. He worked as a wedding photographer: sometimes he'd leave his work on one of the two computers he kept in the lounge. He never took pictures of us, though. And, oddly, I thought, he didn't have a TV.

Aarif wasn't the sort to tell us much about himself, but I know he had kids because sometimes he'd speak to them on the phone, saying it was his son or daughter. Some of his friends called him Khan.

The flat had just the one bedroom that you got into by taking a step up. There was a double bed in there. The bathroom had a shower but no bath.

Aarif was there on his own.

As soon as we arrived, Emma told me I had to go and sleep with him. I said, 'No, you promised this wouldn't happen again.' So she actually went into the bedroom with him herself, '... to show that it's OK.'

I stayed in the living room, feeling glad that I'd not had to sleep with him. But while we waited, Tariq started complaining that 'it wasn't fair' on Emma. Next time, he said, I should do what I was told.

Emma came out a few minutes later and we went home. We'd been in the flat for no more than a quarter of an hour.

The next night it really was my turn. There were four of them there this time: Aarif, Saj, a guy from Jo Baxi's Taxis who told us to call him Joe. I have no idea what his real name was. There was another man too who I never got a name for.

Emma made me go with the first three, one after the other.

I remember there were clothes hanging on the handles of the wardrobe, and a table next to the bed with a drawer. There were condoms inside it and they all got one out before they attacked the sobbing girl at their mercy on the bed: one by one, turn by turn.

I assume Tariq, or maybe Aarif, had told them about the condoms before each of them came in. Either way, I got the impression they'd been to the flat before, with other girls. It seemed normal to them. They all knew each other; they were friendly with each other.

I knew I was trapped and that I couldn't stop them. If I had, I think they would have attacked me in a different way. Aarif came in first, then Saj, then Joe, while Emma just sat in the lounge.

It was sick. How can a man get any pleasure from something like that? As far as I know they all had wives, so why do that to a kid? All I could wonder was what they could find attractive about me? An under-age girl who just lay there, sobbing, looking up at them … as they come to her one by one.

I don't know whether all the men knew my age, but Tariq certainly did, and I'm sure the fact that I was under age was the main reason they wanted me.

That night, Aarif handed Emma the money for having raped me: I don't know how much it was. Afterwards, they all went for a meal with Tariq. When they got back, Emma gave the money to him and he gave her £10 of it back.

On the way home, Tariq kept saying: 'Hannah, you're a good girl.' While I sobbed in the back, Emma was just laughing.

I felt numb. Why hadn't I just run out into the street, anywhere? Just to get away from them. Looking back, I know that's what I should have done. But the kid I was then was frozen with fear and just kept on thinking that they would make things even worse for me if I resisted. And I also thought just what Emma had hoped I'd think: that it was hopeless, that no one would believe me. 'What, that you've been raped dozens of times?' she scoffed. 'They'll just laugh at you.'

They would, I thought. A girl who goes to the police about being raped, and a few days later is going in cars to be abused again by loads of other men? They'd fall about laughing and then kick me out. And to go where? The gang would have just picked me up again. In my mind, they were just too strong and too ruthless to resist. I thought it would be me who'd be blamed, not them, and that afterwards they'd want their revenge.

Chapter Eleven
You've Got To Get Away

I couldn't believe what was happening to me – all within a few days of going to the police. In the police station I thought I was saved, that it would end. Now I was thinking, *It's never going to go away. Not even the police can protect me. It's just happening again.*

I'd told the police about Emma and how she'd organised it all with Daddy and Immy, so I thought they'd investigate her. But as far as I know they didn't – and that meant she could just go on doing what she'd been doing, only with different men instead of Daddy, and with Tariq now mostly pulling the strings.

From that point on, it just got worse. It would happen most days, with up to five different men in a day. And not even just in one house or one flat: I'd be taken to one house, then another, then a third. It might be Rochdale one night, Bradford the next, or Nelson or Oldham.

Wherever I was taken, there was a set routine, in which they'd give me alcohol to get me drunk and then come at me, one after the other, until they'd had enough of me. Then I'd be taken back to Harry's to await the next call.

In the flats and houses where I'd be taken, I'd feel I was looking down on myself: lying there, huddled and crying, naked from the waist down, with Emma bringing in a new man every time the previous one had finished with me. She would be laughing. It was still all just a joke to her.

Maybe it was the trauma of it all, but I felt myself losing track of what was normal. Lying spread-eagled on a bed so a succession of men could abuse me just became routine. I became used to it, I suppose. I stopped feeling disgusted, and felt it was almost a challenge – a challenge to see if I could somehow cope with the pain and humiliation, no matter how many men Emma made me sleep with. I tried to convince myself that just by coping with the sheer numbers I was becoming stronger. It was a way to make things seem better than they were: I could feel my mind and all my thought processes distorting. It was like an illness.

With Emma around me 24/7, I began to sense I was being brainwashed. At Harry's place, she'd even use her hold over me to get me to do chores. Whereas at home with Mum and Dad, I'd resisted, here I felt I had to do as she told me. She knew I had no money to pay rent, or to buy food, so she'd come down in the mornings and tell me what to do. If I didn't, she said she'd get Harry to chuck me out.

The softest she ever appeared were the times she'd sit on the loo seat while I was bathing and chat about some of the men she planned to take me to later.

'You'll be OK with him cos he's good looking,' she might say. 'So it won't be as bad and you won't have to mess up by being a mard ass.'

The fifteen-year-old me didn't even know that what she was doing was a crime. All the time it was happening, I never thought of it as such. I didn't know about 'grooming' – where grown-ups become friends with children so they can have sex with them. I knew it was wrong, but I didn't know that what the men were doing to me, and what Emma was arranging for them to do to me, was against the law. I didn't know there was a name for it. I just knew that if I resisted, they would come and get me. I could see Tariq and Emma getting money for what was happening to me, but I couldn't see a way of stopping it.

Emma was pimping me like a prostitute in a niche market, a prostitute for paedophiles. She had such control that she didn't even need to pay me. She could just hawk me around, night after night, and charge them for raping me in their seedy flats.

I came to realise that Emma had recruited me to something evil, but it was something I couldn't fight off. The crucial thing for her was that I'd fallen into the trap of going to live at Harry's place. Once I was there, she immediately knew she could use me and convince me there was no escape. She was powerful enough on her own, but with Daddy, and then Tariq, behind her, she seemed to me to be invincible.

I'd become a piece of merchandise for her to sell. She was constantly checking on me to make sure I'd always obey: I was so submissive towards her that I'd even find myself apologising to her whenever I burst into tears.

So much of her hardness had come from what I sensed was being born into a family that didn't care for her. None of them had had a job in generations, and her mum wasn't bothered whether she stayed with her or at Harry's. Emma used to have one of her little sisters over for a couple of nights a week, and their mum would drop her off. Sometimes she'd stay for tea. I'd be sitting there, thinking: *Surely she must know what her daughter's up to?*

But if she did, she didn't seem to care.

My depression and desperation were made deeper by the fact that going to the police had made no difference to my life whatsoever. The disclosures I'd given, together with the long and detailed video interview, were now a distant memory and looked like a huge, sick joke. There was no rescue. There was no protection. *I've already told them*, I thought, *but I'm still here and it's still happening to me.* I was once again beyond rescue – and pretty much beyond reason.

There was only Emma and the gang.

* * *

I turned to the only refuge I could find – alcohol. At first Emma had used the vodka to make me more malleable; now it was me who was desperate for its raw edge, drinking it as quickly as I could to numb the horrors of each night, and hope they would stay somewhere near the surface rather than searing a path into my soul.

I'd sometimes be so drunk that I'd forget where I'd been or precisely how many paedophiles had forced themselves on me. Only the jagged pain I'd feel the next morning would remind me of the abuse I'd suffered.

September brought with it the start of the new school term – the year I was supposed to be doing my GCSEs.

Visits to Mum and Dad's were becoming more infrequent, but the day before school started I went home to collect my uniform. As usual, I felt they didn't really want me around, so I only stayed for a few minutes.

There'd be no lift to the school gates from Dad. Instead, I caught the bus from Harry's place with Ricky and Hayley's old flame, Wayne. Emma was still in bed as we set off.

It seemed so strange to see the boys in school uniform again, and even stranger when we got to school. Hayley was there, and we said hi, but it was different. Everyone else seemed so happy and so normal. All I could think was, *None of these kids has any idea what's happened to me these summer holidays.*

And how could they know? How could they even guess? For them there might have been a bit of teenage fumbling; for me, it had been first one rape in a bedroom over a takeaway, and after that so many more that I'd actually lost count. Forty? Fifty? I had no idea. All I knew was that my life was ruined and there was no way I could ever fit in somewhere that was so achingly, wonderfully normal.

The first lesson of term was Art, and I sat at the back next to Wayne. He lived around the corner from Harry's place, and because he was there so often, he'd got to know how Emma was using me.

Away from Ricky now, and far enough away from the other kids in the class to whisper unheard as he drew, he started to try and help me.

'You've got to tell someone, Hannah,' he said, leaning towards me. 'Tell one of the teachers and they'll sort it out. They'll get you away from Emma, honest they will.' He looked up to check the teacher wasn't looking, then continued: 'You act like she's your mate, but she's not. She's just a fat bitch and she's using you, Hannah. You've got to get away.'

Somewhere inside I felt myself trying to respond, trying to understand the sense of what he was saying, but I couldn't. I just wiped away a tear and carried on drawing.

He kept on at me for the entire lesson, telling me I was a victim and that if I could tell someone it would all be over. 'All those men need locking up, Hannah. Go on, tell someone.' All I could find to say in reply was a petulant: 'You just don't understand! Now leave me alone.'

Later that morning, Miss Crabtree, the mentor for kids the school thought were struggling, called me into her office.

'Hannah,' she said quietly, 'we've heard from the police about the allegation you've made about being raped.' She paused. 'Do you want to talk about it? I'd be happy to do anything I can to help.'

'No,' I said in a whisper, deliberately looking beyond her deep green eyes at a spot over her shoulder. 'I really can't.'

She seemed crestfallen, almost hurt. 'Well, if you ever change your mind, I'll be here, OK? And if you don't want to speak to me, we'll find someone else for you to talk to. A counsellor, maybe.' She gave me a hesitant smile. 'Just don't feel alone, Hannah. We're here to help you, we really are.'

I shuffled out of her office and into a corridor crammed with kids heading towards their next lessons. I'd wanted to tell her, but I knew I just couldn't. I was in too deep, and no one, just no one, could rescue me.

* * *

By the end of that first week back at school, Tariq was regularly picking me up from near the top gates where, a lifetime ago, I'd smoked my first illicit cigarette. Sometimes Emma was with him, and together they'd take me off somewhere.

Normally at the end of the school day teachers would gather by the gates so they could watch out for any fights – kids were always fighting at our school, either among themselves or against the rival schools in our area.

I'm guessing that some of the teachers had seen me getting into a taxi, Tariq's taxi, and had begun to put two and two together. They began to question me about it, but I'd just shrug them off.

I then made the mistake of telling Emma that some of my teachers were becoming suspicious. So, instead of being picked up at the end of school, I'd get a phone call or a text to tell me to come out fifteen minutes early.

Emma had hated the idea of me going to school in the first place: she couldn't see the point of it. Her theory was that by me wagging lessons a quarter of an hour early, the teachers would lose the scent. They'd still be in class and I'd be off, not exactly free like all the other kids off wagging, but out of their sight, sitting in the back of a taxi taking me to a hell they couldn't begin to imagine.

I'd feel a sense of impending dread as the last lesson of the day came to an end. I knew there'd be a phone call from Emma, or maybe Tariq. It was always a phone call; maybe they thought it safer that way, rather than leaving a trail of text messages.

It wasn't difficult to leave early. The school regime didn't help. You might have thought they'd lock the school gates so that once the kids were in they couldn't get out. What they actually did was leave the gates open all day, so the kids could walk out whenever they wanted: otherwise they knew they'd kick off and they'd have to deal with it.

When it came down to it, the teachers couldn't control anyone and they knew it. In fact, the staff lived pretty much in fear of the kids they were supposed to be teaching – they would be assaulted on a weekly basis, so you can't really blame them. The school even gave up trying to exclude the tearaways because they realised some of them were getting excluded deliberately.

It was tough. There were kids at school with pretty chaotic backgrounds. I'd been given values by my parents, but those counted for nothing when I had the gang to contend with.

The school was like a war zone: so tough that they had a policeman on site who had his own office. Maybe I should have gone to him, but I never did.

I didn't realise then, but Rochdale Social Services knew all about me by this time. Staff at my school – Miss Crabtree, I think – had started ringing Social Services to say I was coming in smelly and dirty and smelling of alcohol, as well as being picked up in taxis.

Social Services also knew about lots of other girls like me, and how they'd been exploited by similar gangs in the local area.

They'd known for years.

They knew because Jane and her boss at Crisis Intervention, Sara, kept on telling them, in report after report, letter after letter. And what had Social Services done for all those girls?

Nothing.

Some of the details about my case would have been put on Social Service desks within hours of me telling police how Daddy and some of the others in the gang had raped me. So it should have rung alarm bells with them, and it should have made them think of all the other cases of under-age kids being exploited by networks of paedophiles. And then they should have done something to try to stop it.

Actually, they did do one thing. That September, they held a strategy meeting at their offices in John Street, Rochdale.

It was either in that meeting, or else just before it, that members of the Safeguarding Children board were given copies of a letter sent to them by Sara. The letter, dated 10 September, marked 'Private and Confidential', was a plea for Crisis Intervention to be kept fully in the loop. It mentioned both me and Daddy. It also repeated something Social Services already knew – that one of the places Rochdale Council sent its young mums to live for a bit after giving birth was being targeted by predatory men, almost all of whom were Pakistani, who wanted these vulnerable girls for easy sex. These men were calling at a local single mothers' housing unit, to either 'visit' girls, or else collect girls and young women.

Social Services, however, sat on their hands. They didn't tell my parents any of what Sara had told them in her letter – Dad was on to Social Services by this time, telling them he and Mum needed help because they'd lost control of me and were worried. They said that for all that I might be unruly, they couldn't do anything because I was fifteen, nearly sixteen, and therefore nearly an adult. In their minds, it was up to me if I was off with men – nothing to do with abuse, just me making a 'lifestyle' choice.

* * *

I'd convinced myself that Mum and Dad didn't care; that they still just saw me as a wild teenager and didn't have a clue about me being passed around for sex with the gang.

In fact, it had begun to dawn on them that Harry's place was evil and they were beginning to get frantic. True, I'd stay at home some nights now, but would leave again when I got Emma's siren call. They would hear my phone vibrating and count the minutes before I tried to bolt to the door and be away. I was so desperate not to upset the gang that I'd sometimes climb out of a bedroom window, shimmy down to the eaves above the front door, and run out into the night. Back to purgatory.

Dad would go to Harry's house himself to look for me sometimes, though more often than not it would be left to Mum to reclaim her 'lost' daughter because he didn't trust himself not to hit someone. She'd drive up and then wait outside in the car for a glimpse of me, because they'd always deny I was there.

One time she called at the front door to be told I'd left, but with the door ajar she could see me nipping out of the back door. She shouted at me to stop and managed to grab me and bundle me into the car. I went home that time, but soon I was back again, reeled in by Emma's unhealthy control over what passed as my life.

In the early days, Dad had reacted to my swearing at them by throwing me out of the house – not in a, 'Here are your belongings, now off you go,' sort of way, but in an attempt to calm me down and shock me into thinking about how I was behaving.

Now he and Mum just wanted to persuade me to stay at home because they sensed something was horribly wrong. All these years later, they say they'll never forgive themselves for not trying harder. But there was only so much they could do.

Some nights, when Mum and Dad would ask the police or Social Services to get me away from Harry's place, the police might turn up, but they'd just put me in a van and dump me back at home. They never seemed to care whether I was OK, whether the gang had any hold on me. There was never any, 'Look, sweetheart, if these people threaten you again, you've got to come to us.'

At first I had thought the police were like my parents, thinking it was only Daddy and Immy who were involved. But then I remembered telling them about being attacked by the other men as well, and about Emma, and how it all worked.

I felt betrayed by them, as though after all I'd been through I was just a joke to be laughed at – by the gang, the police, by Social Services. I was locked into the life Emma and the gang were forcing on me. Part of me told me it was my own fault for keeping on going back: I should have had more courage, or strength, or just common sense. I should have told someone rather than waiting for somebody to rescue me. But Emma had that hold over me and wasn't about to let me go.

From that point on, I sank to a new level of despair. I was effectively owned by a gang who felt they were immune to justice.

For their part, the police either knew I was still being abused or should have guessed. They'd called at Harry's place for the underwear they needed for forensics, and I'd told them how Emma had been controlling me for the gang. They also knew, as the autumn wore on and I remained at Harry's place, that I was still massively at risk, because my parents would ring them in despair to ask them to bring me back from there. They'd do it, but, as I said, they never did anything to make me stay at home – or sit me down and ask why I was doing it. The police were the ones investigating Daddy over the rape, so surely they should have taken more of an interest in me? After all, I was the victim and the main witness.

Chapter Twelve
Don't I Deserve Something?

And so the days rolled on. Some days we'd go back to Emma's so I could change out of my school uniform, but other times we'd go straight to wherever Tariq and Emma had agreed to meet the gang. People have said since that kids shouldn't be out that late, all indignant, thinking these things always happen at night. But this was in daylight, three o'clock in the afternoon, with me being picked up still in my uniform to be taken to God knows where, straight from the school gates.

If I did get a chance to change, I'd wear a tracksuit or jeans and a T-shirt. I deliberately dressed down, knowing that whatever I wore, it wouldn't matter. My clothes came off anyway.

Emma would be trying to hurry me as I got changed, though sometimes she'd wait in the car for me outside Harry's, chatting with Tariq while I got ready. Normally it would take about two minutes: no make-up, no hair do, not even the Poundshop powder I used as foundation when I could afford it. Anything not to encourage them.

Once I was ready, we'd get back into the taxi and I'd be driven to Rochdale, Oldham or wherever. I never went anywhere on my own; Emma was always there.

As soon as we got to where we were headed, I'd know what was coming and try to get it over with so I could go home. I'd go onto autopilot.

Sometimes we'd go to a place and stay there for a few hours while a succession of different men came to have their so-called fun. Other times we'd go somewhere, stay a short time, go back to Harry's place, and then there'd be another phone call to her mobile and we'd be picked up again to go somewhere else. It could be anywhere, just as long as they were getting paid and Emma was getting paid both for what she was doing and for selling me.

Escort girls want to do it – and have the choice to do it – and Emma, by then, it seemed, wanted to do it. But for me it was rape, because I didn't want to do it.

I knew from magazines that girls from other countries were trafficked into Britain for sex, and that they might end up in brothels, unable to escape. These stories were quite high profile. But what about *this* story, that was happening to me? What was happening here was still trafficking, except there were no air fares to pay, no girls to pay. Domestic trafficking, as the police call it. And you still couldn't escape because of what they'd do to you. It was ruthless and evil, and they didn't care whether they were destroying the lives of kids like me.

I think if they were threatening me now, I wouldn't believe it – at least not the worst of it. But at fifteen, I thought they were totally invincible and totally beyond the reach of the law. So when they said they'd burn my parents' house down, beat the shit out of me or my parents, and rape my sisters, I believed them. And, as a kid, once you've convinced yourself that they'll do what they say, they don't need to keep repeating themselves: you see the threat in their eyes every time they look at you. It doesn't go away.

With the men, it was always brutal, always at the most basic level that sex can be. They were animals. They didn't bother with anything that might make it easier for me; nothing like using a lubricant. They were prepared to hurt me because all they wanted was what they'd paid for. I just had to suffer the pain. By then I wasn't bleeding or anything any more, but because up to six men a night were raping me, one after the other, I'd often feel terribly sore inside.

They knew we weren't prostitutes because they could have found those for themselves. They needed this specialised market that people like Daddy and Tariq, in their separate gangs, had carved out for them to enjoy: the forbidden market in which they could turn up at a stranger's flat or house, violate an under-age girl – a white girl – and then go back to their wives as if nothing had happened.

I'm guessing that they'd see a prostitute as dirty and disgusting, but a young girl as clean, innocent and somehow pure. It must have been a turn-on for them – it *was* a turn-on for them, as some of them asked for even younger girls than me, younger even than Roxanne at thirteen.

I still can't understand how they could be turned on by a sobbing child who was indifferent to them. A prostitute will put on a show if she knows that if she does she may get more money. And she'll play an active part in it, again because of the money. But when they attacked me, it was just a kid taking her leggings and knickers off with everything else still on, lying there on the bed and looking at the wall while they did it. No conversation, just Tariq having told them, 'She's young and tight,' and giving them a price.

Where was the fun in that for these men? Maybe it's the power, the control. There's no power with a prostitute, but there is with a child, even if she could just as easily be your daughter.

It was one huge circle of activity, a bit like when you throw a stone into the middle of a lake and the ripples keep going out towards the edges. Obviously there are paedophiles from all races, but almost all those who attacked me were Pakistani. I've heard since that white paedophiles operate mostly on their own. To my knowledge they don't usually do what these guys did: ring their mates and say, 'We've got a fourteen-year-old here, come on round.'

It's almost as if they don't see it as wrong. There were so many of them, all friends, or friends of friends, all passing on numbers to each other so they could have sex with a young white girl. They'd think it was normal to go to someone else's house, walk into a room where three schoolgirls were being plied with drink, and then a few minutes later force them to have sex.

Some of them, and men like them, had been going through the same vile ritual for years.

* * *

Through all this, it was Harry who'd been the one to distract me, however briefly, from the nightmare that I was living with Emma and the gang. For all his weirdness with Emma, he was like a father figure to me, friendly, happy, with a knack of taking me out of myself when things became too much. It was as if he understood.

But when he saw me getting into taxis, the same taxis with Emma, he must have put two and two together. Everyone else in the house seemed to know, so I suppose it was inevitable that he'd realise, too. And, of course, Emma would have been happy to give him all the lurid details.

There began to be a disturbing change in the way Harry behaved around me. He'd never talked about sex in front of me before, and I wouldn't have expected him to – not an old guy in his fifties, who could have been my granddad. But now he did, whenever any of the girls were around.

Emma and Roxanne seemed to love it, and actually thought it funny when he pointed at the top of my legs and said, 'You know what that's for, don't you? Make whatever you can out of it.'

I would go red and shrink away, mortified that someone like him, someone I looked up to, could have said such a thing. It got worse, though, as he started asking me weird questions when we were alone, maybe when *Coronation Street* was on, or *EastEnders*, which he loved. And they always seemed to have something to do with sex.

'What's your bra size, Hannah?' he asked once.

'Do you shave down there?'

And then, out of the blue: 'Have you ever come?'

One day I'd gone to school without some of the books I needed. When I returned to the house at around 10 a.m.

to pick them up, the other people in the house were asleep, but Harry obviously wasn't: I could hear the television in his room was on.

At first I was glad. The door to my room was closed but it didn't have a handle on the outside, so I knocked on Harry's to ask him if he had anything I could use to open it.

He told me to come in. His room was painted red. The TV was in the corner and Harry's double bed was opposite the window. Daylight was streaming in.

'Come and sit down,' he said, patting the side of the bed. I did, and he shifted towards me.

The things he said next took me back to the day my whole nightmare had started. The more he said, the sicker I felt.

Just like Daddy had done, he was saying how much he liked me. But then the twist.

'You've been living here for free, haven't you, my darling?'

'Yes,' I mumbled.

'And you've had my food and my cider and all the other things for free too, haven't you?'

I didn't reply, but then, I hardly needed to. I knew where the conversation was headed, and no matter what I said, it wasn't going to change anything. Unless I wanted to pay rent or else go back home, I'd have to 'treat' him.

'I've always wanted to do things to you,' he breathed, 'right from the first day you came here. Don't you think I deserve something?'

His words hung in the air. He knew I was trapped, knew I'd feel I had nowhere else I could go, and that no matter what he did to me no one would believe me.

It was another betrayal. I wanted to yell at him and scream: 'You're a pervert, get lost!' But I knew that if I did he'd throw me out. And then what?

I was in my school uniform and I shuddered as his hand crept towards me, brushing my knee as it slid under my skirt. The tears were welling up, but I wouldn't let them fall. I tried desperately to keep my legs crossed so he couldn't get to me. Then he changed tack, withdrawing his hand and instead pushing back the quilt. I could see he was naked and had an erection. Slowly, he reached out to take my hand and put it on him.

'I've been told you give good blow jobs,' he said quietly, 'so suck it, there's a good girl, and then you can stay.'

I felt the same sense of hopelessness that engulfed me every time Emma took me to the men. I'd been so conditioned that I couldn't fight them – any of them. It had got to the point that all I could ever think of by then was to get it over and done with as soon as possible, and cling to the idea that it wasn't me doing it but some other girl, some other victim.

When it was over, Harry looked down at me and said, 'Get a roll-up if you want. Then get your stuff and get off to school.'

I felt horrible. Doing that with Harry was worse than when I was with the other men because I was living with him. I had to see him every day. I'd trusted him. I thought he was a surrogate father in some ways. And now this. Another paedophile to ruin my life, and another layer of misery to try to shut out.

There would be other times with Harry, of course. And I always did it because Harry, just like Emma, knew everything ... including where I lived.

That night, when I told Emma about it, she said she did it to him, too, when she was skint, and he'd give her £10. Roxanne did it as well. To them it was just normal. *Normal.*

I dreaded the thought that one day it might seem normal to me.

* * *

I now had no sanctuary, only differing levels of pain and misery. Harry's place was a prison filled with hopeless, feral creatures I knew cared less for me than for the fleas that infested their mangy dogs – some nights, after that first time with Harry, I would sit down with a glass of water, picking up scores of fleas and drowning them. I wanted to drown, too.

I was full of self-loathing. I hated myself for letting it all happen, but I didn't know how to stop it. All the time Emma was telling me my parents would be ashamed of me so I could never go back home, and all the time I was having to do things that would make it even more difficult to return.

I knew that I needed protecting from myself because I'd been making the wrong decisions. I was like a different person. I didn't have a life any more. It was all a blur, a different world. I didn't really know how to cope with anything and just blanked everything out. I didn't have the power to resist the men because they were so intimidating. I needed someone to do it for me – to stop it for me.

I became increasingly unkempt: I smelt, and my hair was always dirty and lank. I was almost feral myself. The men who were abusing me didn't care what I was wearing, and I didn't care what I was wearing, so I'd generally just keep on the same tracksuit day after day. I'd go around stinking of alcohol and with wee on my jacket, but not having a clue how it had got there. Sometimes I'd wear boys' clothes, but it still didn't bother them – just so long as they could do what they wanted with me.

* * *

Aarif's flat was the gang's favourite haunt. I was taken there about four times a week from August, through September and October and into November.

The arrangements would be made by Tariq, who would tell Emma what time to get there and how many men were likely to be waiting. He'd then come and pick us up from Harry's house.

We'd arrive at the flat at about 8 p.m. or 9 p.m. There would usually be food and always vodka. Because I knew what was coming I'd drink as much as I could – usually about half a litre. Once I was drunk, either Tariq or Emma would tell me who I'd be sleeping with and send me into the bedroom.

I had to have sex with Aarif every time. There would usually be three or four others, sometimes five, but he would always go first. Tariq never said why it had to be that way, he'd just tell me to go and have sex with him.

It was the same routine. I'd go into the bedroom and lie on the bed. Aarif, and then the others, would come in, get naked and climb on top of me. I'd just lie there. Afterwards the man who'd just raped me would go back into the living room and the next one would come in.

Usually Saj was there, and Cassie from Castleton Taxis, Joe from Jo Baxi's Taxis, and another of the drivers, who, for some reason – that I never wanted to know – was called Megamuncher. Sometimes there were other girls there too: Roxanne, Paige, a third girl who was introduced to me as Darcy, and a fourth I didn't know who was half-Asian, half-white. I only saw her that one time.

Roxanne only came to Aarif's flat at weekends that winter, because during the week she was away from Harry's. She was thirteen but looked younger. She was with us about a dozen times.

I know she slept with Megamuncher, and I think with Cassie as well. I never actually saw her have proper sex, but I'd seen her give Aarif a blow job. It was on a night that Tariq wouldn't take us home because he'd been arguing with Emma. He threw us out of his car at a garage near Aarif's flat. So we walked there and rang the buzzer. Emma asked Aarif: 'If one of them gives you a blow job, will you give us the taxi money to get home?'

He said, 'Yeah.'

I don't know why it ended up being Roxanne, but I remember Emma telling her she'd batter her if she didn't do it. Roxanne just did it, while Emma and I sat there on the other sofa. Nothing was said, though I was squirming.

I felt tight about Roxanne having to do it, but at the same time I was so relieved it wasn't me.

For all that I'd been through myself, the sight of that thirteen-year-old girl giving a middle-aged man a blow job will haunt me for ever. She'd barely taken on a woman's body, and yet there she was, leaning over him with a smile, giving the sort of performance that would have made you think she was a porn star.

At thirteen.

I shuddered when I thought about how much practice, how many encounters, she must have been through to become so proficient, so convincing. As if it was something she'd been doing since she was a kid. And would there ever have been any love?

All Emma could do was laugh at her, and him, as they went through the whole horrific pantomime.

To Roxanne, it was absolutely, entirely normal: just something she did, a trick in the repertoire, that she was happy to do for any bloke at all, just so long as she could have a few swigs of vodka and end up with a fiver or a taxi home. What did she get from it? A feeling that she was being appreciated? Valued? *Loved?* What was her life normally that she had to come here to get that? At the time, though, I never stopped to ask those questions of myself.

Most of the time at Aarif's, though, it was just me and Emma, both of us lying there, in turns, being abused by however many of them had paid. Whenever it was all over for me I'd put my leggings on again and go back into the living room. Without fail I'd feel ashamed and dead inside.

If ever I refused to lie there for them they'd throw me out and I'd have to make my own way home. But I was usually too numb, too cowed, to refuse.

They didn't bother talking to us. Every night it happened, they would just chat among themselves in their own language until they'd finished and it was time for us to go home. We never stayed the night; we were always back home by sunrise and usually much earlier.

The worst times with Aarif were when he wanted me 'the other way'. When he did it the first time, he promised me he wouldn't but, of course, he did, suddenly and without warning, and the pain of it shot right through my body.

The first time it happened, Emma had just been with him and had then shouted me into the bedroom to sleep with him. They ended up dragging me in.

At first I lay on my back, but then he told me to turn over. When it happened I tried to arch away from him as the first sobs welled up deep within me. I was screaming and shouting at him to get off me. I shouted for Emma, too, and she came in, followed by Darcy, who'd seen me being dragged into the bedroom and who was asking if I was all right.

Aarif had just carried on the attack until they came in, me sobbing from the searing pain and humiliation, trying desperately to fend him off. Darcy had a friend there that night and because I was crying so much she was saying, 'Should I stay for her?' Emma was telling them to go, that'd I'd be all right. She was laughing. I think she got a buzz from knowing I'd been attacked that way.

Slowly, painfully, I put my clothes back on and a few minutes later Tariq arrived to pick us up. When Emma told him what had happened, he showed not an ounce of sympathy.

In his mind it was all about practicalities. 'If it's your period, you have to do it that way because otherwise it's unclean for the man,' he said. 'There's no point crying about it.'

Most of the other men liked to do that to me as well, especially if I was on my period. As Tariq had made clear, it meant they stayed 'clean' while they were raping me. Lucky them.

There were lots of times I had to sleep with Megamuncher, who was in his thirties, with long hair swept back over his shoulders. He sometimes used a silver BMW. I think he worked part-time in an Asian clothes shop. We went past it once, on a big road with a lot of takeaways, and Emma pointed it out.

Megamuncher had sex with Emma more times than with me, but for me it was still so often I can't add them all up. It's the same with most of them.

I think Joe from Jo Baxi's and Cassie from Castleton Taxis were friends, because they'd usually turn up at the flat together. Usually I was dead drunk, but I remember the first time with Joe. Aarif just told me to sleep with him and I did because I was used to it. I didn't want to, and I didn't like it, but I was used to having sex with all these men. I knew it was wrong because they were old and I was only young – and because I didn't want them to do it. Every time I'd just want them to hurry up, hurry up, for God's sake, hurry up and get it over with.

That first time with Joe, and all the other times, I'd just turn my head away from him and towards the wall. He must have known – they all must have known – that I didn't like doing it, because why else would I have just lain there and stared at the wall?

I tried not to think about anything any more. It was better that way. I was there in that world, I was living it, but I wasn't thinking. I'd walk down the street like a zombie, emotionally shut down, with everything in my vision moving in slow motion. I could hear things going on around me, but I couldn't distinguish what they were, and I couldn't respond, because I wasn't actually listening.

It was like a dream state. I didn't want to contribute to the world around me any more, and even if I had, I wouldn't have been capable of doing so. My dignity and self-respect had both been ripped away, leaving me an emotionally empty shell. I could feel my brain and all my senses shutting down, leaving just numbness.

And I *welcomed* it.

Gradually, I had come to feel that the worst things were happening not to me but to someone else. I wasn't sad any more, I wasn't angry any more, and I wasn't happy. Ever.

* * *

Thankfully, however, I had the occasional respite, as well as school. Most Thursdays would mean the walk into the Crisis Intervention place in Taylor Street with Emma. I'd always try to just sit there, hoping not to have to speak. I think Jane could tell I was intimidated by the huge girl next to me. Right from the start, Emma had done the talking for me, trying to lay a smokescreen, making up stories about men I supposedly loved to sleep with, saying, 'Yeah, she's a slag,' and things like that.

But soon I wasn't even embarrassed. I'd gone past that. I had other things to worry about, so what was the point?

As I say, Jane sensed that Emma had a hold over me – though at that time she had no idea quite how strong that was or how deep it went. Sometimes, if Emma had gone out to do a test or do a wee, Jane would ask: 'Is there anything you'd like to tell me while she's not here?' I always said no. Jane would then suggest I could see her alone. I wanted to, but again I would say no.

At that stage I couldn't engage with anyone. All I could do was try to beat back the pressure and pain I was in.

On those Thursday nights we'd come away from Taylor Street with a bag of condoms, usually around ten of them, always in a white bag. Emma would get them for herself or she'd get a bag for me as well. Out we'd go onto the street – her singing or whistling, me silent and shuffling beside her.

Chapter Thirteen
Disturbia

Emma never rested in her quest to find more and more men for us – obviously, the more men I slept with, the more money she got. Over those next few weeks she found lots of new faces that I'd never seen before. I first met Billy at Aarif's. He was a skinny Asian man with short hair and, according to Emma, he was good looking.

'So it'll be easier with him,' she said one day, me in the bath, her sitting on the loo seat so she could keep an eye on me and make sure I'd shaved.

Actually, it wasn't easier with him because rather than just get on with it, he'd always want to touch me, like I meant something to him. I told him if he was going to have sex with me then just to do it and not touch me.

He'd have sex with Roxanne, too, and one night she told me she loved him. I couldn't believe it – and one day nor will she, hopefully. How could she decide she loved someone who'd do that to her and all the other under-age girls? It was sick. But at the same time, I guess it was the ultimate clue as to just how brainwashed we girls had become by these monsters.

We'd been seeing Cassie for a few weeks at Aarif's when he started to ring Emma and say he wanted to take us somewhere else. Maybe he got us cheaper that way, I don't know.

He'd turn up in his people-carrier, a VW Sharan, before driving us out to Ashworth Valley. It's all open moorland there, but it was still quite public – we were close to Rossendale School – but he'd park up on a track away from the main road.

He always wanted to have the two of us together, one after the other. Usually he didn't mind which way round it was, so we'd have to make the choice. Some choice. I always wanted to go first because it was quicker and cleaner – and easier, because the second time always took him longer to get through it.

Emma usually had her way, though, and would go first, while I sat in the front trying to ignore the sound of cheap sex and him groaning. Then it would be my turn to get out of the front passenger seat and swap places with Emma in the back of his car. It's shaming to say it, I know, but I didn't care any more that he'd just been with someone else, with Emma. I was past that point; I felt disgusted enough without analysing every sordid thing that was happening to me. Sitting in the front, dreading my turn, I would try to concentrate on the hum of the huge wind turbines looking down on us. I often wondered what the local dog walkers and runners made of this taxi parking up on the moors in the early morning.

I know that he knew our ages because Emma once told him when we were in his taxi. Instead of being shamed by this, straight away he had asked if she knew any girls who were younger, and Emma had told him about Roxanne and Paige. He asked her to bring them next time.

I thought he was beyond perverted for saying that, though part of me was relieved, thinking that if they came it would mean I'd not have to have sex with him. I know it sounds awful, but that's what I was thinking – what I had been reduced to.

Tariq was all right about him picking us up and, anyway, Emma used to give him some of the money that Cassie gave her. Cassie would give her £30 or £40 after he'd had sex with us. Sometimes he said he was too tired to sleep with Emma, so then it would be just £20. But Emma would always give some of it to Tariq. Then she'd give me £5 or £10 or buy me a beer out of it.

The money didn't always go to Tariq and Emma, however. By now, Harry was having trouble paying his mortgage, and one night I saw the two of them talking. A while later Emma came over to me and said, 'Go and get ready. I need to make some money for Harry.' That night, I remember I had to sleep with five men. They all paid Emma and when we got back, she gave all the money to Harry. I think it was a couple of hundred quid.

After a while, Billy started taking us to a flat in the Falinge area of Rochdale. It belonged to a guy called Jamal, who said he owned the franchise of a big shop somewhere in town. One night, after the men there had had sex with us, they were then going to throw us out. For some reason, Emma started to kick off – perhaps they hadn't paid? Jamal hit her and she punched him back. We ended up having to walk home.

Billy would also take us to the home of a guy called Safeer. It would be just Safeer there with another of the men, Tiger. Billy and Tiger would sleep with us, but never Safeer.

On one occasion, there were four men there. Emma slept with two of them and wanted me to sleep with the other two, but I said I wasn't going to do it. So she started telling me, 'Just do it, just do it, because if I have to you're not getting into my taxi.'

I slept with one of them, but point-blank refused to do it with the other. He called me a white bitch and I called him a bastard. But I wasn't going to sleep with him.

* * *

Sometimes it felt as though there were gangs within gangs, or maybe splinter groups of men who'd then fall out with each other. I know that every time Billy took us out, Tariq used to get mad and threaten Emma.

He and Emma fell out over Juicy too, when he started picking us up in September. Juicy would pick us up in Peel Lane, near the Britannia Mill Industrial Estate in Heywood. He drove a light blue BMW and would take us into Ashworth Valley, though not as far into the lanes as Cassie did.

The first time he was on his own, the next with a man he called Boss. Juicy was in his fifties, fat, balding, with a big, bent nose and a moustache, while Boss was younger, in his thirties, tall with short black hair. He usually wore Western clothes, and Juicy was always in Asian ones.

We both had to have sex with them, one at a time. Whichever one wasn't having sex would get out of the car and wait. It was mostly me with Boss and Emma with Juicy. I'd tell her I didn't like it and she'd say, 'So?' Just like all the others, I felt I didn't have a choice.

I was with Juicy three or four times, with Boss six or seven times. Emma would get paid.

After a while we started going to another flat in Falinge. Juicy said it was his auntie's. It had one bedroom and they'd have sex with both of us.

One time, Boss was having sex with me and said he'd give me £40 if I'd take all my clothes off, but I wouldn't. He said, 'Come on, come on, take your top off, and your bra.' He started trying to lift the top off and I was saying no.

I pretended I needed to go to the toilet, and when I came back Emma was having sex with him instead.

The next time we saw Tariq, he hit Emma because he'd found out about Juicy and Boss. He was mad with her, saying to never do it again, because she was only supposed to meet the men he knew. I guess it was an issue over money – Tariq wouldn't get his cut if Emma, and not him, started finding men for us to sleep with.

* * *

It was late October that something that chills me to the bone happened.

Emma tried to get one of my sisters involved.

Every time I'd go back home with her, Emma would ask Lizzie if she wanted to come out with her one night, making it sound like just a few drinks and some fun. But I knew it would be more than that.

I was so deeply traumatised by then, I just couldn't find a way to warn Lizzie, to tell her: 'You can't come, sis. If you do, you'll be raped.' Instead, I just played the role of older sister, telling my parents there was no way she was coming out with me because she'd spoil all my fun.

Fun. A good joke, eh? Though at least it saved my little sister.

Emma really knew no bounds. She seemed to have saturated every part of my life. The sight of her made me shudder, but it was the sound of the ring tone of her phone that became a thing of real terror for me. Typically for her, and fittingly for the situation I now found myself in, she'd chosen a song filled with dark piano chords and even darker lyrics.

In other circumstances, Rihanna's 'Disturbia' might have become an anthem to my teenage years. But here, in this shadow world, it served as the calling card of pain, violence and degradation.

Bum-bum, be-dum, bum-bum be dum-dum ...

Day or night, her phone would come to life: the discordant sound of piano as someone runs their fingers along the keys, then Rihanna's moody vocal filling me with dread as I began to visualise the darkness that lay ahead. As Rihanna sang about going crazy, I'd feel my mind begin to whir as Emma took the call.

I knew we'd be climbing into Tariq's taxi within minutes, Emma in the front, me, as usual, in the back; heading into a scene that in my imagination was a mirror image of the one portrayed in the music video. For Rihanna's act, it was a prison cell and a gas chamber: a girl tied to a burning stake, or caressing a mannequin on a steel-framed bed, or else trying to break free of the chains that held her fast. But that was all it was: an act.

For me, it was rape in the feral, urban landscape that neither the police nor the local social workers seemed prepared to acknowledge even existed.

Disturbia.

And so I'd hear that brilliant, awful song on so many occasions as I set off to be raped, hunched up in the back of a people-carrier that looked for all the world like just another taxi.

Even when we'd returned to Emma's house there would be no let-up. Emma loved the song so much that she'd play it endlessly on her phone.

Disturbia.

* * *

Mixed in with the hell of Aarif's flat and all the other places I'd be taken to, there were occasional times I could feel almost human. It still wasn't the sort of stuff Mum and Dad would have approved of, but it just about kept me together.

One Friday in October, Emma hurried me out of the bathroom and said we were going to meet a new guy. We left the house, me thinking the worst, Emma swaggering towards the black Toyota Lucida that had pulled up outside, carrying the name 'Eagle Taxis' on the side. The same firm as Tariq's.

You could hear the music pumping out of the stereo even before you got into the car. Pop music, chart stuff. The taxi's driver leaned back and introduced himself. 'Hi,' he beamed. 'I'm Car Zero.'

Another guy, another nickname, I thought. And then there were the drinks he'd brought: whisky for him, vodka for us, and two mixers, one of cola, the other lemonade. 'So you can pick,' he said, smiling.

He'd take us out, usually on a Friday or a Saturday. This went on for weeks, through into November. It seems so weird, but I grew to like him. Sometimes we'd go to Ashworth Valley, other times he'd just park up in an empty car park or industrial site. He'd drink his whisky and cola in the front, while we had the vodka – Glen's, of course – in a litre bottle.

Everything seemed just as it did with all the other men, the paedos who'd attack me; everything except the end result. All Car Zero wanted to do was party. He loved the same sort of music we did, and he also loved to drink. He even brought little plastic cups each time for us to drink out of.

While he drank, he'd talk to us about normal things – as if he was one of us. It meant that whenever Emma said, 'We're going out with Car Zero tonight,' I'd be relieved because unlike all the other nights, with all those other men, I knew I wasn't going to be attacked. I felt safe. It might even be fun.

He didn't get drunk the way we did in the back, but even so I knew he must still have been way over the limit. In the old days it would have worried me. Now I couldn't care less: if we crashed, we crashed.

The last night I saw Car Zero he picked us up from Harry's house as normal, before heading out to Ashworth Valley close to where Cassie would take us.

We'd been drinking for about an hour, laughing, being stupid, when Emma said she needed a wee.

'Will you come with me?' she asked.

I got out of the car and we both had a wee.

As I headed back to the car she pulled at my sleeve and said, 'Are you going to sleep with him, then?'

'No,' I said, almost laughing. 'We've never had to sleep with him. He's not like the others.'

Emma gave me her look, the controlling look; the look that tells you you've got to do something.

'But, Emma, he never tries to sleep with us. He doesn't want to. He just wants to drink and chill with us.' I could hear my voice starting to sound panicky.

It was no good. 'He's bought all this stuff for us, Hannah. You can't just expect never to do anything for him. So get back in the car and do it.'

So he really was just like all the others. The penny dropped, and I suddenly realised she must have struck a deal with him. It made me feel worse than I'd felt in a long time. With the others, I'd just got used to it. With him, I thought I'd found someone in Emma's world who was normal and safe. But it was just another betrayal. *Stupid*, I thought, *I should have expected it*. I knew I had no option.

It had started to rain as I climbed into the front passenger seat. Car Zero knew full well what our conversation outside had been about, and he just said, quietly, and a bit sheepishly, 'Get in the back.'

As I did what I was told I could see Emma outside, drawing on a cigarette and pulling up the hood of her tracksuit to keep out the rain. She didn't have long to wait. Once he'd joined me in the back he told me to take my pants off and lie down, so that's what I did.

The music was still blaring out of the speakers as he drove us home, but no one was talking. Once we were at Harry's place, the two of us got out and he drove away.

I never saw him again because Emma deleted his details from her phone. 'The bastard wouldn't pay me cos of all the beer he'd bought,' she explained.

I went upstairs to the bathroom, feeling sick.

* * *

So there I was, this poor, stupid teenager, locked in a world I'd walked into and now wanted more than anything to escape.

Maybe I was naïve to think I'd be rescued; that the police would do everything they could to protect me.

What I needed most was to be protected from myself: however anyone might judge me, I was still only fifteen. A child. The police must have suspected from the interview I'd done that it was still going on, and knowing that still makes me feel gutted.

I know they couldn't have stopped Daddy from raping me those four times, and Immy, with his 'treat', but, once

I'd told them, surely they could have done something to protect me? Surely they could have made sure I went home, and stayed home, and kept me away from the gang?

Instead, the taxis kept on coming to Harry's place, turning up, bang on cue, within minutes of me hearing the Rihanna ring tone chime out from Emma's phone. Usually it was Tariq's car 40. There were many other men in this sick conspiracy, but so often I couldn't remember their names. Either that or the descriptions I gave police – the nicknames they'd told me, or that I'd made up for them, and the detail of how they looked and how they behaved – led to a blind alley, a cold trail.

In the days of my long-forgotten innocence Dad used to give me a lift to school and collect me when he could. Once I'd moved in to Harry's place, my attendance at school dropped, but whenever I did go I'd either walk or get a taxi. Tariq's taxi, usually. If I somehow persuaded Emma to let me go to school, she would ring up Eagle Taxis and ask for a cab, saying 'Can you make sure it's car 40?' And he'd come, and I'd get in and we'd head off to school.

It was always weird. Tariq usually had a smile on his face, as if he was hugely chuffed about something. As soon as I was in the taxi he'd say, 'Hello, Hannah, how are you today? You're coming to see me later and I'll pick you up.' As if it was all a laugh. 'I'll pick you up at seven o'clock. Be ready. Be a good girl for me tonight.' Back at home, my parents were receiving letters from school about my behaviour, most of it about unauthorised absences, others about turning up still drunk from the gang's vodka.

Sometimes the teachers would take me to Food Tech and give me toast and a cup of tea because they realised I needed it. I was always dead tired because I was so often out late, getting to bed at 3 a.m. or 4 a.m. and getting up again at 8 a.m. so I could pretend to be a vaguely normal schoolgirl.

I think it was Miss Nuttall, the Food Tech teacher, who grassed to Miss Crabtree about me. I actually felt OK that day, but she must have smelled the alcohol, left the class, and gone off to fetch Miss Crabtree.

'Hannah,' she said, when she arrived, 'I can smell alcohol on you. Are you drunk?'

'No, Miss,' I said. I admitted to having had a couple of drinks, but no, I wasn't drunk.

'I think you are, young lady,' said Miss Crabtree, quietly, not cross, almost sympathetic, it seemed. Then, 'How much sleep have you had?'

'I had an early night!'

She looked at my sunken eyes, my pallid skin, and must have known it was another lie.

'And where did you sleep?'

'At my dad's house,' I said.

'Well, I'm going to ring your dad now and ask him to collect you, because we both know you're drunk and we also both know you can't come into school in that state.'

So my dad came and that time I went home to safety. I still got texts from Emma later on, though, and I think I climbed out of a window and out over the porch roof again so I could head back to Harry's house. Maybe that was the time that Dad threatened to superglue my bedroom door shut.

At school, I did occasionally tell teachers I was hungry, and maybe that's why they'd feed me. But I think they knew: knew something, at least. In Food Tech there was a jar of one pound coins that was used to pay for the ingredients of dishes they wanted us to cook. Sometimes they'd give me a a pound coin and say, 'Go on, quick, get yourself something from the shop.'

Miss Crabtree was one of those who kept trying with me. I think it was in November that she took me to one side after hearing me rowing with another girl who'd called me a 'Paki-shagger'. Miss Crabtree had overheard it and called me into her office.

She sat me down across the desk from her, saying she wanted to know if I was OK. She said she'd heard what the other girl had called me, and wanted to know why, wanted me to open up to her.

I didn't, though. I just couldn't. Up to then I'd just explained the 'Paki-shagger' thing as a rumour because my mate had an Asian boyfriend, but now, in Miss Crabtree's office, I was too frightened to tell her.

I was crying, sitting there in that school chair, but for all that she tried to coax me into talking to her, I couldn't. All the time, in my pocket, I could feel my phone vibrating because it was on silent. Even without looking I knew it was Emma ringing me. I guessed she'd be close by, wanting to go somewhere with the gang.

In front of me, Miss Crabtree was saying something about a Pandora's box. How it needed to be opened, and how, for all that it might be scary, it needed to be opened so she could help me.

It didn't work. In the end she said, 'Look, I'll go and buy you a big bag of Haribo and leave them in my office. You come and pick them up at the end of the day and go home, and share them with your family.' She paused and looked at me. 'Have a proper chat with your parents, Hannah. You need to – and everyone wants to help you.'

I wanted so desperately to say, 'Yes, I'll do that, I really will.' But of course I couldn't – not then. I'm so sorry, Miss Crabtree.

And all the time she'd been talking to me, being nice, my phone – the new one Emma had 'allowed' me – had kept on vibrating in my pocket.

I was still in tears as I fled Miss Crabtree's office, heading for the exit and taking the phone out of my pocket as I ran. I could see I had loads of missed calls, all from Emma. When she rang again, I answered.

'We're outside,' she said. 'Come to the front.'

It was Tariq's taxi. I sat in the back as he drove to Harry's so I could get changed. Half an hour later, we were on our way to some disgusting flat that didn't know the world of Haribos and kindness.

When I next saw Miss Crabtree she asked me why I hadn't collected the sweets.

'Sorry, I forgot,' I said. Just deadpan.

Chapter Fourteen
Jane

By now I'd come to know every yard of the journey to Aarif's flat. If the condoms weren't already there, Emma would always have her supply from the Taylor Street clinic to fall back on. Billy was the only one who didn't use a condom, but I wouldn't dare object; and usually, if I was lucky, I was too drunk to realise, anyway.

Apart from Billy, there wasn't any pawing, not really. It was usually just quick, as if it was nothing – which, really, it was, I told myself. All I had to do was go into a bedroom with whomever – someone I'd never even spoken to – and let him do things to me until he was finished.

Normally, as I say, it was in twos or threes. Sometimes it was up to five at a time, one after the other. They'd slap me and grab me sometimes. Once, at Safeer's place, I got grabbed by the throat. I'd already slept with three of them and I told the next guy that I wouldn't sleep with him. So he got me by the throat and threatened me and called me a 'white bitch' and a slag.

I came to learn not to aggravate them. I knew they were going to have sex with me anyway, so it was best if I just let them. That way it would be easier. But even now I panic if someone shouts near me, especially if it's a man.

You never know what goes on behind closed doors, but I got the impression Asian girls are safe from them. Maybe it's because they wanted them to be pure so they could marry them off, and maybe it's partly about availability. Their girls are different because they're generally so covered up. They don't drink, they don't go out walking the streets at night; they're protected to the nth degree.

Safeer was in his forties, but he had a much younger 'girlfriend'; a half-white, half-black girl who looked the same age as me. Like the other mixed-race girl I'd seen, the one at Aarif's flat, she was something of an exception, because in the time I was being passed around by the gang it was usually just white girls. We were the ones who were available. It might have been black girls or Chinese girls, or girls of any other race, but around our way, we were the ones who were available.

I first met this particular girl on an evening when I'd already been raped, at a house in Nelson. Emma, Roxanne and I had walked to Morrison's car park in Heywood, and been picked up by Saj and Aarif. We headed off to the motorway and then up into Lancashire, where we ended up at Saj's place. As soon as we got there he gave us some gin. I wanted to get drunk because I knew what was coming, but I'd only managed two glasses before Emma told me to go upstairs. As usual, I didn't want to, but as usual she just said, 'You're already here now, and if you don't, how the fuck do you think you're going to get home?'

The sheets on the bed were brown and smelt of grease and sweat. There were Asian-style pictures on the walls; one of them with what looked like a poem and a scroll.

Saj was in traditional Asian clothes with baggy trousers. It was all either white or light blue.

He tried to take my leggings off for me, but I did it myself because I didn't want him touching me. Then he put a condom on and started. He was doing it really slowly, which filled me with revulsion because I just wanted it to be over with. Doing it slow like that, it's like the way you'd do it with your boyfriend or something – something loving.

I just shut my eyes, and thought, *Hurry up, hurry up and get it over with.* Times like this had become more of a mental torture than a physical one. I could deal with what was happening to my body, but in my head I just felt disgusted: sex is supposed to be with someone you love or, if not, then at least someone you want to be with, even if it's lust.

Above me, Saj was saying that he really liked me and that he wanted me to stay overnight. God, I could never do that! I couldn't cope with lying next to some creature like that for an entire night.

He kept trying to persuade me, saying he had enough money to pay Emma. I just kept saying no, and that I'd have to let Tariq know and he wouldn't allow it.

When he'd finished, Emma brought Aarif into the room and said I'd have to sleep with him as well. I was crying again by now, saying, 'No, I want to go home. I've done it now, can you take me home?'

Emma said, 'You can't just go with Saj and not Aarif when he's here as well.' But she then tried to appease him by saying he could have Roxanne. He moaned about it because for all that she was only thirteen, Roxanne was almost as big as Emma then. Eventually, though, he agreed to go into the bedroom with her.

It was Aarif who took us back to Morrison's car park, and from there, almost immediately, we were picked up by Tiger. Billy was with him in the car. As we sped away towards Safeer's place, Emma told me we had to go with them because I'd only slept with one person that night. Unbelievably, I found myself wondering if I would have been safer staying the night with Saj.

They'd given us a bottle of vodka, and even though the journey couldn't have taken much longer than ten minutes, I tried to drink as much as I could. As ever, I knew that if I was drunk I wouldn't feel as bad afterwards: it was always worse when I was sober, as I had been with Saj. The vodka was making me feel sick, but I kept forcing it down so I could get drunk.

Safeer's 'girlfriend' sat with us in the living room in an awkward silence. We'd been there for maybe ten minutes before Emma told Roxanne to go into the bathroom with Tiger and give him a blow job.

I assume that was what she started doing, but after only a short time, Roxanne came out and said Tiger wanted to speak to Emma. They had a hushed conversation before Emma came to me and told me I had to go into the bathroom and finish him off. He didn't like Roxanne: she was too fat.

Emma pushed me through the doorway but once I'd got there, trapped and shaking, I told him I didn't want to do it. He laughed at me, and then started trying to have sex with me but he decided the room was too cramped for that, so he ordered me to do what Roxanne had started. When it was over, he got up and left. I just sat there, staring at the wall, half-drunk, completely violated, angry that I'd had to do something Roxanne was supposed to have done. And then feeling guilty because I'd dared have that thought.

Safeer's 'girlfriend' stayed in the living room the whole time. I guess for her it was normal, and besides, maybe it was her turn later. I never saw her again.

* * *

As the days wore on, I began to wonder about Jane. She clearly wasn't stupid, and I sensed she was becoming suspicious. She'd seen the way Emma behaved around me, and she must have wondered why I was so quiet and seemingly under her thumb.

I didn't give it that much thought, though, because my retreat into alcohol was pretty much complete by the middle of November 2008: even on the days and nights that I wasn't being abused – which wasn't many – I'd try to drink myself into oblivion so I could forget.

Jane came in to see me at school on a Wednesday, midway through November. She was there partly to explain that I'd been referred to Childcare Services, because everyone was worried for me.

We began talking about drinking, and I let slip that when I was drunk I'd do things I'd never even think about doing when I was sober.

'I'll sleep with anyone when I'm drunk,' I said. It was meant to be a joke, but Jane latched on to it and the conversation went deeper: a lot deeper.

I suddenly found myself telling her how controlling Emma was, and how she'd deliberately get me drunk so she could take advantage of me and make money from me. She'd take me to meet men who'd then sleep with me. And she'd rarely let me have a mobile phone, partly because she wanted to control me and partly because she was paranoid about me having the men's numbers for myself. As if I'd want to.

At one point Jane looked up and asked: 'Did you ever see money changing hands?'

I nodded. Emma always had at least £60 on her at any one time, I said, and I'd seen her force Roxanne to sleep with a man. Emma got £20 for it, and she gave Roxanne a fiver.

It was a day for confessions, and for the rest of that meeting I couldn't help but confide in her, as maybe I should have done a long time before. I suppose I saw it as my only chance. I told her a lot about what I'd been going through, and how, for all that Emma and Roxanne seemed to enjoy what they were doing, I always felt scarred and damaged. And how I wanted it to end so that I could have my life back.

The one thing I didn't tell her about was Courtney's involvement in it all. I thought she'd been attacked, but I wasn't sure.

Sitting there with Jane, I told her that despite all that was going on in my own life I'd made a new friend at school. Her name was Robyn, and she was the sort of girl who right from the start would try her best to look after me.

Fat chance, but Jane still smiled. I said I felt ashamed about what was happening to me, and that I didn't want any of the other kids at school to find out.

It reminded me of Harry's house. 'There's sick graffiti about me on the walls outside,' I said. 'And in one of the bedrooms … it's like it's been written about someone else, someone I've never met.'

But of course, I had.

While I was with Jane that day, she got me to fill in some forms about relationships and respect. The first page was called, 'My life as a young woman in Rochdale', and after that came some headings where she asked me to give her answers. This is how I filled it in:

Something nice: *Hanging around with mates*

Something horrible: *School*

My mates: *Robyn*

How do I spend my time: *Drinking and going out*

Where do I go: *Friends' houses*

What do I do: *Party*

What do I want to do in
the future: *Be rich*

What risks have I taken: *Loads*

After that, she wanted me to make a list under two headings: 'Good things about being a girl' and 'Bad things about being a girl'.

In the first column I wrote down the usual suspects: *Boys, make-up, getting hair done and shopping.*

In the second I wrote:

Losing your virginity, periods, having a baby, responsibility, being used, being in love, vulnerability.

I thought we were finished, but then she asked me to do one more of the things she did with kids like me. 'Perfect Partners', she called it, and I had to describe the sort of lad I dreamed about.

Looking back, I think she was trying to make me think about Jake (she still didn't know he hadn't been a real, proper boyfriend). She said she wanted it to be all about respect: how you'd look at the qualities a lad had to offer and aim for someone with good ones, because that would make you feel good about yourself and good about life.

So I thought about that. And I realised that while I was being ravaged by the men, and flipped this way and that way – treated as though I might have been one of those naked, plastic models they have in department-store windows – Jake had come on to me and he had used me too.

And, finally, I tried desperately hard to imagine that I was leading a normal life and could actually choose someone to be my partner – someone to love and to look after me; someone to value and respect me.

All of that was beyond me for ever, I thought. I could feel Jane studying me as I scribbled my list of 'Perfect

Partner' words for her, but she had only an inkling of why I was wiping away tears.

I'd written:

Caring
Nice body
Honest
Fit
Nice
Money
Drinks
Car
Funny
Trustworthy
Good looking
Kind
Job
Romantic

'Well done, Hannah,' she said. 'It looks a lovely list.'

A week later, on 28 November, Jane was back in school, and this time she asked me the question I'd been pushing to the back of my mind – it filled me with dread and fear.

Would I talk to the police again? she asked. Would I tell them what the gang had been doing to me since the days with Daddy?

'No way,' I said. 'I only told you because I'm not involved any more. And it's confidential.'

Inside, I was shuddering, and wondering how the hell she could even ask such a question – even though I was bluffing, and was actually still caught up by the gang.

I'd reported it all to the police nearly four months earlier, and what had happened? Nothing. Who was Jane to be suggesting that I talk to them again now?

'No,' I said again.

Jane realised she'd crossed a line with me that I wasn't about to go over, and held up her hands as if to say, 'I surrender.' Then, while I sat there, sullen, eyes down, staring into my lap, she changed the subject.

She talked for what seemed like ages, and, slowly, as I came round from being angry with her, I gradually began to take in what she was saying.

She was talking about exploitation, sexual exploitation, of girls like me who some men saw as easy meat. They were young and they were vulnerable, and they were afraid to come forward and tell people who could help them.

'It's happening to lots of girls, Hannah,' she said softly.

I looked up, but only for a second.

She carried on. 'I've seen them over the years, talked to them, and all of us at Crisis have tried to help them. And, Hannah ...' She paused. 'Hannah, I know it's still happening to you, and that you don't want it to be. It's fine that you don't want to speak to the police again for now, but maybe one day you will. And if that happens, then I'll help you with that. Do you understand?'

I understood, but it was still difficult for me to deal with. We sat there in silence for a couple of minutes, me undecided, one moment raising my head to speak, the next lowering it again, too frightened, too ashamed.

Eventually, though, I found my tongue. 'I'm still not going to the police,' I whispered, 'but I'll tell you.'

So for the next few minutes I gave her some of the pieces of the awful, broken jigsaw that Emma had made of my life.

I told her about the flats and houses I'd been to, the ones in Rochdale, Bradford, Leeds and Oldham. 'The men don't usually live in these places,' I said. 'They just meet there. Sometimes they're just empty.' And then: 'Did you know I've been raped?'

'I'm not sure ...' she said, her voice trailing off to a silence.

So I told her, told her about that first time with Daddy, and the room above the Balti House, and the clock, the children's clock, that kept on ticking, and how he'd forced me even after I'd said no. I told her how I'd been shouting for Emma, whose only response had been to tell me to shut up.

I told her how Daddy had made me feel sick, and how after that first rape it had all got into sort of a pattern that always had Emma at the heart of it.

I told her about the time I'd gone with Emma and Roxanne to a flat in Rochdale where I'd been slapped for refusing to have sex with one of the men. And the time a taxi driver I'd never met pulled off the road onto a dirt track. Emma had told me to give him oral sex and I'd refused. Why couldn't she do it? 'Because we can't get home if you don't – and he wants you to do it.' And, shamed and humiliated, I told her I'd done what Emma had told me to do and the driver had dropped us off in Heywood.

I told Jane what a bully Emma was, and how scared of her I was. I told her how sorry I felt for Roxanne and Paige because they didn't stand up to her. As if I ever did.

Jane seemed to be on the verge of tears herself when I told her about the time Emma had told Roxanne to sleep with two men, but had handed over her mobile so she would be safe – as if a girl of thirteen could be safe with two paedophiles four times her age. That night, Emma had tried to ring Roxanne to check on her but the phone had been switched off. When we'd finally found her, Emma had gone mad with the kid because she'd only got £5 for sleeping with each of the men, twice. Emma had screamed at her and hit her.

I told Jane about Tariq, and that even though Emma's mum knew what he was up to, she'd let him drive her around in his taxi. I also told her how Emma had gleefully confessed to blackmailing another man by telling him she was pregnant, even though that couldn't have been true because she'd had the hormone implant.

In the middle of that heart-to-heart, Jane got to know how the people at Harry's place knew exactly what Emma was doing, and didn't lift a finger when she'd take little kids with her when she went to meet the men in the Asian gang. She'd say one of them was her kid. Around this time, in fact, Emma was mad with Crisis Intervention for telling Childcare Services that she sometimes took a little niece of hers with her when she was out 'partying'. It wasn't Crisis Intervention, as it turned out, but that's what she thought.

I was also really worried for Paige, I said, because she looked so young and I knew she was still involved with Emma. In the same way she'd softened me up, she was taking Paige out. Though in her case, because at that time she was still only thirteen and a virgin, Emma just made her give the men blow jobs.

She was also making her stay at Harry's new house – one we'd all moved into a couple of weeks earlier. Later, I learnt that Paige's sister was worried for her, but she hadn't got the new address and so couldn't rescue her.

Both school and social services knew that Paige was massively at risk. Miss Crabtree and a social worker called Anne had even had a meeting about her, because there was talk of her and other girls meeting Eagle taxi drivers at the Lidl car park in Heywood.

I looked Jane in the eye when I told her how firmly in Emma's grip she was. 'Paige won't say no to her,' I said.

And I should know, of course.

Eventually, the school bell rang and it was time for me to head away. Jane looked as though she wanted to carry on talking, but for me it was a welcome break.

As I left the room, I caught sight of Paige walking away up the corridor, quicker than she would normally. Suddenly, I wondered whether she'd been listening at the door and had overheard our conversation: heard me talking to Jane like I was a grass.

I decided I couldn't face any more school that day, and ran out through the gates, terrified my cover was blown. I was thinking, *Now Emma will know I've been talking to Jane. Paige will tell her.*

My conversation with Jane left me confused and more than a little scared: each day I wondered whether Paige would grass on me to Emma.

It was December now, and I was missing yet more school. Despite telling Jane I wasn't being taken to the gang any more, I was. Maybe she guessed as much, but she didn't let on and I wasn't about to tell her. I'd discovered that there's only so much you can tell people, no matter how much they may be trying to help you.

Chapter Fifteen
Two Blue Lines

Christmas was fast approaching. As if my life couldn't get any worse, on 11 December – when the cheerful, festive Iceland and Asda adverts were running back-to-back on TV – came another event that threw me into an even deeper despair.

I'd gone to Crisis Intervention in Taylor Street, though this time with Robyn rather than Emma because she'd gone off to see a 'boyfriend' on her own. I had a pregnancy test, and I remember Jane sitting there with the testing kit in her hand, her hand over the panel that gives the result. 'What will you do if it's positive?' she asked, with a gentle smile. It was an innocent question, but in my mind I started to panic. It must have shown on my face.

Slowly she opened her hand, looked for the tell-tale lines, and suddenly stopped smiling. She looked flustered, rising to her feet and saying, 'I just need a second opinion on this.'

As she left the room I thought, *It will be fine. If she's not sure, it must be all right.*

She came back a couple of minutes later and said, 'Look Hannah, I think it's positive, but I can't be sure. We'll have to do a second test in the morning.'

The plan was for her to meet me at school the next day, and carry out the second test. I wasn't to have a wee in the morning when I woke up, she said, because the first of the day was always strongest. That way there would be no doubt.

I was back and forth between Harry's place and home at that time (Emma must have realised I was in the gang's grip so fast it didn't matter if I went home occasionally) and a queasy feeling took hold of me as I walked home. I didn't know what to think.

When I woke up the next morning, Mum thought I looked a bit peaky and asked if I wanted to stay off school – I could help her with the shopping, if I wanted.

'No,' I said. 'I need to go to school.'

She looked astonished and exasperated all at once. 'But normally we can't get you there,' she said. Then I told her I was seeing Jane, and she started to catch on. She knew who Jane was, and what her job involved, and she knew school wasn't exactly my favourite place.

Her face clouded. 'You're not pregnant, are you?' she asked.

'No, no,' I said, but not with any real conviction.

So she told Dad, and Dad sent Lizzie off to the local shops to buy a tester kit. She came back with two, in fact. Maybe she thought the second one would come in handy another time.

Mum wasn't taking any chances. A few weeks before I'd had another scare, but that time I had dipped it in the toilet bowl to make sure it said negative. Mum never said anything, but this time Dad said: 'Make sure she does it properly.' I was so wayward then, he knew he couldn't trust me.

Mum came into the bathroom with me and made me wee into a cup, and then she dipped the tester in the cup. Then she dipped the second one in. They both said positive.

So there I was: chaotic, exploited and abused – and now pregnant. It was a fact, proved twice over.

It was just the identity of the father that was unknown.

Given the abuse I'd suffered, and was still going through, a nightmare scenario seared through my mind: the thought that this baby was one of *theirs*, was one of the men who'd been abusing me over these past months. Billy's? It could be. He didn't use condoms. *Oh God, it could be.*

Mum broke down as we came downstairs, but I was in too much shock to cry. Dad had been waiting in the living room. The TV was on, but someone – I've no idea who, as I was out of it by then – switched it off. The rest of the family were sent upstairs, confused, upset, and then Dad gave Mum a hug and told her everything would work out fine.

All I could think was, *Please, God, don't let it be one of theirs.*

I knew there were two possibilities. Either it was the offspring of one or other of maybe four middle-aged paedophiles, or else Jake's. The first was unbearable; the second an indicator that I'd let my mum down, despite all her strictures about saving myself for the right sort of lad. If the lad was the father, it had been less a seduction and more of a mauling. But at least it was more 'normal', because he was at least around the same age as me.

There were no hugs for me; instead, a cold anger that I could have done this, that I could have got myself pregnant by someone, anyone, at the age of fifteen. And, equal to that, the shame of it. My parents still didn't know about the gang. They just thought I'd been stupid and careless.

Upstairs in my bedroom I broke down, holding my stomach, wanting to love the tiny life inside me but not daring to. At least not until I knew the identity of his or her father.

In amongst the rows of the next few days, I told Mum and Dad the baby's father was the teenage lad, because to tell them anything else would have aroused suspicion about what was still happening to me. That was torture as well. I thought, *I can't even tell them. They think it's this boy's, but it might not be.* It was another worry I would carry all the way through the pregnancy, right up until the baby's birth. I tried desperately to convince myself that it was his; that of these two possibilities, this was by far the best. I couldn't face the thought that it might be one of *theirs*.

I know you're supposed to know the identity of your baby's dad, along with his favourite football team, the way he'd hold you, his favourite drink, and all the other things about him, but I didn't. I might not even know his name.

Over the previous few days, Lizzie had started calling me a 'Paki-shagger' – she was at the same school as me and had picked up on the rumours that I was sleeping with Asian men: old Asian men. I'd tried to shut her up, but she'd told Mum and Dad. Now that I was pregnant, things started clicking into place. I could tell from their faces that they were both wondering just how wayward their daughter had become.

Dad now started asking difficult questions, his face reddening with fury as each of them left his lips.

'This baby's nothing to do with any Asian men, is it?' he asked. 'We've heard some of the rumours.' Despite knowing about Daddy and Immy, like the kids in the playground he must have thought that if I'd done it, it was out of choice.

I felt trapped. I kept on denying it, of course. I just stuck to the story that the baby was my 'boyfriend's'. Inside I was in turmoil. I had no idea who the father was, and as Dad shouted and Mum joined in, I was eaten up by the feeling that I'd let them down; that my whole family was ashamed of me.

And I had no idea how Emma would react. The thought of that made me feel sick.

At my next meeting with Jane I told her I desperately hoped it would be the lad's baby. If the dad turned out to be one of my abusers I'd still have it, I'd still give it that chance of life; I'd just never be able to keep it. It was a total, total nightmare – another example of the chaotic hell my life had become.

Worse than all this, however, was the news that my being pregnant hadn't gone down well with Rochdale Social Services.

* * *

Christmas was barely a fortnight away when two social workers called at home, having made an appointment to see me and my family. I'd just got home and changed out of my school uniform and was sitting in the living room with Mum and Dad, when we heard them walking up the path.

Once they were inside, and sitting down with a cup of tea, one of them, Anne – the same social worker who'd been dealing with Paige – looked over at me and said, 'You know why we're here, don't you, Hannah?'

'About the baby?' I asked nervously, fearful of how the meeting was going to go. 'And about me being at Harry's place?'

But it wasn't that simple. They were also there because they knew I was sleeping with lots of men. Right there in front of my mum and dad, she talked about me being a prostitute, saying I was sleeping with men for money.

'No,' I said. 'It's nothing like that. They're raping me. Just like Daddy did.'

Beside me on the sofa, I could sense my dad getting angry. Mum was wiping away tears, doing everything she could to avoid looking at me.

The social worker carried on. 'Hannah, this is really serious. Our main priority has to be the baby, and we have to warn you that if you carry on staying at Harry's place, we'll have to do a pre-birth assessment. And that could mean us taking your baby into care as soon as it's born.'

I was sobbing now, scared at what might happen to the baby and mortified that my parents were hearing all this from a social worker.

Anne didn't seem interested in what I was going through: when I talked about the video interview I'd done for the police and the evidence I'd given about the situation I was in, she said it had nothing to do with Social Services. The police investigation was separate; she was here to see me about the baby.

I felt so helpless that some of the detail I'd hidden for so long started to spill out. I told them frantically that it was specifically Asian men from takeaways and taxi firms who were either organising it or attacking me. I went on desperately, trying to convince them, convince my parents, that it was not my fault.

To this day I am convinced that Social Services knew full well what was going on. They knew about Emma because she'd had a social worker from the age of about ten. And they knew about Roxanne being with the Asian men as well.

The pair of them were only in the house for half an hour, but it felt like a lifetime.

Once they'd gone Dad's rage – and Mum's – erupted. For ten minutes they just ranted at me, saying how ashamed they were of me, how I'd let the whole family down, and how none of their other kids would ever have behaved like this.

It seemed they trusted the 'professional' social worker's opinion over mine. They'd been led into thinking I was a prostitute. Even though I was only fifteen.

Weirdly, rather than that making me angry, it made me sad. I felt like I *had* let them down, but I just couldn't get them to understand how trapped I'd been – and how I still was. The underworld I'd fallen into had a grip so strong that not even they would have been able to rescue me, or so I thought.

Right at the peak of his rage, Dad said something that cut me to the core. 'Not only are you a prostitute,' he said coldly, 'but you're a prostitute to fucking Pakis!'

He deeply regrets it now, I know. But whatever his reaction, in the heat of the moment, all my fears about how my parents would react seemed to have come true: they were sickened by me, ashamed of me.

I fled to my room, totally distraught. I now felt there was no one out there for me: not my family, not the police, not Social Services.

The social workers must have known from the police that I'd done video interviews about being raped back in August. But it had only been now, in December, that they had come to see me; and that was only because Crisis Intervention had told them I was pregnant. They weren't worried about me – just the baby. Once again, I'd learn later that they thought I was making a 'lifestyle choice' to sleep specifically with Asian men.

Anne even complained to Jane about her huge workload, saying she needed to focus more on other girls. True, there were younger girls being abused, but I was a kid too, still only fifteen, still under the age of consent. Yet Social Services did nothing to help me, and certainly nothing to help me get away from Harry's place. They did ask what I'd do if the baby was half-Asian, and when I said I didn't know, they told me to give them a call once it was born if I decided I didn't want it. That was it. They just didn't seem interested.

* * *

Over the next few days, feelings of despair washed over me like waves over a shipwreck: one wave fear, one wave guilt, and every now and again a swell of panic and revulsion as I realised I might be carrying the baby of a paedophile who had paid money to attack me.

Physically, the pregnancy was fine. No morning sickness, no cramps, just a craving for fried tomatoes and Philadelphia cheese. Together! But, emotionally, as the infant grew, I was in turmoil, bound to a nine-month purgatory that might yet condemn me to the hell of raising my abuser's offspring.

I know that some mums, some parents, have a pet name for their baby until they decide what they'll call it once it's born. But I had none of that. For me it was just there, inside me, and I didn't want it to be. I had no interaction with it because I didn't want to be pregnant at all. I wasn't interested in it.

I didn't want to harm it, but why would I want a baby, at fifteen, with my life in a mess and all the time being raped by this paedophile gang? In my mixed-up head, part of me wanted to have a miscarriage, and yet … and yet … something held me back from asking for a termination. It was offered, of course, but for all that I hated myself, and hated my abusers, I couldn't bring myself to condemn the unborn child inside me. It wasn't its fault that its life had begun in a moment of sickening depravity.

And that depravity hadn't ended. Emma still had her sickening hold over me and so, for all that Mum and Dad tried desperately to keep me at home, I would still break away and end up at back at Harry's place.

I told Emma about it one tea time. In fact, I told Harry first. He was sitting doing his crossword in the kitchen and I sat at the table with him to have one of the cigarettes I'd vowed to give up for the sake of the baby, but was struggling to with all of the pressure.

'Well, aren't you daft?' he said, after I'd told him. He wasn't nasty, but he wasn't sympathetic either. When he asked me what I was going to do with it, I said, 'I don't know yet.'

Emma came in and asked what we were talking about. I just told her straight off: 'I'm pregnant.'

At first she starting saying, 'You're lying, you're lying,' and then she was having a go at me: 'You little slag, you won't even know who the dad is. You'll have to get rid of it.'

She was the one who'd been touting me around, and yet here she was getting angry with me. Maybe she was worried she wouldn't be able to sell me to the men any more. Whatever it was, she picked up a plate of chips that had been lying there and threw them at me. I just sat there, blank, while Harry told her to calm down.

Emma stormed out, but came back a few minutes later and said something that chilled me to the core: 'Well, you can't tell you're pregnant, so you can still go out.'

* * *

The phone calls from the gang kept coming all the way up to Christmas and, as usual, I'd be forced to go with her. Then, more than ever, it felt as though they were doing those things to someone other than me; that it wasn't my body they were abusing, but someone else's. I was in no state to defend myself. My will had gone. I was living inside a body that didn't seem able to reach out.

Mum and Dad would try to keep me at home, but I'd still either escape or just lie by saying I was going to see one of my old friends. I knew they were suspicious, and sometimes they'd check up on me and catch me out. But the bottom line was that they couldn't watch me 24/7 and I was too brainwashed to resist Emma's hold over me.

I carried on drinking in those early weeks – to start with because I didn't know I was pregnant, and later on because I didn't care. Everything was still going on with the gang and it helped to make me forget.

I felt disgusted with myself and so ashamed. I hated myself all through the pregnancy, and spent hour after hour wondering who the father could be. It would be worse if it was a boy, I reasoned, because then the thought loomed, *What if he turns out to be like them?*

So for all those months, I never felt any excitement or elation. I didn't want it at all. I hated the baby, and I hated seeing people putting pictures of their bumps on Facebook and writing about how excited they were and how they were buying this and that for their babies. When my baby kicked, I loathed it. The hospital did give me some ultrasound pictures, but I lost those. Looking back, I just think that shows how desolate I'd become. It seems so tragic now to know that I didn't really care for the baby. I feel ashamed now, but that's the way I felt. That's the truth.

In the meantime, I still had school to cope with and, as soon as term ended, Christmas to get through. By the time school broke up, I was taking more and more time away from lessons: partly because of the gang, partly because education seemed totally irrelevant to me. What future did I have?

By Christmas there was still no bump, though finally my breasts had begun to swell. *How ironic*, I thought, *that I've had to get pregnant for that to happen.*

None of the men still paying Emma and Tariq so they could clamber on top of me noticed. I was still slim, still almost boyish. Only I knew, wincing as they assaulted me, and I tried with every sickening thrust to shut out the knowledge that I was carrying a child. I wanted to scream out, to protect my baby, but the paralysis I felt – the sense that there was nothing I could do to protect myself, let alone the infant – still gripped me. I pushed to the back of my mind that he or she was having to endure it, too.

I was at least able to spend Christmas Day with my family. It wasn't anything special for me, except a temporary reprieve from the gang, though everyone at home was glad to have me back with them. They thought things were settling down for me. Dad actually said, 'This is great. We've got our girl back.'

Mum and Dad gave me a new phone that Christmas – the latest Sony Ericsson with a really cool music player. It was black, an MP3 phone.

Sitting around the tree opening presents with the little ones was weird. I felt totally out of place. I tried to enjoy it, but I kept thinking of what would be happening to me straight afterwards.

I was back at Harry's on Boxing Day and out with Emma and the gang that night. Juicy picked us up, and she told him I was pregnant as he drove. 'Well, you don't look pregnant,' he said, once we'd parked. It didn't bother either him or Boss. They just did what they always did to me, and when it was over took us home. Once again, I tried to block out the fact that I was carrying a baby.

The new year began with me living partly at home but still in the clutches of the gang, still being hawked around at any number of seedy addresses. Emma, as manipulative as ever, was trying her best to keep her grip on me. Within a week or two of me getting the new phone, she'd stolen it and had then sold it. I knew she'd have wanted the money, but it also gave her more control over me. Even on the nights I wasn't with her, she'd be messaging me on Facebook to say she couldn't wait for the baby to be born. It just made me feel more bewildered and helpless than ever.

But Jane was trying to help. She rang Mum and Dad one day, introducing herself and saying she'd been working with me over the past few months. Dad told her it would be fine for Jane to meet up with me later in the week. And, now that he and Mum had come down from their initial rage, they'd work with her. They'd do all they possibly could to keep me away from Harry's place. They were on the team now: Mum, Dad and Jane. The three of them laid it on the line. Harry's place was out of bounds.

Jane picked me up early on the Friday morning so we could go for breakfast at the big Asda in Pilsworth.

'What do you fancy?' she asked, as we joined the queue.

'Actually, I'm starving,' I said. 'Is it OK if I have the full English? Oh, and hot chocolate, please.'

We carried our trays to a table in the far corner, her sitting opposite me. It started off with just chit-chat, but then she asked how I'd got involved with Emma, Roxanne and Paige.

I hesitated, blowing at the froth on my hot chocolate, but then told her about how Emma had told me it was a girl called Carla who had got Emma involved with it all when she was still really young. Carla had then dropped out of the scene, leaving Emma to take over. I hadn't known any of this at the time, I said, and hadn't known how dangerous Emma was. She had broken me into her world by letting Daddy rape me.

We talked about the baby and who the dad was. It was definitely Jake's, I said. She asked if I was sure. I just shrugged.

I was still struggling with that question – and the feelings it prompted – when Jane asked the question she'd asked before Christmas: would I go to the police?

'Jane,' I said, anger bubbling up in me, 'I've already told you I don't want to speak to the police. Emma would go mad, and they won't go through with my rape case against Daddy if they think I'm a prostitute.'

She told me I wasn't, and then began to tell me about something called 'a controlled abusive relationship'. As she spoke, she rummaged in her bag for a piece of paper. She began reading from it as she asked me a series of questions.

'Just think about how things are between you and Emma,' she said, before she started. 'OK?'

I nodded, wondering what was coming, trying to shut out the sight of a mum breastfeeding her baby across the room from us. I couldn't bear the reminder.

'Are you scared to say "no" to Emma?' Jane asked.

'Well, yes,' I said tentatively. 'I can never cross her, I wouldn't dare.'

'Does she upset you for no reason?'

'Yeah, she's always doing that,' I whispered.

'And do you find yourself saying sorry, when it's actually her who should be saying sorry to you?'

I nodded. I was always apologising to Emma. I didn't even know why, really – not always. For getting upset, I supposed.

'I'd apologise for getting upset,' I told Jane. 'Like one time at Aarif's, the first time he … you know … did it that way. Darcy had run in, but all Emma did was laugh at me and then start going mad. She was telling me to go back in the bedroom and I was so scared I even said "please" to her – "please don't make me, Emma! Please!" She called me pathetic, said I was a useless mardy ass. It was me who ended up saying sorry, just like always. And I'd always end up doing what she wanted me to do, even if it was, you know, *that*.'

'And does she try to alienate you from other people? Keep you away from them?'

'Yes,' I said, thinking of all the times Emma had taken my mobile phone, or come with me to my parents.

Jane reached across to me, brushing my hand with hers. Then she looked back down at her sheet of paper and started reading more of the points there, about people who were abused and the ones that abused.

She made it sound so scary but, deep within me, something started to click. The people she was talking about sounded familiar. Finally, I looked up, feeling, almost with a sense of awe, that I finally understood something about myself.

'It sounds just like the way Emma is with me,' I said. 'She wants to make it so I have no one in the world but her.'

Jane met up with me again the following week, in her office, after I'd had time to think about Emma and how she'd controlled me over all these months.

'She's a lot bigger than me,' I began, timidly. 'And she scares me. It's like she gives me this look, and if I don't do what she says I know she'll batter me. That's how she got me, and that's how she got me to go with her to all those men. And once it started, I've not been able to stop it.'

I told Jane how betrayed I'd felt by the first police investigation, but then, through my tears, I made the decision I never thought I'd make: I suddenly blurted out, 'I'll do it. I'll talk to the police again.'

And then, still doubting what I'd just said, and still wondering whether I'd really go through with it, I added, 'But only if I can tell it to you first.'

For the next two hours she sat there at her desk taking notes while I poured my heart out to her, in the sort of detail that made me cringe, and probably her, too. But she kept reassuring me that it would be fine and that I was doing the right thing. When I told her I felt like a prostitute, she said 'No, you're a child who's been sexually abused and exploited.'

Maybe I found it easier to speak to Jane, or maybe the police weren't asking me the right questions.

I gave her as much of an insight as I dared into what was happening to me and some of the other girls, and how Emma was operating.

I told her about the time a girl called Alesha slept with two Asian men when she went out with Emma, and had had to go to hospital.

'How do you know that?' she asked.

'Emma and Jake both told me,' I replied.

I couldn't bring myself to tell her what Harry was making me do whenever I was alone with him, but I whispered: 'It's not just with the Asians she's doing things – and the same with Roxanne.

'Both of them keep giving Harry blow jobs, you know, when they're skint. She and Emma just laugh about what they do with Harry. They don't see it as wrong.' I paused, then continued, 'And with the Asian men, both of them love the sex. On the way home, they'll say it was good. They never seem to feel the way I feel …'

I trailed off, but then added: 'It always makes me feel so sick. I hate it. I always turn my face away.'

She'd filled nearly seven pages by the time we'd got to the end. Each of them was A4, lined, filled with names and addresses, and the accounts of what the men had done to me.

Together, they made it clear that the gang was still out there, still attacking me and other girls, whether it was in Rochdale or Heywood or beyond.

I signed every page to say that what Jane had written was true. She made us both a cup of tea then – to calm us down, I think. It had been an emotional time.

'Will I have to stand up in court?' I asked, sipping tea.

'It's very unlikely,' she said. 'But the important thing is that you've been brave enough to get this far. I'm sure it will get easier now.'

Through all this trauma, the baby grew inside me, innocently oblivious to the fact that it would be born to a mother who felt that she was totally inadequate and completely incapable of looking after it.

Chapter Sixteen
Speaking to the Authorities

The statement Jane had taken down for me was dated 14 January. Just over a week later, on 22 January 2009, after she'd passed on copies to both Social Services and the police, I was on my way to do another video interview with detectives.

Jane came with me to the police station. She was driving, and for most of the journey we were pretty quiet: me, pensive, wondering how on earth it would all go; her, I sensed, equally nervous, anxious to get me there before I changed my mind.

Which, in my still-fragmented state, I was always likely to do.

Walking into the police station, however, my mind switched on to what I was about to go through. I realised I was terrified.

Jane waited outside while I went into the interview room. It was John again. He ushered me – a thin street kid in grey turned-up jeans, a low white top, dark chequered jacket and flat black shoes – into the same room. You still wouldn't have known I was pregnant: I looked far too young and, anyway, the still-tiny bump was hidden by my top. My hair was short, but a strand of it sometimes flopped over onto my cheek until I'd brush it away. I sat on the sofa, my legs crossed, biting my lip.

John started with some small talk, thinking it would put me at my ease: 'What have you been doing since I last saw you?' he asked. 'Anything good?'

'Not really,' I said, thinking, *If only he knew!* 'I'm not allowed at Harry's house to see Emma,' I said simply. And yes, I was still at school, though I hadn't been going for a month because I was pregnant.

'What have you been doing with yourself? Sitting around at home?'

Mostly, I said, or going out sometimes.

What we both knew was that the 'going out' had been with members of a gang of paedophiles.

It wasn't the easiest start to an interview. But it was a relief when he told me I wouldn't have to talk about Daddy.

I told him how I'd been switched from Daddy's control to Tariq's, how he'd already started picking me and Emma up before the main police interview I'd done the previous August.

I'd seen him in the Balti House ages before, near the end of what had been going on with Daddy. He'd come in one night and just started talking to us. I think Daddy already knew him.

'He asked us if we wanted to come to Tasty Bites later, and the next day Emma just said, "Tariq's picking us up today." It just started there. At first he'd take us for a drive, then to Aarif's. He drove a silver minibus for Eagle Taxis. It's car 40, the airport one with a picture of a plane on the side.'

John asked: 'How does Tariq know you're prepared to sleep with men?'

'Emma sorted it out,' I said. 'In his car, he'd talk about anything. What have you been doing? Where do you live? Who do you live with? How old are you? We told him we were both fifteen.'

I recalled the time at Tasty Bites where about half a dozen of the men had been trying to persuade Emma, Paige and me to drink their vodka, and asking me whether I'd have sex with them. It was the time Emma had given me £2 to go home. Later, I told John, her fabulous boyfriend was talking about the money he got for us. I asked Emma what he was on about, and she replied: 'Don't you know? He gets paid for us shagging people.'

John looked up from the papers he was shuffling in his lap and asked quietly, 'Why did you do it, Hannah?'

'I don't know,' I replied. 'I felt scared of Emma, and scared of Tariq as well. Because I've seen what he's done to Emma and what he says to her.'

I didn't tell him, but I was thinking of the times I'd seen the two of them together, and how, for all her 'strength', all her control, Emma was actually subservient to Tariq – a bit like I was with her. It was as if she was really scared of him and had met her match. Tariq had an aura about him that said 'Don't mess with me.' Emma did as well, of course, but at the end of the day she was still only five months older than me. To him, she was just a kid; a fat, difficult, lumbering kid, but still only a kid. A kid he was using, just as she was using me.

Lost in thought, I dragged myself back to the real world: a police station a million light years from 'Disturbia' and gangs and Harry's house. John was asking another question. I forced myself to focus.

'Why go back to Tasty Bites?' he was asking. 'Why go back with those other men, given what you'd been through before?'

'I don't know,' I said again. And then I opened up just enough to give him an insight into the way I'd been groomed.

'Emma kept telling me to go,' I said. 'She kept telling me "They're dangerous." When I kept refusing, she'd threaten me. She used to say she'd tell my mum and dad. That she'd get me battered.'

I gave John a list of the men who'd attacked me, and then he wanted me to tell him about each specific incident.

I knew I couldn't.

'There's too many,' I said. 'Tariq would just tell the two of us who we were sleeping with, and then he'd send us off. Afterwards he'd collect all the money. Usually we just had to give them a blow job and then lie down and let them do it,' I said.

Then I took a deep breath and said, 'If we were on our period they used to tell us to do it up the bum.' I told John I hated it, that it had really hurt, but that they used to tell me that I had to do it.

John asked gently: 'Did they take steps to make it not painful for you?'

I shook my head, then forced myself to speak. 'No,' I whispered. 'They'd just slam it in.'

He asked me to rate how much it hurt me on a scale of nought to ten.

'I don't know ... seven? eight?' My head lowered, I started to shake. I felt my hair fall over my face. But I went on. 'At first it was, like, really painful, but after they'd done it a few times it didn't hurt as much.'

If I thought telling him that was bad enough, there was more trauma to come: John wanted to go through the number of times each of them had attacked me, and how.

'Aarif?' he asked.

'Every time we went there,' I replied.

'Up the bum?'

'Eight or something.'

'Megamuncher?'

'About twice, because Emma always used to go with him.'

'Joe?'

'About six times or something.'

'Anally?'

'I think it was just once.'

He asked about Cassie. How often with him?

'Lots of times,' I said. 'About twenty, thirty times because he used to pick us up in the car as well.'

'And anally?'

'I can't remember.'

'Saj?'

'About ten times.'

'Anally?'

'About three times.'

My head stayed down.

* * *

They let me have a break so that I could get some food with Jane. I started off telling her how embarrassed I'd been about some of the questions I'd had to answer, and then I told her that Emma and Roxanne had started to hang around with a girl called Nadine, who went to Roxanne's school.

'I've mentioned her to you before,' I said. 'She already does it – I've seen her at the houses I've been to. Her best friend does it as well, but Nadine's involved with loads of Pakistanis. She tells Roxanne how much she loves them.' I knew it would be more information for Jane to pass along, more evidence to build a case against these men.

Just before I went back into the room, Jane told me to carry on being honest with the police. That's what I did, but they didn't ask me many more questions – and there was nothing about Nadine.

The interview over, as we drove away I told Jane how at the main interview in August, once the tapes had been switched off, John had asked me if I'd done it for the money. He had also said this time he didn't believe me when I said I was scared of Emma.

Jane was furious. 'How dare he?' she said. 'It's disgusting that he would say that – even if he didn't believe you, which obviously he should! That's no way to treat a girl who's been through what you'd been through.'

I was truly grateful to her, but the memory of how my stomach and heart had both dropped the instant he'd spoken came flooding back. I wondered whether it was all going to happen again – that despite overcoming my fear, and choking on every word I'd spoken as I'd recalled the horrors I'd been through, the police still wouldn't believe me.

Was it going to be a rerun of what had gone on before when I told the police about Daddy? That I'd be dismissed and ignored by the very people who should be helping me?

Then what? Emma and the gang would drag me and my unborn child back into their dark world.

* * *

For all that I'd done my best to help the police, I was still living a double life. With the gang all still free, all still able to hurt me, I had to make it look to them that everything was normal: as normal as it could be in this world of theirs. I was trying desperately hard to find an escape route from Emma and the gang, but I was terrified they'd guess that I'd gone to the police again – just as I'd done in August.

And so it was that I felt I had no option but to allow Emma to give me to the gang the very same day I'd done the second video interview. I'd managed to talk to the police about Tariq and lots of others, but I couldn't resist her threats that night. So immediately I was back in the worst of danger. This was rock bottom.

Perhaps even more dangerous than this, Social Services' intensive support team closed their case on me that same day. They said Anne, my social worker, had told them that as far as she was concerned, I wasn't at any more risk. Mary, from intensive support, said it was felt I had enough support from Crisis Intervention, and that in the future I'd also have Maternity Services. I could get back in touch with the intensive support team if I ever felt I needed them.

Miss Crabtree, my teacher, told Jane she was disgusted with the decision and very worried about the safety of both me and my baby.

For me, it felt as though every last flame of ambition to fight my attackers had been extinguished. What was the point? There was no escape. There would never be any escape.

* * *

I really can't remember now, but one of the people I may have told the police about during that interview was Parvez. Or maybe he just came later – with so much happening to me, I simply couldn't keep track of it all.

Emma introduced him to me as another of her 'boyfriends'. By then, I'd learned that a guy she thought of as a boyfriend was actually just one of the gang she actually fancied.

We only went to his flat a few times. He'd sleep with Emma, and Roxanne or I would have to sleep with the other guy there. I slept with Parvez once. After that, he said he just wanted Roxanne because she was more into it; he thought she actually enjoyed it.

This didn't stop her helping me to rob him one night – or at least try to. We'd been at his flat and Emma had rung a taxi to take us on to someone else's house. Roxanne and I didn't want to go so, just as we were leaving, I grabbed his wallet and we ran off.

We got out of the flat OK, but he caught up with us in the road. He slapped me in the face and took his wallet back. A minute later, Emma arrived in the taxi she'd booked, laughing at us.

Not getting away with the money meant Roxanne and I had to go with her, otherwise we wouldn't have been able to get home. I think we went on to Billy's house.

Either way, I was to have to tell Jane about Parvez for one very important reason.

Towards the end of January, the various agencies in Heywood and Rochdale – the police, the social workers, and Crisis Intervention – suddenly had something very worrying to concentrate on; something else that should have alerted each and every one of them to the increasing power of the gang.

On or around 26 January, two local girls had gone missing from home. A girl called Ruth had just vanished, and Paige had not come home after telling her family she was going babysitting.

Jane was really worried, and asked me if I knew anything that might help. We met in the Asda café again.

'Well, I saw Paige getting on a bus with Emma,' I said, once we'd got settled with some tea. I wanted to help, but was scared about telling Jane too much – especially about Emma. 'But that was last week,' I went on, a little too quickly.

'Hannah,' said Jane, patiently. 'I know you still see Emma, so you really don't have to lie to me.'

I reddened, then smiled at her in relief. 'OK, OK, it was yesterday.'

She smiled back. 'Thanks, Hannah. And what about Ruth? Do you know anything about her? Is she involved with Emma? With Paige?'

I shook my head. 'Not that I know of,' I said tentatively, holding out on her again.

Jane looked serious, studying my face, trying, it seemed, to gauge just how much I really did know.

'Paige hasn't been home in days,' she said, 'and people are very, very worried about her. So, come on, Hannah, tell me. You know how important this is.'

I did, and so I told her the bit that might help Jane find her. 'She will be with Emma,' I said. 'And, most likely, they'll be with Parvez.' Once the words were out, I felt better. 'I'll take you there if you like – to show you.'

She declined the offer, saying it would be best to wait for the police to take me.

The waitress came over to clear up the empty plates then, so the conversation ended. As we headed off, out past McDonalds before stopping at the traffic lights beside the motorway, I kept thinking about Paige.

'Jane,' I said. 'Will you ring me if she doesn't come home?'

It turned out there was no need, because the next day the police found Paige – not at Parvez's place, but at Harry's. I never did find out what happened to Ruth.

* * *

I'm guessing Paige was found around the same time as I was going out in an unmarked car with a detective sergeant called Daniel; another police officer, Susan; and Jane.

I'd been at my parents' house for a few nights, so Jane called there to pick me up and take me to the police station.

The idea was for us to drive around, with me pointing out as many of the gang's hang-outs as I could.

It was frightening to drive around the town in the daytime, especially because we looked so obvious – two police officers, admittedly out of uniform, with a teenage girl and a woman who looked like a social worker. I kept thinking we'd see some of the gang because this was their territory.

I'd pointed out seven different addresses by the time we pulled back into the police station car park.

'You've been very brave.' Jane smiled gently as we came to a standstill. 'You should be very proud of yourself.'

I didn't feel proud.

It had been a huge thing for me to go out with the police, because I still thought that if the gang found out they would kill me.

It didn't occur to me to ask the detectives for help because I simply didn't know you could do that – however much I may have wished to. I didn't know they could help a girl like me beyond doing the normal police things.

Once I'd told the police, and once we'd been out in the car looking at addresses, they set up a big surveillance operation. At one stage one of the detectives told me: 'Even if we don't get them to court, at least we'll have disrupted them; at least they'll know we're on to them, and that may have a deterrent effect' – as if surveillance alone could combat a gang who put no value on human suffering.

I felt sick – I knew that wouldn't help me. Quite the opposite. In the days and weeks that followed, I lived in constant fear that I'd put myself in an even worse situation.

I felt I'd been let down so terribly by the police the first time around, I just prayed it wasn't going to happen again. They wouldn't abandon me a second time, surely?

Chapter Seventeen
Escape

Ultimately, it was my baby who ended the abuse that had taken over my life.

As February 2009 approached, the gang seemed to be growing tired of me. It's one thing forcing yourself on a girl in a padded bra, but when she's pregnant and her breasts have finally begun to develop there's a problem: at least, for a paedophile. There were fewer and fewer phone calls telling Emma to take me to whichever address, and more for the new girls she was trying to recruit. If I did go, I'd hear members of the gang telling Emma she had to bring younger girls next time, and not one who was pregnant.

The baby had been growing in my womb for nearly three months now, content, oblivious to the fact that he or she was the accidental offspring of an under-age girl whose only reason to carry on was to protect the life inside her. In quiet moments, I'd look down at the now distinct, visible bump and stroke it.

Whenever I went home to Mum and Dad I was still a nightmare: stubbing out cigarettes on the floor and the kitchen worktops, swearing and, one night, drunk, dancing in the front room and saying to my dad – I am so ashamed now to think of it – 'Do you want me to dance naked for you, Dad?'

He had looked utterly appalled that I could have said so vile a thing. And me? The next morning I just thought: *Your mind's not right, Hannah. How could you have said that to your own dad?*

It got to the stage where he couldn't bear to be in the same room as me, and Mum felt the same.

I'd also scared both of them by saying the baby could have any one of five fathers. It's not the sort of thing your mum and dad want to hear. They were worried, too, that I was still heading off to stay at Harry's place whenever I could. I'd just wait for the chance to climb out of a window, onto the roof of the porch, and away into the night.

I still wanted to break away from Harry's place, but the brainwashing effect Emma had on me was too strong.

Jane, wonderful, patient Jane, tried her best to help me find the courage.

A week or so before my sixteenth birthday, close to Valentine's Day, the two of us were at Asda again, her drinking tea, me hot chocolate, when out of the blue she said: 'Hannah, I know you've been going to Harry's again – and I know you've been staying overnight there.' She let it sink in. 'So stop lying to me, and please, for your own safety, stay away from there. It's all being dealt with by the police. Just let them get on with it while you concentrate on looking after yourself and the little one.'

She said she'd spoken to my parents, and that they were worried sick. 'You do realise, don't you,' she said slowly, deliberately, 'that even when you're sixteen you can be referred to Childcare Services if people think you're putting your baby at risk?

'And you can't expect your mum and dad to do all the looking-after of it once the baby is born.'

As she went back to sipping her tea, I tried to focus on the significance of what she'd just said. She was right – I knew I had to get away from Emma, from Harry's place, if not for me then for the baby. It was doing me no good – and could I really picture a baby living there? The thought of it made me shudder.

As I thought about the baby, I tried to picture it – wondering whether it was a boy or a girl, and wondering, too, whether it was half-Asian. Another worry rose to the surface of my mind.

'I've worked out my dates,' I said, 'and I'm really worried the dad might be one of those men. If it is, I won't be able to feel the same about it – not ever, because I'd know it was from being raped. I'm really not sure I could keep it.'

For the next few minutes I sat there, morose, trying to block out the turmoil I felt about my baby's identity.

* * *

My sixteenth birthday was actually a laugh. I spent most of it with Lizzie, heading off to Manchester on the bus and spending some money Mum and Dad had given me as a present.

We spent ages in Primark across from the Arndale shopping centre, with me eventually buying some pyjamas, a few tops and a pair of leggings. We had a KFC in the food court, chatting like two sisters should chat: about the baby, about the future.

At one point I remember thinking, *This is normal. It's what I should be doing – not meeting up with old men.* On the way home, I thought about my life and how sick it had become. From somewhere, I began to feel a sense of resolve building inside me, telling the stupid, hopeless part of my mind that with the baby coming I really, finally, needed to break away from Emma and the gang.

But then came the following day.

I was over at my parents' when, about one o'clock in the afternoon, Emma knocked at the front door for me. I answered it, and she sounded the way she always did when she thought my family might be listening – all cheery, all matey.

'So you're sixteen now, eh? Join the club.'

She must have thought the coast was clear, because she lowered her voice a bit and then said, 'Right, are you coming? We've got people for you to meet, so let's get back to Harry's.'

She must have seen me hesitate, because she went on, louder now: 'You don't have to answer to your folks now. You can live where you want, sleep with who you want. They can't stop you.'

I was about to send her away, but just at that moment I felt a rush of air as my mum came storming up behind me; I guess she'd been listening from the living room. The front door had only just been ajar, but she yanked it wide open, clawing at me and pushing me outside.

'Go on, then,' she screamed. 'You go with her. You're sixteen. You go off with your men – just don't ever come back here!'

And with that she slammed the door, leaving me bewildered and frightened on the garden path. Emma just thought it was the funniest thing she'd seen in ages, but I was aghast.

'Mum,' I wailed. 'Don't do this. What am I supposed to do now?'

There was no reply. All I could hear was Mum crashing about upstairs. I sat on the lawn in shock and disbelief. Then, I heard her coming down the stairs. Again the front door was flung open and this time a bin bag was dumped unceremoniously at my feet. Some of my clothes spilled out as it landed.

'Now, go!' screamed Mum. 'I've had enough of all this. Just leave us in peace!'

I tried to reach out to her, but she was gone. The emotion of what she thought she'd heard too much for her. Emma didn't hesitate. Laughing, she bent down, picked up the bags and set off towards the road, shouting: 'Come on, let's go. Taxi's waiting!'

Distraught, I followed, crying as I staggered away from my home and from my family. I'd wanted to stay; I'd dared to hope I could finally break away from Emma. Now I was heading back to misery with her because I didn't know what else to do.

Back at Harry's, Emma was soon on the phone to Tariq. I was in the kitchen, quiet, smoking, when I overheard part of the conversation. 'It's all right,' she was saying, 'she's sixteen now. So they don't have to worry. She's legal.' Her voice sounded cold.

With the call over, she came to find me, suddenly all breathless and cheery. 'You'll be fine here, Hannah. You and the baby can stay. Harry will give you the money for a cot, and we'll get a new double bed we can share. I'll help you get your address changed. We'll sort it out tomorrow. You can stay for ever and no one will be able to stop you.'

But I realised I wasn't listening to her. I was focusing hard on what she'd just said – and what she'd said to Tariq a few moments earlier. My mind flashed back to the times I'd been with Jane, when she'd spoken of her fears for me, the way she'd talked to me about controlling relationships, and how it seemed Emma wanted to isolate me from everyone else so that I'd have no one to turn to but her. 'You have to really think about this, Hannah,' she'd said. 'Until you do, you'll never truly break free.'

The words I'd overheard Emma saying to Tariq a few moments earlier bubbled up again in my mind. That I was sixteen now, so there'd be no problem with the men; that it would be totally legal for them all to have sex with me.

For ever?

I couldn't bear that. I really couldn't bear that.

* * *

The next day, Mum drove to Harry's place, knocked on the door and dropped off another bin bag full of my belongings. I saw her and ran after her. She was just opening the car door when I got to her.

I was sobbing. 'Mum, Mum, I don't want this,' I said, clutching at her arm, her shoulder. 'Let me come home. *Please!*'

'No,' she said coldly, her voice at odds with the tears I could see welling up in her eyes. 'You've made your decision now – and so have we.'

A moment later, she was at the wheel and driving away, leaving me standing forlornly on the pavement.

Thanks to Emma, I still didn't have a phone, but that night Emma's mobile rang and, as she answered it, she scoffed. It was Dad – he must have kept the number from when he thought she and I were just proper, ordinary mates. 'Yeah, yeah,' she said, 'I'll put her on. I'm sure she'd love to speak to you.'

Dad spoke to me for nearly five minutes. First, he told me to go where Emma couldn't hear me, then he said he'd talked Mum round and they wanted to give me one last chance. 'Come home now and we'll take you back,' he said. 'But if you don't, that's it. For ever. You choose.'

A sob – more of relief than anguish – caught in my throat. So I could still go home! But I hesitated. I was more canny, now that I knew what Emma was about. I knew I had to throw her off the scent.

'I can't come home now, Dad,' I whispered. 'But tomorrow – let me come home tomorrow. It's my scan …'

A plan had begun to form in my mind. I started to explain it to Dad. He was up for it, he said, but there could be no turning back. A few moments later he was off the line, and I joined Emma in the living room.

'Got rid of him, then?' she asked.

'Yeah,' I replied, as nonchalantly as I could. 'They're off my back now.'

But as she turned away, I allowed myself a faint smile. I glanced for reassurance at the two bin bags full of my clothes, lying by the front door.

I tried to make it as normal a night at Harry's as it could be. Mercifully, there were no calls from the gang and I was able to slip off to bed just after 10 p.m.

'It's the baby,' I explained to Emma. 'I feel really tired.'

For a while I lay awake, holding the bump as I thought of the misery I'd endured those past seven months, wondering whether this was the moment I could finally summon up the courage to break free. Because that is what it would take – immense courage. I was still so scared of Emma, and of what she could do to me if I didn't keep in with her.

Would she batter me, and risk hurting the baby? In my last few days with the gang, I'd begun to stand up to her. Being pregnant actually helped me, because I didn't think that even she would do anything to hurt my baby. But how safe were my parents and sisters and brothers? How would the rest of the gang react? Would Emma just let me go now, after all this time?

I cradled my bump, wondering if it would be the one thing that changed her mind – that I was now no use to her, and she would just let me go.

The next morning, the strains of 'Disturbia' ringing out from Emma's room woke me up. A few minutes later, she was banging on my door, telling me to get up.

'Quick,' she shouted. 'We've got to meet Cassie. Get up.'

It was 17 February 2009, the day of my three-month scan, and yet I was beginning it with my customary feelings of dread and despair. But this time I was determined to somehow get away.

It would prove to be a hopeless thought.

Once I was dressed, Emma walked me down to Morrison's to meet Cassie. He was meant to be on a shift for Castleton Taxis, but just after 9 a.m. his black people-carrier pulled into the supermarket car park and we climbed in so he could take us to his favourite lane in Ashworth Park.

Cassie was even more disgusting than the others: he liked to kiss the whole of my face, and I hated that. With just sex I could manage to detach myself from it, but all his touching and kissing just made me feel even more sick.

This last time, in fact, Cassie's fun was interrupted by a couple driving down the lane towards us in a Ford Focus. Emma saw them first and shouted, 'Someone's coming.' Cassie got up, with no trousers on, and climbed into the front, pretending nothing was happening. The couple must have seen us but they didn't stop or say anything. As soon as they were gone, he climbed over onto the back seat and just carried on.

That time Emma had gone first. When it was my turn, I just kept thinking, *This is the last time. After this it will be over and you'll be going home. So just get through it, just get through it.*

Somehow I did.

Emma had a plan as well as me that day. Hers was to go into the college she'd been referred to because of her appalling attendance record at school, and then to go with me to the scan.

'It'll be the two of us together,' she'd said, sounding as sincere as I'd ever heard her. 'Seeing the baby.'

I pretended to agree.

So, after the early-morning encounter with Cassie, he dropped her off at a bus stop in Heywood and then carried on to Harry's place with me.

I got back at around 10.30 a.m., slipping quietly into the house, taking a shower, and then going into the still-empty living room to wait for Mum.

It seemed I was waiting there for ages, every now and then glancing at the bin bags tucked just inside the doorway, and all the time feeling a growing sense of excitement.

I was going to do this. I was finally going to be free!

Finally, Mum's car drew up outside and I bounded out of the house, grabbing the bags as I left and piling them onto the back seat. Then I ran round to the passenger side, climbed in, and said, 'Go, Mum. Let's go.'

I kept looking back at the house, wondering if any of them had seen us leave, and then feeling the finality of it all. Soon, I knew, Emma would be getting back. When would she notice the bin bags gone? When would she realise that this really was the end? That finally I'd left her world behind?

We stopped off at a chippy on the way home to pick up an order – chips and curry sauce for me, fish and chips for Mum and Dad. Back at the house, it felt so deliciously normal to be eating soggy chips and looking forward to the scan.

There was still time for a lecture from Mum and Dad about this being my absolutely last chance – understandably – but then Mum and I were off again in the car, heading to the hospital.

* * *

As I lay back on the hospital bed ready for my scan, my breath caught as a tiny black and white image flickered onto the screen. I stared in disbelief at the tiny little form. I could see little limbs, a beating heart. Suddenly, a delicious warm feeling spread through my weary body.

It was the most beautiful thing I'd ever seen.

I looked at Mum with tears in my eyes and she reached for my hand and gave it a gentle squeeze. 'It's time to come home, Hannah,' she said, tearfully.

It was a moment I'll never forget; the moment I felt I was finally being dragged out of the dark and murky world I'd been living in for seven months and back into the real world. This tiny life gave me the connection I needed.

The intense fear that had gripped me during every waking moment of the day for seven months drained away. Suddenly, it didn't matter who the father of my baby was, or about the gang or Emma. What they could do to me didn't scare me any more. There was only one thing I needed to do – I had to get out and stay out whatever the cost. If this baby stood any chance at all, I had to use every last part of energy I had to fight; to make sure it had a good start in life and protect it from any wrong-doing in the world.

I realised, too, just how hideous those seven months must have been for Mum and Dad: to be worried all day, every day, about what their own baby girl was doing and what harm she was coming to. The confusion over why I was doing it in the first place. None of it must have made any sense to them.

Mum was so right. It was time to go home. I just had to figure out a way to make that happen for good.

As we stared at the screen, a nurse approached, smiling, and asked, 'Would you like to know the baby's sex? Whether it's a boy or a girl?'

I wasn't sure, and looked at Mum.

'It's up to you, Hannah,' she said.

Maybe I should know, I thought, *maybe it will help*. Even if I don't know the baby's colour, at least I'd know something about it that might bring it closer.

'OK,' I said. 'Tell me.'

The nurse, tall, in her late thirties, must have had the same conversation a thousand times, but she wiped a tear from her eye as she said, 'You're carrying a little girl.'

A girl! Instantly I felt a flood of happiness…a girl … but then suddenly, I became fearful. How would life go for her? Would she be used by men, as I'd been? Or would she be safe and free? Would she be happy?

I blinked back tears, trying to focus on the ultrasound image again, looking at the tiny arms and legs, trying to imagine my growing baby as a girl. Gently, I touched the bump and smiled up at my mum.

She drove me straight home, with no thought of going to Harry's: I was still so programmed into being with Emma that that had worried me – that I'd want to go over to hers and 'impress' her with my baby news.

I'd like to say it was a happy homecoming, but it wasn't – the topsy-turvy relationship I had at home saw to that. For all that Mum and Dad tried their best to reach out to me, I was still a mess. I'd hit rock bottom by then, a feral creature living a half-life, abused by the gang, abandoned by both the police and Social Services. My parents had also been let down, and they were both confused and incredibly angry.

Mum had given my room a spring clean in the hope that I'd finally be coming back to stay for good but, as usual, we ended up rowing. She threw a cup of lukewarm tea in my face and I tipped the bed over. She then kicked me out of the house. I sat on the steps at the back for a while, but went back inside when Dad rang me on my sister's phone. He told me to go in but to stay upstairs away from Mum.

When it had all kicked off again, Mum had rung Jane in tears to say – not for the first time – that she'd had enough. She and Dad had seen going to the scan of the baby as a pivotal moment for me, a wake-up call I suppose, to finally take charge of my life. Jane told her to ring Social Services and said she'd do the same.

If they were looking for help, it was a waste of time because now that I'd reached sixteen, Social Services were able to completely cast me adrift.

I had always felt as though Social Services were always trying to make me look like the one in the wrong: the prostitute, the silly, drunk schoolgirl who was messing everyone about. In some of their reports they talked about drugs, making it look as though I took them. But I never did – not beyond trying them and deciding I didn't like them. But it felt as though in their eyes I was always the bad person. I know that I drank, and I'd drunk in the early months of the pregnancy, but I only started drinking when it was all going on with the gang. To block it out.

The girl who'd become the bane of their lives – they had never understood the hold Emma had over me, and had never seen why I kept going back to Harry's place – was legally over the age of consent, and so they closed the file on me. Despite still being a child in need, from now on, in their eyes, I would just be another wayward, dysfunctional girl making the wrong life choices and 'hanging around with the wrong crowd'.

So when Jane put the call in to Social Services on 17 February, Anne, my social worker, wouldn't even speak to her. The case was closed, she told a colleague, and Jane would have to contact the referral officer. My dad got the same treatment a bit later on. 'I rang her, but she wouldn't accept my call,' he said. Rochdale Council had officially washed its hands of me.

For days after my return home, to my shame, the house was filled with the sound of terrible rows; most of them between me and my mum. She still didn't see me as a victim, and nor did Dad, because Social Services had never told them what was really going on. And, of course, I hadn't either. So in all those rows I was told time after time that I was a slag and that I disgusted them.

* * *

I still felt I was living a nightmare, but coming home did at least one huge thing for me: it finally ended the long cycle of abuse. From that point on, I never went back to the gang, and, instead, my mind focused – or tried to focus – on one day bringing them all to justice.

For Emma, too, there was a change, because although she didn't know it yet, she had lost the girl she'd recruited for the gang seven months earlier. She would have to use other victims. At the time, I didn't actually realise that would be the case – I was still just relieved to be away from her. It was only later that I would come to realise what my escape meant – another girl's imprisonment.

I'd never speak to Emma again and yet, bizarrely, in those final weeks with her at Harry's house, and sometimes later, much later, I felt a connection with her in some sick, weird sort of a way.

For all that she was evil and skewed, she was perhaps the only person in the world who knew the hell that I'd been through: I can only guess she had been through it herself when Carla had first taken her on. The twist was that I think she got a buzz from then doing it to me. And, once I'd escaped, girls like Paige – who wouldn't, or couldn't break away – and Nadine.

After a couple of weeks, things became a bit easier at home. In fact, the house itself became a bit of a sanctuary.

For a time, Emma and Tariq would come up onto the estate and drive around. They'd park up behind my parents' house and try to get me to go out. But I resisted. Finally, in my own head, it was over.

My parents never knew, but Tariq even kept the house under surveillance for a while. There were many times I'd peek out from my bedroom window and see his taxi, car 40, parked outside. Sometimes Emma would be with him; she'd even call my mobile. I'd keep changing my sim card, but each time, somehow, she'd find me.

They also followed me when I was out of the house. The first time it happened I'd been out shopping and was on my way home. Tariq shouted, 'Hannah!' and I recognised his voice straight away. I thought, *Oh my God, I'm going to get shot or something*. I got back to the house as quickly as I could, my heart beating. Mum and Dad were at home, completely oblivious to it. For a long time I wouldn't go out on my own.

Time went on and we were into March. I was about to set off for school one morning when Dad took a call on his mobile.

I could hear a man's voice at the other end of the line. It sounded like one of the detectives I'd spoken to.

'Wow,' said Dad, then, 'that's great news.' He broke off for a moment. 'Hannah,' he said. 'They've arrested Harry.'

Yes, it was great news. It turned out that Harry, once a father figure to me, later a disgusting paedophile, had opened his front door in his boxer shorts to find two plainclothes officers standing there. By all accounts, he had gone quietly, knowing, I hope, that his days of sick perversion were over. While I was walking to school that frosty March morning, Harry, finally dressed in crumpled jeans, a cheap checked shirt and off-white, slip-on shoes, was being led into a police station by a detective trying desperately to hide her smile.

He would be there a long time because he had a lot of questions to answer. And this time he wasn't dealing with kids.

I had to eat dinner on my own that day because I couldn't see any of my friends around, like Robyn or Hayley – the Hayley I suspected had been abused by the gang along with me. But it didn't matter because I still felt good. I felt safer than I'd done for ages.

And it got better – some time after that, the police moved in to question Emma.

Knowing this was strangely difficult for me. How could I explain to myself, let alone them, that in the darkest days I'd begun to see her as my only friend, as if I was bound to her by the secret we shared about the men she took me to? But the ties between us had loosened, and now, realising this, and knowing that she was being interviewed, I actually felt a new wave of freedom wash over me.

It made me feel as good as the day Harry was arrested.

There was yet more news. The police called to ask me to identify someone who knew Daddy from the Balti House – this was on the same day I heard they were questioning people from the halal meat shop. I'd been taken there with Emma, Roxanne and sometimes Paige. It was suddenly all coming together, and I felt great that it seemed they were all being rounded up.

The forensic tests, however, weren't as simple as the police had first thought. They'd sent away my knickers for testing back in August, but then asked for a second test – and these weren't finished until 18 March.

The results blew away Daddy's alibi. All this time he had been saying that the only reason they'd found his DNA on my knickers was that Emma and I had swapped after the two of them had had sex and that she had consented to the sex. But they never did have sex – at least, not as far as I know.

The second test proved beyond doubt that Emma hadn't worn those knickers. When the police put this new evidence to him, Daddy couldn't give them an answer. He just told them he had nothing else to say.

It seemed that, just like me over all those months, he had nowhere else to run. I thought a date for his trial would be just around the corner.

Chapter Eighteen
Chloe

My parents were really supporting me now, and I began to daydream about the sort of future that other sixteen-year-olds take for granted: going to college and maybe, just maybe, university. Except that I would soon have a baby to look after. Despite that, I decided to make a real effort with school now. *Miss Crabtree will be shocked*, I thought.

Emma remained a threat, though, as she still sometimes came onto the estate and, one time, to the back of the house with a girl who'd started coming to the house, Taliah. She had tried to get my sister to get me to go out, but I wouldn't. Sometimes, when I looked out of my bedroom window, I could see Emma standing at the corner and Taliah a bit further down the street. It was chilling.

Unfortunately, just when the bond between me and Jane seemed to be at its best, it began to unravel.

'We're going on a family day out to a theme park,' I told her one day, oblivious to the fact that I was about to cross a line with my rescuer. 'The BNP have organised it.'

She looked at me, aghast. 'Sorry, Hannah,' she said, as if she hadn't quite heard properly. 'The BNP?'

Sadly, Dad's bitterness about what had happened to me had turned into an irrational – and, thankfully, temporary – hatred of all things Asian.

'Yes, I said. 'Dad's joined. He reckons that if the BNP get in to Parliament, they'll give all the foreigners money to go back to their own country.'

Jane, gentle, lovely Jane, had a face like thunder.

'That's racism, Hannah,' she said, as levelly as she could. 'I think you need to think very, very seriously about what you're saying here. Your own baby may be half-Asian, mightn't she? And would you like her to grow up facing any sort of racial abuse?' She paused and looked at me. 'And, honestly, do you really think that what your dad seems to want is even possible? That people should be given money to go to a country they may never even have seen? *This* is their country!'

I think we both felt uncomfortable when we parted that day, When I got home I told Dad about it and he was livid, telling me I mustn't see Jane again.

The summer would be over by the time the drip-drip of this BNP-fuelled poison between me and Jane would take full effect, but in the meantime I was feeling strong enough to push really hard with my GCSEs. I wanted to show the world, but especially myself and my parents, that I still had some kind of worth and could make some kind of contribution to the normal society I'd been locked away from. That I wasn't just going to be a victim for the rest of my life.

So I put up with the sidelong glances and the ribbings and name-calling in the classrooms and corridors, and tried my damnedest to re-engage with education.

English lessons had never been a pleasure, but Maths was good, and I even started looking forward to Resistant Materials class. School as a whole was still a war zone but it was my war zone, and suddenly I began to feel I belonged.

There were still moments of terror that summer, though, as the gang's taxis weaved their way through the streets of Heywood, Rochdale, Nelson, Bradford, and all the other towns where they had friends and relatives. I'd feel a sense of foreboding every time a taxi came into view or pulled up suddenly close by.

I'd wonder whether this was the moment they'd chosen to come back for me.

I left school once my exams were over, but didn't do much beyond staying at home with Mum and Dad.

I missed the School Leavers' Ball. I'd been invited, just like everyone else, but I was seven months pregnant and couldn't face anybody. Part of me wanted to put on a nice dress and go to a ball, but I couldn't do it. Apart from anything else, I felt ashamed that my life was such a mess: at times, I'd have another wobble and wouldn't be sure I even wanted the baby I was carrying.

I saw the pictures of the ball on Facebook – a sea of bright, shiny faces, all scrubbed up and wearing smart suits and outrageous summer dresses. Not for the first time, I felt like I'd missed out.

I was beginning to miss out on Jane, too. She kept trying to call me but I kept putting her off. I'd be in the bath when she called, or busy, or something. Whatever. At the time, still a kid, I'd thought Dad was right. I'd become so used to just believing what others told me to believe. We've both changed our minds now. I can't believe either of us truly believed it at the time.

Over the months, Mum's initial horror at her eldest daughter's pregnancy had mellowed. As my due date approached, she was more excited than anyone.

I, of course, was terrified, still not knowing whether my baby was the daughter of a paedophile rapist and not knowing how I would react if she was. Would I blame her and want to have her adopted? Or would I just accept her, whatever her colouring, whatever the way she was conceived? All through the pregnancy, the exams, the meetings with social workers about the baby, these were the thoughts that were always at the forefront of my mind.

Despite accepting the baby, and the fact that I was going to be a mum, I never felt much excitement or elation. Sometimes I'd convince myself that I hated the baby, that I didn't want her at all. And I still so hated those mothers who were full of how wonderful their babies were, oh, and look at the pictures, and come and see the clothes we've bought …

It was, in fact, me that I hated the most: me and Emma and those men.

The girl who had loved dressing her Barbie dolls had shrivelled up and died long ago. I didn't buy anything for the baby until a week before I was due, and even then I just bought a cot, a pram, bouncy chair, sterilising stuff and some nappies. I think part of me wanted to love the baby, but until I knew who the father was, it was too difficult, so I slipped into some sort of weird denial. Only, I knew there was no stopping Mother Nature, and soon I would have to confront reality.

* * *

The contractions were coming every five minutes when Mum and I set off for the hospital.

It was around 6 p.m., a cold, blustery day, and by then the midwife had already been out to see me.

When we got to the hospital, though, they weren't sure. 'Well, you don't look to be in pain,' said one of the nurses, 'so we'll probably have to send you home.'

She changed her mind when I had a contraction just as she was checking the dilation. 'Crikey, Hannah, you must have a high pain threshold – you're six centimetres! You can stay in.'

So for the next six hours I lay there, Mum wanting to rub my back, me not wanting her to, while, slowly, I dilated to eight centimetres. By then I was in pain, for all that the nurse had said about my threshold, and asking for an epidural.

They suggested instead breaking my waters to speed things up, but in the end agreed to give me the epidural. Mum and I both nodded off for a while then – me in the bed, her in the chair beside me.

At 6 a.m. I started pushing, and for the next half-hour I felt panic-stricken, wondering what colour the baby would be. I'd looked on the internet and, to my shock, read that even when a baby looks white when it's born, the skin can change colour later on. I still wouldn't know for sure, even when I saw her for the first time.

'What will I do if it's one of theirs?' I whispered to Mum, after one of the later contractions.

But by then Mum was trying desperately to forget how this baby might have been conceived, and how abused I'd been. She'd been taken over by the excitement of it all: worried, too, but mostly excited. 'You'll do what's right, Hannah, that's what you'll do. So don't worry. Let's just help her to be born.'

I wanted to be happy, to enjoy the moment like all the other mums on the ward that day. Instead, I was beside myself, almost with a feeling of grief, as I pushed one more time.

In the moment she was born, I looked away. I didn't want to hold her or anything until I was sure, until I'd had a chance to have a proper look at her, to see if she was the daughter of one of my attackers. Tears were pouring down my face, and inside I was screaming: '*What colour is she? What colour is she? Is she one of theirs?*'

I remember still looking away, looking anywhere, frantic, as one of the nurses put her to my breast. Through my tears I screamed at Mum, 'Get her off me, get her off me!'

Thankfully she was calm, sweeping this warm, soft little bundle of humanity into her arms and giving her a kiss. A first kiss.

Then she was trying to get me to focus. 'Hannah, Hannah,' I heard her saying, my eyes still turned away, 'She's not one of theirs, sweetheart, she's not one of theirs. She's just yours, and she's beautiful.'

So that was Mum's reaction: normal, happy, just enjoying the moment of her granddaughter's birth. I still couldn't look, still couldn't hold her. Not for another two hours.

And then, tentatively, I eased the shawl from the side of her face and looked down at her, as she lay in her cot next to my bed. Slowly, I took in her features: the shock of black hair; her nose, just like mine; her lips; those beautiful blue eyes gazing back at me.

'Hello, Chloe,' I whispered.

Until that moment, I'd convinced myself that I didn't really care for her at all. Now, seeing her, holding her, all that changed. 'What did she weigh, Mum?'

'Seven pounds, one ounce,' said Chloe's proud grandma. 'She's perfect, isn't she?'

I lay there for what seemed an age, holding my baby, pressing my nose against her cheek so that I could inhale her wonderful, unique scent, my mind flooding with the relief of knowing that we could both have a fresh start.

For her, there would be the steadily gathering, simple joy of life while for me, still only sixteen, there was the chance to rebuild my own life away from the misery and pain that had engulfed me for so long. I knew there would be difficult times ahead, but I would try my hardest for her to put the past behind me and give her a future.

As I drifted off to sleep, I recognised there was a part of me that was still damaged, still desolate and still frightened, but I saw, too, that none of that was her fault. An inner certainty told me that no matter how she'd been conceived, she was her own person and fully deserved to have her chance.

The next time I woke up, Dad was there, Chloe in his arms, smiling at me. He'd brought with him a pink blanket that would be so adored by my little girl. It had the image of a teddy bear in the middle, and, as she grew older, she'd take it everywhere with her, always hating to give it up, even to be washed, as if she had a fear of feeling alone in the world. I think she knew instinctively that it wouldn't be all plain sailing and that with a kid like me as her mum, she'd need that blanket.

My brothers and sisters weren't allowed to come and visit in the hospital, so they only got to meet her when I came home the next day.

Jane sent me a New Baby card and wrote her number inside, to let me know she still cared and was still there for me. I didn't feel ready to reply, but I felt glad inside.

Chapter Nineteen
Trying Again

I was asleep with my new baby when the letter from Greater Manchester Police arrived.

It landed on the hall floor like an unexploded bomb that detonated the moment my dad unfolded it and began to read.

I woke up to the sound of Dad ranting and raving downstairs in the living room. Bleary-eyed and aching, I went downstairs to see him waving an A4 piece of paper in his hand. He was crimson with rage.

'They've stopped the case, Hannah! The Crown Prosecution Service say it's not strong enough. They're not going to put that bastard on trial. They're just going to let him go.'

Dad held his arms out to me and I collapsed into them, sobbing, suddenly terrified that my abusers would be free to attack me again.

As my tears soaked into his dressing gown, Dad went on reading bits of the letter out loud. It was dated 25 August, though it turned out the CPS lawyers had actually reached their decision almost a month earlier. The police had taken until July 28 to send them the file and they made their decision not to prosecute the following day.

I could feel Dad shaking with rage as he talked about the DNA the police had from my knickers. 'You were *fifteen*, for God's sake, and he was nearly sixty,' he said, his voice breaking. 'How could any jury ignore that? You were under age. They'd have to convict. They'd have no option!'

I was in shock. What would happen to me now, with Daddy and the others completely free?

Mum had come into the room too, and while we sat in a huddle on the sofa Dad rang one of the detectives on the case. He was raging at him about the decision, and then went suddenly quiet as the police officer at the other end of the line explained what he knew about it.

When he came off the phone, Dad said, 'They didn't think you'd make a credible witness, kid. And that the men would have just claimed it had been nothing more than consensual sex with a girl who'd gone off the rails.'

I thought of all the evidence the police had gathered: the DNA, the interviews I'd put myself through, the names I'd given them, the addresses, and the detailed, harrowing accounts of being passed carelessly around like a broken doll. They knew about Daddy, about Tariq, and Billy, and Cassie, and all the others.

What more evidence did they want? Why bother interviewing me again in the January if it was going to come to this? Why bother driving around with the police to show them the addresses they'd all taken me to? Why the resulting identity parades?

The identity parades were among the worst things I had had to do.

From the surveillance operations the police had set up of the addresses I'd given them, as well as the locations from the day we'd spent driving around, the police were gradually arresting the men they thought had attacked me. Every so often they would ring and say, 'We've got some more, please come in.'

It made me sick every time.

I did three or four identity parades, or VIPER sessions as they were called, involving about fifteen suspects. I found these VIPER parades, which is a form of identity parade that allows a victim to see line-ups by video, really stressful.

At each VIPER, it was down to me to say whether or not I recognised any of the men in the images that flashed up in front of me. There's always a suspect in each group of pictures – you're shown the men's faces randomly, nine on each disc, I think – and you have to pick the suspect out. If you don't, they're allowed to go free. If you're sure it's them you say so, and another paedophile is hopefully off the streets. Quite a lot of responsibility, then.

And yet, here I was, back at square one. Why hadn't the CPS believed me? Or the police? Wasn't it obvious that I'd been raped? And trafficked?

All in all, at this point it was as if nobody believed me. I thought about all the months it had taken for the police to even get the file to the CPS. I thought about their attitude at the time they were interviewing me; as if they thought that whatever had happened to me I'd brought it upon myself. There was also the fact that Social Services had told my Mum and Dad I was a prostitute; that'd I'd made a 'lifestyle' choice.

In their eyes I was just a wayward teenager who'd made the choice to sleep with takeaway workers and taxi drivers in their forties and fifties; to have sex with them one after the other, this way and that way, and then be driven back to a fleapit of a house to recover in time for the next round of 'fun'.

I felt as though the whole world was laughing at me: the lawyers in their flash offices, the police down at the station, and the men in their taxis and takeaways and grubby flats and houses.

My life had been destroyed, and yet no one was going to pay but me. No one had even bothered to come and see me to break the news. I realised, in those moments, that I'd been abandoned. Again. All that remained for me was a life sentence of fear and ruin.

As Dad threw the letter into the bin in total disgust, I headed back to bed, distraught, paralysed by the fear that now gripped me.

I couldn't believe it. The police had taken almost a year to get a file to the CPS and the lawyers had decided – in a day, as it turned out – that there was no case against Daddy and Immy. Never mind all the other abusers who'd followed them. Here we were, within days of the anniversary of me first telling the police what Daddy had done to me, and it was all being thrown out.

I knew that Jane believed me, and that she knew I was only one of dozens of girls being picked off and broken by the gang every night of the week. She thought she'd done the right thing by persuading me to go to the police. She'd coaxed me, reassured me, helped me through it all. And for what? So that the people in suits, and the people with social-work degrees, could throw it back in my face and turn a blind eye to what was going on in my home town. I should have trusted my instincts when I thought it would come to nothing.

I didn't blame Jane, and for all that I'd lost touch with her now I knew she'd be bitterly disappointed by the decision. She'd feel she had let me down, I knew. But it wasn't her. It was all the others. I'd told Jane right at the start that no one in any kind of authority would believe me, and now I'd been proved right.

A whole year to decide the case was too shaky. A whole year to decide that it wouldn't be in the interests of justice to put a gang of paedophile rapists on trial. It was a joke, and it made me weep.

The injustice of the Crown Prosecution Service decision wasn't lost on some of the detectives involved in the case. One had once hinted to Dad that it might come to this because he'd seen it happen in the past. That same officer came to see him now. He was shaking his head, saying: 'I don't believe it. If it had been up to me I would definitely have prosecuted.'

It would ultimately come out that even at that late stage, Greater Manchester Police could have contested the decision, but the top brass decided not to. I'm guessing they didn't want to upset the CPS. Or that they, just like the lawyers, had decided to take the safe, more politically correct route, rather than face up to the fact that gangs of Asian men were preying on kids like me.

At the time I had no idea they could have appealed, and there was never any talk about it.

* * *

All that was left was a deep, impenetrable silence. The whole investigation stopped. Just like that.

I was left feeling devastated and frightened out of my wits. With no trial, there would be no justice. And, worse than that, the gang would feel the police couldn't touch them and so they'd be free to carry on with an ever-widening pool of victims.

I kept hearing of other girls they were using.

The system had allowed my abusers free to roam, completely beyond the law. I looked down at Chloe, almost for comfort, shuddering at the thought of what the future might bring.

Two days after I was abandoned by the Crown Prosecution Service, Dad drove me to school so I could get my GCSE results. I'd made a huge effort with them, but as I slipped into the hall to learn my fate I really couldn't be bothered. What did exam results matter now?

Miss Crabtree was there, and she came up to me, really friendly, asking how I was and the baby and what did Chloe weigh? When I showed her a picture of her she gave me a hug and started to well up.

All the GCSE results were in brown envelopes on the stage, and I opened mine with Miss Crabtree. I couldn't help but smile when I read the sheet inside. I'd got C grades in everything! Not bad for a no-hoper who'd just been dumped back into hell! And it meant I could go to college.

Miss Crabtree was really, really pleased for me. 'Oh, Hannah,' she said, and then her voice cracked. She actually started crying, properly crying.

I couldn't believe that someone was crying for me, crying because I'd done something good. For one of the few times in my life, if only for a moment, I actually felt proud of myself.

* * *

Even with the bounce of my GCSE results, the rejection of my case sent me into another downward spiral. It was even worse this time around as I'd started a college course and also had the baby to care for.

I struggled, I really did. I wasn't breastfeeding Chloe. The nurses at the hospital had given me the usual encouragement but left me to make the final decision. I had decided I didn't want to. It just didn't appeal to me. I don't regret it – I think she's turned out fine without it – but it did make things more difficult, with sterilising and mixing the formula and everything. Doing all that on your own, as well as nappy changing, bathing, dressing, winding and comforting Chloe, while trying to do my college work, was stressing me out.

Chloe and I stayed at my parents' home through the autumn and winter and into the new year of 2010 and of course my parents helped out. But Chloe was my ultimate responsibility – the buck stopped with me, and I wanted to get it right.

A couple of weeks into January, I decided I was ready to call in to see Jane at the clinic, and to show Chloe off to

her. She was great, and said she looked so like me. I told her
I was sorry I'd stopped seeing her.

'How's college?' Jane asked, delicately changing the
subject.

'It's great,' I said, jiggling the baby. 'I'm doing pretty
well, too, I think. It's just tough with this one.'

'And home?'

It felt as though a cloud passed over my face. While the
gang was history now, so was any court case that might have
put Daddy and them in prison. Plus, life with my parents was
getting more and more stressful again. Dad was always on at
me, saying I was living there rent-free, and if I ever went out
with my mates both of them would start on at me, accusing
me of having sex with people all over the place. It had got to
the stage where I could really only speak to my sister, Lizzie.

Jane had been waiting patiently for my reply. 'It's pretty
rubbish,' I whispered. 'I could do with trying to get my
own place.'

She said she'd have a word with a woman from Rochdale
Connexions, who I'd already spoken to about money and
my screwed-up home life.

When we talked about how the case had been thrown
out by the CPS, Jane said she was disgusted. She still looked
at my file every day, she said, because it reminded her to
keep going. She wanted to keep pushing and pushing for
me, and not give up.

Jane's chat with Connexions meant I was put on the
waiting list for a place at a single mothers' housing unit
– the same apartment block for young girls that back in

2008 was being targeted by abusers. Sara, Jane's boss at Crisis Intervention, had told Social Services so in one of her letters, and who knows whether that was still the case when Chloe and I – a fragile, inadequate teenager and her infant daughter – moved in towards the end of June 2010?

At the time I had no idea what potential danger I was in. I was just relieved and I think Mum and Dad were too.

But I wonder now whether I and some of the other girls might have been targeted by the very people who'd abused the 15-year-old me; either them or members of a new gang.

To be honest, there were too many bad memories around Mum and Dad's place, and I'd liked to have moved away from the Rochdale area altogether. But I didn't have the money, and the council would only let me move locally.

Close to a park and Rochdale town centre, the housing unit didn't seem a bad place to be because I was with other young mums trying to cope with things and to try to be independent. Well, not totally independent, because there are staff in the block twenty-four hours a day and CCTV to watch out for anyone kicking off.

There are a dozen flats there, and mine was on the top floor, overlooking a park. It had just the one bedroom for Chloe and me, but that was fine. And at least, unlike the flats on the two lower floors, there were no grilles over the windows.

I had a living room, and they gave me a starter pack to fit out the bathroom, the bedroom and the kitchen: a beige duvet cover with white circles, white sheets, pots and pans, cutlery, towels, toothpaste and shampoo, all of it from Asda.

Next to the single bed I put Chloe's cot; just a cheap one, wooden, from Argos.

At first it felt good to feel a little bit free. Chloe and I settled into a routine that worked for us. But, after a few weeks, the loneliness started to kick in. There were other girls to talk to, I suppose, but I was shy and I found it hard. And with Chloe only being a baby still, I felt pretty much alone.

It was then that I started to have a drink in the evenings. And then another. As a kid of fourteen and fifteen I'd been drinking normally like teenagers do – getting drunk on a Friday night, maybe, and having a laugh. Getting drunk that is, but not too drunk. With the gang, I'd knocked back the vodka as quickly as I could and it was this thought that remained – that alcohol could numb you.

Now, in my own place, I started to drink more because I felt lonely. There was more, however – I started to rake over what had happened – or rather was not happening – with the gang. I felt abandoned, and it made me scared again because I knew the men were all still out there, and all still free. Then there was Emma. She didn't know where I lived, but she kept emailing me to get in touch. She still must have wanted me back. I ignored her, but it just made me feel more scared.

I started drinking more and more. Just like before, I drank to forget: the abuse, the abandoned case, everything.

Some mornings I'd wake up and feel as though I was trying to drink myself into oblivion. It didn't matter what I drank – anything really. Lambrini sometimes – you know, the cider: 'Lambrini girls just wanna have fun.' Except that this girl wasn't having fun. Most of the time it would actually be the very cheapest cider I could find – White Star, which they sold around the corner and was a favourite among all the local alcoholics.

I'd get a three-litre bottle and drink it on its own. On a normal day, I'd start drinking as soon as I'd finished college and collected Chloe from nursery. It could be about four o'clock in the afternoon or maybe even earlier. But I wouldn't let myself get drunk until the baby had gone to bed. I wanted to drink, you see, but I didn't want to be too drunk.

So I'd pour myself a glass and then wait an hour for the next one – the way I was thinking by then was that messed up! I mean, who does that? Having one drink and then trying to wait an hour before having the next one?

Part of it was because I knew I'd never survive if the drinking really took hold, but part of it was also because I wanted to be responsible for Chloe.

Through no fault of her own, however, Chloe was part of the problem, too. I was with her 24/7 with no help and no one to talk to. All I had then were different staff workers coming in and out, just checking on me for this and that.

In all the time I was at the housing unit, my mum and dad never came to see me. I thought that with no trial coming up, they must have gone back to seeing me as a prostitute (or, at least, that's what my crowded head was telling me). After all, that was what everyone was saying, wasn't it? They'd not disowned me, but I felt they weren't really interested. I'd speak to them on the phone sometimes, and every now and then go around for tea. But they never came to the flat or offered to look after Chloe. That was part of why I was so depressed – my own mum and dad didn't seem to want to know.

All the other girls in the flats would be going round to their mum and dad's, or else their mums would be coming round helping them out and taking the babies out. But my mum and dad never did any of that. I think I was a bit jealous. I was angry as well, that they were only like that because of what they thought I was. Thanks to Social Services, they thought of me as a prostitute and not a victim. That was the conclusion I reached; they might have had their own reasons.

I drank because I couldn't cope with all the different things going on in my life. Everything was just going around and around in my head. I was trying to live a life after being abused for months and months, but with nothing having happened about it.

I gradually made friends with most of the girls at the housing unit. They didn't know what had happened to me, and I didn't know why they were there, either – apart from having got pregnant. Sometimes I'd wonder whether any of them had been caught up in the gang, but it seemed too far-fetched and, anyway, I doubted that any of them would have admitted to it. I wouldn't have – it was too shaming.

On my bad days, I'd just stare at the walls, completely ignoring Chloe. I'd feed her and clean her and dress her and all those other things, but too many other times I'd blank her out. It got so bad that she'd bang her head on the floor just to get my attention. I could see that her little heart was breaking. It breaks my own heart now to think of it.

Somehow I just didn't seem to have the motivation to do anything, and I started to feel depressed almost all the time. I could feel myself slipping down into a world away from normal society.

I felt I was being tortured day in, day out. I still couldn't believe that Daddy and Immy had been allowed to remain free for all that time. It was horrible. I thought, *They've done this to me and they've won. Everyone thinks I'm a prostitute.*

And I was still worried that they would come after me. I was in Rochdale, where so much of it had happened. I was just worried in case I bumped into any of them.

I actually did see one of the men, Saj, as I was pushing Chloe through Rochdale town centre in her pushchair once. My stomach dropped to the ground and I thought I was going to be sick. I remember turning around as quickly as I could and pushing the buggy as fast as possible in the other direction. I don't think he saw me.

I bumped into Emma once, too, in Rochdale town centre. She was with her mum, and her mum shouted across the street, 'There's the slut!' They were calling me a liar, saying I'd tried to send innocent men to jail.

And that, I knew, was exactly what the rest of the world thought about me. That Daddy and Immy were innocent, and that all those other creeps, who would pay their money so they could rape me, were innocent, too.

And so, on days like those, I would nip out to the shop around the corner and buy another three litres of White

Star, put it in the fridge, and try to put off the moment I'd walk back into the kitchen area and open it.

* * *

Social Services knew about the drinking, and they gave me an alcohol worker who started coming once a week. She was nice enough, but all she really did was have a chat and give me tips on how to cut down. I knew, and I think she knew, that in my case especially, I had to do it myself. And I wasn't ready to.

The social workers also got me to go to a young parents' group, where they help you to cope with your baby and train you in how to look after them.

By now my little girl was walking. She'd started off by hauling herself up whenever she reached a chair, then gradually getting the coordination to set off. I used to love to see her tottering towards me, a big smile on her face, desperate to succeed, falling into my arms and giggling with pride and satisfaction. It made me feel good, too.

The young parents' session on 10 August 2010 should have been as dull and uneventful as the rest, but instead it was terrifying.

I'd just sat down when the last girl in the world that I wanted to see walked in. Emma. I hadn't even known she was pregnant.

Her eyes locked onto me and I felt a wave of revulsion and fear. A moment later, I was flying out of the door, pushing my way past the staff who were trying to get me to stay.

Stay in a room with the girl who'd controlled me for all those months? Never. Terrified, I fled back to the flat, looking over my shoulder in case she'd decided to follow me.

She hadn't, but the next day I heard that Social Services were thinking of giving her a place at my housing unit.

I told them I'd leave if they did. How could I feel safe if she was there, too? Because if she knew I was there, so would the men. Thankfully, they held a meeting about it and decided she wouldn't be allowed to come.

Still scared, I rang Jane for an appointment, and met her on 12 August. We had a real heart-to-heart. I told her how upset I'd been to see Emma at the parenting session, and how scared I felt that she might already know where I was living. I told her how dangerous I thought Emma still was, even though she'd been turned down for the place at the housing unit: imagine someone like Emma having such easy access to vulnerable kids, all of them struggling, all of them broke, all of them weak enough to maybe fall into her trap.

She simply nodded when I told her how I'd hated her at the time for telling people what was happening to me. But now I was grateful because it had eventually made my parents realise the truth. I felt different about other things too, including boys. I'd applied to university by then, and I told her how I felt I'd grown up loads since moving into the housing unit.

'From now on I only want to go out with lads who are normal and have a job,' I said with a laugh. And then, almost in triumph: 'And Chloe will have to come first!'

Jane reassured me that everything was fine between us, and then began talking about other things for a while – babies and stuff, families. And then, with one of the faint smiles that let me know she had something up her sleeve, she moved on to talking about the police, and how they wanted to re-interview me.

I could hardly believe it. After all this time, and all the rejections and all the failings, the police wanted to take me through it all *again*. Two years had passed since I'd been raped and trafficked by Daddy; two years since I'd told the police about it; and two years since they'd collected the DNA evidence that proved I was telling the truth.

But the delay had also given me time to ask myself about why they'd not brought the case to court. I knew some of the reasons, but I had also begun to wonder whether it was partly my fault. Had I not given them enough detail? Had I been too scared to give all the names, all the addresses, for fear of what they'd do to me? Should I have cried more? By the time I spoke to the police I'd become so used to it – de-sensitised, my dad says – that maybe I had come over as a kid who just wasn't as obviously upset as they had expected I should be. I thought about that a lot, but the bottom line was, I'd done all the crying I could do.

Sitting in Jane's office that day part of me, an ever-increasing part of me, wanted to try one more time. In fact, if Jane hadn't mentioned it, I realised I would have found a way of trying, anyway. It was weird. I think that sometimes in your life you have to be totally ready to do something, and it just seemed to be fate when Jane put it to me, as I was ready, finally.

I thought it was high time Daddy paid for what he'd done, and that Emma paid for taking me to him, knowing I'd be raped. And it was time for Tariq, too, and all the others.

Maybe I'd matured over the last two years. Maybe living on my own, being a mum, had changed my perception. I felt braver. Hindsight had given me a clearer picture of everything.

Jane held out a hand to me. I held it, just briefly.

In the silence, I thought about the girl who'd recruited me for all those men. I'd been away from Emma for ages by then, and I think I'd finally begun to understand the hold she'd had on me: that so much of it was down to my vulnerability at the time – my youth, my need to find some kind of life for myself, no matter how on the edge it might have been.

The difference all the way through was that Emma loved the sex and I didn't. In my mind, I had known it was wrong.

'She liked to be abused,' I said now slowly, out loud, 'because in her mind it wasn't abuse.'

Maybe not just then, but with that realisation I could see a time when I'd stop being afraid of her and stand up for myself. She wasn't my mate. Looking back, she'd never been my mate. She'd just used me.

I realised I still hadn't answered Jane's question, about whether I'd speak to the police again.

The more I thought about that, the more I felt I was doing the right thing. I knew that if I helped the police now I could help to save other girls from suffering the same fate as me.

So in the end I said yes, I'd go ahead with it. Jane looked so pleased, and so sad, too, in a way, as if she was thinking of all the previous disappointments. But then, briskly, she picked up the phone, dialled a number and waited for it to be answered.

'Hi, Susan,' she said. 'I'm with Hannah now, and she'll be happy to meet you. Can we say next week?' She glanced at me. I nodded. It was agreed.

Chapter Twenty
Calpol and Paracetamol

A few days later Susan, the detective Jane had been speaking to, turned up at the flat and began to explain it all in detail. She and Jane's boss, Sara, worked together on the Sunrise team – the people from different agencies who were trying to get a grip on things.

I warmed to Susan straight away. I think she has that effect on people because she's really level, really reassuring. She told me how she'd been investigating other cases, and when she looked back at the video interviews I'd done, she could tell I'd been telling the truth.

She knew how much I'd felt let down, the way I'd not been kept informed the way I'd wanted to be. 'We're looking at it from a different perspective this time,' she said. 'I can't give you absolute guarantees that we'll get convictions, but we'll be doing our very best to gather all the evidence together so that it can be presented in court.

'What we'd like you to do is to be patient and just keep telling the truth.'

Apparently other girls had come forward, so this time around there would be more witnesses, and not just me. She asked me if I'd be OK to go through it all again – my story was the biggest one, but with all the girls together, it all looked really hopeful.

I felt an immediate difference between her and the police I'd dealt with before. It helped that this time around it was women officers who were dealing with me. What's the word? Empathy? Maybe it's because Susan was a woman, with the same body, but I felt she understood more. I thought, *They have the same bodies as me, and maybe more of the same emotions.* I felt there was more of a connection, because no matter how sensitive a man might be, he's still a man. And so were the people who'd attacked me.

I wanted to know what Emma's situation would be. 'Will she be in the dock with the men?' I asked Susan.

'No,' she said, gathering herself. She looked at me. 'She won't be in the dock because she's a victim herself. I'm not dealing with her. One of my colleagues is doing that. But remember, Hannah, she was fifteen too, and a lot of the things that were happening to you were happening to her too.'

Part of me was furious about that, but then I thought about how long Emma must have been involved with all the men. She'd have been really young when she started, maybe even younger than Roxanne and Paige when they got involved. Everything about her had been skewed. She'd always say how much she loved shagging all those men. But had she? Had she really? I just think she never knew anything different.

I listened as Susan told me how she wanted me to give another video interview, and how important it was to think about what I wanted to say so I could give them as much detail as I could possibly remember. I told her I'd try, but that some of it had been so long ago I might struggle. But I felt I could do it.

There would be a number of video interviews to get through, in fact. Over the next couple of months, I got into a routine of doing them after I'd dropped Chloe off at nursery. Jane would always be there, supportive, a shoulder to cry on in the rest breaks after I'd given the detail of all those harrowing attacks in such detail it made me cringe.

All the way through, at the back of my mind, was the thought that my abusers deserved what, hopefully, was coming to them. Jane said I was brave, but to be honest I didn't always feel it, and it still helped to have a drink.

Life was tough, but the crucial difference this time around was that right from the start I felt Susan and the others in her team believed me, and wanted to hear what I had to say. They were immediately sympathetic. I wasn't some kind of child prostitute wasting their time with made-up stories.

* * *

Unbeknown to me, there'd been a huge change in the way the police looked at the sort of abuse and grooming I'd been through. Susan's investigation had involved just a few girls, me included. Now, it turned out, Greater Manchester Police were going to spend millions of pounds on helping kids like me – and cracking down on the gangs exploiting them. So detectives like Susan were taken into a new, much wider investigation. They called it 'Operation Span', though I wouldn't know that until my involvement in it was over.

Most of the early cases looked at by Operation Span were in Rochdale but, gradually, once more and more detectives knew what they were looking for, the operation would expand. And, in time, other police forces would start to do the same. It was a ball that would keep on rolling.

While Susan was speaking to me, and constantly reassuring me, other detectives were trying to track down some of the 'newer' girls who'd been picked up off the street and dumped on the gangs' production lines. Rochdale Social Services didn't want to face up to it, but I knew, and eventually the world would know, that virtually all the girls were white and almost all of the men who paid to rape them were Pakistani.

Sometimes the truth hurts. But it's still the truth.

As for me, I was still confused, still desperately frightened. I was still paranoid about Emma and the others contacting me – I'd hide in the flat and switch my phone off when it got really bad.

With the video interviews, all my memories of the bad times with the gang came flooding back – the pain, the threats, the way they'd pass me around. Then, too, I'd think about the revenge they'd try to take against me if they knew what I was doing.

Even though I didn't know it at the time, Susan and Jane started to talk to the housing unit and Social Services about how they could help me through the process. They all knew how scared and upset I was, and they set up what

I suppose was a safety net to help me through. The police, too, had their own doubts and, unbeknown to me, at least to begin with, they were working behind the scenes to make things a little more bearable for me.

One of the issues they had was that the housing unit was close to the centre of Rochdale, close to where so many things had happened to me, and where so many of my abusers might be lurking. Social Services only seemed to think as far as the town itself; the police thought I'd be safer if I could be found somewhere to live outside the borough.

Little by little, I came to believe that there really would be a trial this time. The only problem was that I was incredibly damaged, and I wondered whether I'd have the strength to stand up to what lay ahead. I still carried with me a huge sense of injustice about being abandoned the first time around, and I was still finding it incredibly hard to do even the normal things in life – like raising my baby and getting on with the college work I hoped would give us a future.

In the end, I suppose I thought that until they were locked away I'd never be free; I'd always be looking over my shoulder, wondering when they'd catch up with me.

No one actually came out and said it, but I could tell that the detectives involved with Operation Span were annoyed with their colleagues who'd dealt with my case before. They kept on saying they were sorry, that the evidence had been there right from the start, and that certain procedures hadn't been carried out when they should have been – basic things, like collecting the knickers as soon as I'd mentioned them, because in a case like this that sort of thing was crucial.

When they'd picked Daddy up, he totally denied having had sex with me, and yet his DNA was on my knickers. Wasn't that enough to convince the police? And the CPS lawyers who looked at the file? It would have been more difficult for them if Daddy had said I'd had sex with him willingly, but he hadn't – he just denied the whole thing.

The Operation Span team had to go through the whole investigation again for themselves, checking and rechecking, testing every single thing that I'd said and that my abusers had said, and reviewing all the forensics.

I'd hear them muttering things like: 'This should all have been done the first time around,' and 'How the hell could they not bring this to court?' Just like me, they couldn't believe that the CPS had sent back the file marked 'No Further Action'.

'It's as if they just didn't want to know,' hissed one detective. 'All in all, Hannah, they had your account and they had the forensic proof. It just looks as though they'd all agreed – the police and the CPS – that they didn't want to pursue it. We can't believe how shoddy a job it's been.'

Operation Span was only a couple of weeks old when the police moved in to start arresting more men who'd attacked either me or some of the other girls they'd groomed.

In quick succession they picked up Tariq, Cassie, Saj, Car Zero and Tiger.

Billy didn't know it then, but he'd be next on the list. He was the one Roxanne thought she was in love with. She'd got pregnant by him, but he'd persuaded her to have an abortion. The police checked all the medical records, traced the remains of the foetus and sent them away for forensic tests. The results proved that Billy had been the father, and he was arrested as soon as the report came back from the lab.

There was one glitch, however, and that was over Aarif. He was arrested, he was questioned, but after being allowed out on bail he went home, packed his bags, and caught a flight to Pakistan. As far as I know he's still there – until the day police can perhaps track him down and bring him back to finally face trial.

* * *

The rest of that winter, 2010 into 2011, was a nightmare for everyone involved with me: my family, the police, social workers, Jane, and the people at the housing unit. And me, of course.

Things had started to get on top of me again. Badly. I felt like I was in a recurring nightmare, with everything from all that time ago bubbling up again.

Locked inside my flat, terrified in case others in the gang came for me, I was heading straight back down the spiral, no matter what Jane or Susan did to try to keep me afloat.

The first time I tried to kill myself is a blur now. I know it was just into the new year, and that I was still conscious when the ambulance arrived, but after that your guess is as good as mine.

Afterwards, staff at the housing unit said I'd locked myself in the flat, and that three litres of cider had turned me mental and aggressive. The night staff shouted at the door for a few minutes, before deciding they had no option but to break in. One went to check on Chloe, lifting her, still asleep, out of her cot and taking her downstairs. The others piled in on me. Restraint they call it, but I needed it.

Drama over, they saw the empty packets of paracetamol and called an ambulance. It hadn't just been cider, either. There was also an empty bottle of Calpol on the sofa. As if anyone tries to commit suicide with Calpol!

For good measure, apparently, I'd cut my wrists; which explains the jagged little scars I still carry there today.

I spent that night in hospital, while Chloe was driven off to Mum and Dad's place in the back of a social worker's car. Nobody visited me in hospital that night, not even my parents. They couldn't bear to. They were livid with me because I'd done it with Chloe helpless in her cot. And me, as I came round – I couldn't believe I'd abandoned her like that.

Once I'd been discharged, I headed home from the hospital in a taxi. Mum and Dad gave me the cold shoulder, thinking I was just attention-seeking. Or, simply not knowing how to cope in this situation; this new turn of events. Chloe, though, ran to me as I came through the door.

As she snuggled into my shoulder I thought, *What they hell have I done? I'll never do that again. It's just not fair to let her grow up without her mum.*

After that, I was sent to the hospital in Manchester where I'd been born. This time, though, it was for counselling about the abuse that had made me try to kill myself.

It didn't do me any good, however, not then. And, back at the housing unit, I was still so paranoid about Emma and the others contacting me that I was still getting drunk all the time.

A few weeks later, I got a final warning. Any more trouble, the staff said, and I'd be out and homeless. But they always said that to girls and nothing ever seemed to happen.

For weeks after that, the police had to file a whole series of reports on the trouble they said I was causing: with my mum, with friends, or the people at the housing unit. Then there was the self-harming. It was always when I was drunk, which was pretty much every night.

The drinking was the worst of my problems, as it exacerbated my paranoia. I felt really low for a lot of the time and was prescribed anti-depressants. Most nights, and sometimes days, I settled for my own anti-depressant: a couple of litres of White Star.

I spent my eighteenth birthday just getting drunk in the flat with a few friends. Mum and Dad, still despairing of me but still trying to reach out, had given me £20. It probably went on cider.

Worse, I couldn't be bothered to go to college much, and my tutor there started to worry about me. Amazingly, I was still on track to pass the course, but only if I started turning up more often.

The police were still trying to help so I'd be in some kind of fit state to give evidence when the case came to court, but it was tough. And Rochdale Social Services weren't a lot of help.

Chapter Twenty-One
It Will Come To Trial

At one point, the head of targeted services, Steve Garner, was asked to give me extra support. His department promptly sent along the two social workers I hated the most. One of them, Anne, came back later, asking me a million questions about Chloe's paternity. I was so angry I wanted to throw her out. It all just added to the pressure, but Rochdale Social Services didn't seem to see it that way. Another time, when professionals met to talk about me in February as the police and Crisis Intervention had said they wanted to give me maximum support because they knew how messed up I was, Social Services didn't even bother to turn up.

It didn't seem to matter to them that I'd been a child at the time I'd been abused by the gang, and that emotionally I was still just a kid. They had ignored all the warnings about me while it was going on; now they were washing their hands of me again. They didn't seem to be able to see me and Chloe as a unit, and that if they helped to sort me out, they'd be sorting things out for her, too.

Jane was still keeping closely in touch with me, though, and every so often the police would ring and say, 'We've got some more, Hannah. Are you okay to come in?'

On 21 February I went to a VIPER parade and identified six men out of eight. It was so difficult, though, because I'd not seen them all for so long. The two who got off must have been thanking their lucky stars.

Most of them had been identified initially from the descriptions I'd given the police – descriptions of their features, their characteristics, the cars they drove, the places they visited or lived. After that, they were put under surveillance, and finally they were picked up.

The police had finally managed to tease some of the information from me in 2011. Some of it, though, went as far back as the earlier, pre-Span investigation of 2008 and 2009.

Three days after that latest VIPER I met up with Susan to do another video interview. I can still remember sitting there in my pink cardigan and the usual black leggings, arms wrapped around my middle, shaking sometimes as the police interviewer, Steph, asked me dozens and dozens of questions.

It was good that it was another woman. She started off by telling me there was nothing I could say that would shock her; I just had to try my best to remember all the details. 'I understand it may be embarrassing,' she said, 'but you can tell me anything.'

My head was down, trying to avoid the cameras I knew were filming me. 'Look, it's nothing to be embarrassed about,' she was saying. 'You were fifteen, you're eighteen now. You learn as you grow older, don't you?'

Yes, I thought. Looking back, I'd been so stupid, so naïve.

I was on the verge of tears as I took her through the way the abuse had started after I'd moved into Harry's house, the way Emma had taken me to the Balti House, and how Daddy had raped me. It was part of the deal, he'd said. He bought me things; I should give him things. I'd felt so scared.

'He said, "We're friends, we do things for each other." I didn't want to because he was old, but I didn't want to say no because I didn't want to look soft to Emma. I just tried to laugh it off.'

Steph leaned forward and asked: 'What were you scared of?'

'Sleeping with him,' I said.

'Why?'

'Because it's disgusting.'

I told Steph how I'd hoped Emma would come in and save me, but she hadn't, and Daddy had started pulling at my pants and I had started trying to look at the wall.

'Could he see the tears?' asked Steph.

I couldn't speak. I just nodded.

We moved on to the time Daddy gave me to Immy as his treat, and how he had told me that in his country, it was tradition for men to have sex with girls as young as eleven.

What had I thought of that? asked Steph. 'I don't even know what I was thinking,' I said. 'I was stupid.'

'How do you feel about it now?'

'Bad.'

'What do you think about Daddy doing this?'

'I think it's sick.'

I said to Steph that I'd been too scared to fight Immy off; scared of Emma because I was living with her and because she was so threatening.

'She'd have battered me,' I said. 'At first she was nice, but then it changed. I didn't like her any more but I couldn't get away from her.'

There had been a time when Chef had been touching me from behind. Wiping away tears, I said: 'Emma told me to let him carry on, but I told him to stop and he stopped'.

A few minutes later Emma had gone upstairs with him. It was the time he'd paid her £20 to let him go down on her. Afterwards, she'd joked about maybe telling someone what had happened. It really was a joke because I don't think she'd ever have said anything, but he didn't take it that way. He went wild, grabbing a kitchen knife and waving it at us, screaming, 'If you tell anyone, I'll kill you two bitches!'

As the questions went on, it felt as though Steph was trying to help me understand how I'd grown up in those three years, and that at eighteen I would have just fought them all off and run away. But, back then, my abusers – whether white, Asian, all of them – knew I was vulnerable and isolated, and that I believed all their threats.

Who could I have told about it? she asked.

I welled up. 'I couldn't have told any of those in the house, in Harry's place. If I'd told my dad, he'd probably have gone mad at me. I couldn't get away.'

Steph asked me if I had spoken to anyone about it. I mentioned Jane, and Steph asked me if anything had changed as a result. I told her no – we both knew how slowly these things happened. But the questions still went on.

I told how Daddy had just kept bringing people to have sex with me, and sometimes he'd give me money to make sure I stayed quiet.

'That's what he used to do. Get people to have sex with me in the places.'

'So why would he do that? What would he gain from doing that?'

'Maybe he was getting money as well,' I said slowly.

A few moments later, to my relief, the interview ended. When the tape and the cameras had been switched off, I looked up at Steph and said: 'There's lots of stuff I could have done, wasn't there? I could have rung the police. I could have stood up for myself. But at the time ...'

She smiled at me sympathetically. I left it there. It had all been said.

When I did the next video interview with her, on 1 March, I told her about some of the other girls I'd seen at different houses, about Daddy's threats to kill me, and how I just got used to being made to sleep with all those men.

'How did you think it could finish?' she asked.

'I thought it would finish after I told the police about Daddy,' I said, biting my nails. 'But it didn't.'

We talked about the mattress they kept at the Balti House so they could sleep with the under-age girls. Me, Emma, Roxanne, whoever else went there.

I gave her a list of names, counting them off on my fingers. 'I don't know if they've all slept with them, but probably,' I said.

'When you'd reported to the police once you'd been arrested at the Balti House for smashing the counter, what did you expect to happen?'

'I thought it would stop.'

'What actually happened? How come it didn't stop?'

'Because Emma got different men instead of them.'

Once Daddy and Immy had been interviewed, I had thought it would stop. But, of course, Emma just went out and found another 'ringleader'.

'What did you think about the fact that it had clearly stopped with these men you've spoken about, but then started again with different ones?'

I wasn't even bothered any more, I said. She wondered what I meant. 'Because it was happening every day, so I didn't bother any more. I didn't feel anything about it. It had been going on for so long. At first I felt dead bad and dead horrible, but then I didn't feel anything any more.'

Steph glanced up from her notes. 'So basically, you've come to the police, you've told us about these men, but what you're saying is that because Emma's got different men that's why it continued with different men?' I simply nodded and Steph continued.

'When Daddy's been arrested, you've been interviewed. What's happened in relation to where you've been living?

'I carried on living at Harry's,' I replied.

'What's happened with your relationship with Mum and Dad?'

I shrugged and explained that nothing had changed. Steph asked why.

'Because they've said it was my own fault for keeping going back,' I explained. 'So I didn't want to live there any more.'

Steph kept on pressing, kept on trying to make me understand the child I'd been; the victim I'd been. 'What do you think about your parents saying it's your fault?' she asked.

I felt a twinge of guilt. 'Well, it is a bit,' I whispered. 'It was my fault for not standing up for myself … and I carried on going.'

I tried my best to explain why; that I was scared, that I felt I had no escape and that Harry and Emma respectively provided me with the food and money I needed to get by. Steph moved the conversation on to the abuse.

I said that Aarif had always been the one to go first with us at his flat. I didn't know why, I said; it just happened that way, no matter how many other men were there. I told Steph how he would rape me and then call the next one through. I'd just let them do it, all the time looking at the wall and hoping it would end soon.

I told her it was him who had first raped me anally. 'I told him not to put it there. He said he wouldn't, but then he did …

'It hurt. I started shouting, telling him to get off me and shouting for Emma. I felt angry and upset because I didn't want to sleep with him anyway, never mind that.'

The next one to rape me that way was Aarif's cousin, Saj, I said. By now I was in tears, but she kept on asking me questions, trying to get the detail the jury would need to hear. I knew it was important, but I couldn't help but feel humiliated.

'I thought at first he would just do it normal,' I said.

'How come it's not been normal?'

'Because Emma's told him I was on my period.'

Steph could see I was distressed, but she kept going, saying she'd just ask me these few more questions and that would be it for the day.

'He asked me if I was on my period,' I sobbed. 'I said no, but he shouted for Emma and she picked up my knickers to show him the pad and the blood. Then he just told me to bend over.'

'How did you feel about that?'

'I didn't want to do it. I wanted to go home.'

'What did you say to him?'

'Nothing. There was no point.'

I told her it had hurt, and she asked how he could tell he was hurting me.

At this point I couldn't help it: my face cracked, and the tears fell down towards my top. 'I was scrunching up my face,' I whispered.

I was back in the video suite again a week later, recalling how Joe from Jo Baxi's Taxis had been friends with Cassie, and that they'd go to Aarif's flat together: if one was there, the other would be.

I said how we'd all just sit there for a couple of hours until the other girls and I were dead drunk. That's when they'd say we had to sleep with them.

Steph asked what I would have wanted to happen if I'd had a choice.

'Stop,' I said.

'Why would you want them to stop?'

'Because I didn't like it. I thought it was wrong.'

'Why did you think it was wrong?'

'Because they're old and I was only young.'

I thought of how I knew they'd come and find me if I refused to do what they wanted, and how Emma would batter me because she was such a thug. All of it was because of her, and all the time it was happening I just never thought it would stop.

Towards the end Steph asked: 'How did you cope?'

'Most of the time I would get drunk so when it happened I wouldn't feel as bad.'

'How do you feel about yourself now?'

I fought back tears, my head down, a hand covering my face.

'I feel horrible about myself,' I said in a whisper. 'That I didn't do anything to stop going.'

Steph was trying to explore the whole issue of me hating the way some of them would touch me – as though they meant it, as though I was special to them.

'It's because it's more intimate,' I mumbled, head down, not wanting to say the word. 'If they just had sex with me, it felt like nothing. I didn't have to…'

And then the dam burst. 'Because I don't want them to feel my "puddy" or touch my body because I don't like them!'

My face was awash with tears. For a few, eerie moments it seemed as though Steph was speaking not to me but to the people – all those unknown people, prosecution lawyers, defence lawyers, police, jurors – who might one day view this video.

I think Steph realised I'd reached my limit, and that to push me any further would leave me damaged. So she eased back, asking me how old the men had thought I was – and how old I thought I'd appeared to them.

'I looked younger than I was,' I said. I hadn't worn make-up then, I said, and I was dead skinny. And I'd had no boobs until I was pregnant.

Steph asked what I thought about Cassie wanting younger girls like Roxanne and Paige.

'I would have been glad,' I said slowly, knowing how bad it would sound but knowing, too, that it had to be said because it was the awful truth. 'It sounds tight, but…'

'Why glad?'

'Because I would not have had to go,' I replied.

'Why tight?'

'Because then it would happen to them, so I'd feel bad.'

I told Steph how towards the end of the abuse I'd be taken to a house in town.

'I'd go there with Emma and Paige,' I said. Then I looked up, wide-eyed, horrified and added: 'They still go and sleep there sometimes.'

* * *

I was trying my hardest to come to terms with the abuse the gang had put me through and how it was still affecting me, but I'd get nervy and lose confidence if I didn't drink. Every time the police asked me to do another identity parade, everything would crowd in on me again: going through all the necessary VIPER parades was bringing ever-more degrading memories rolling back into my already fragmented mind. Of course, I never drank before the interviews, but afterwards I would have to unwind.

It was all a bit up and down, but mostly down, if I'm honest. I was given a provisional offer of a place at university, which was great, but then I got a final warning at the housing unit because they saw me as aggressive, abusive and disruptive. Well, yeah, but wouldn't they have been?

Social Services, having signed me off their books, were still looking closely at Chloe. I never had got on with Christine, my social worker, but at least she wrote one nice thing about me in the core assessment they did on Chloe. She called me 'a lovely young parent' and said she could see I was trying my hardest to give the two of us a better future. They had me marked me down as a 'high risk' to Chloe but, at the same time, another of the professionals dealing with me was calling me 'a devoted young mother'. In one report she wrote: 'Chloe is always well presented. I have observed she has regular baths and is dressed nicely. Chloe is a credit to her.' That felt nice.

As I say, a bit up and down.

A week after I'd gone through the latest video interview with Steph, Susan rang with the news I'd begun to despair of ever hearing. That morning police had finally, finally re-arrested Daddy at his home in Oldham.

'It's an important step, Hannah,' said Susan. 'We still can't give you any guarantees, but we hope it will at least come to trial now.'

Suddenly, the streets seemed a lot safer, and for all my misery, I began to hope I'd see my main abuser brought to justice.

Chapter Twenty-Two
Ups and Downs

If the Crown Prosecution Service had thought I would have been a flaky witness in 2009, they must have loved me two years later. In the time they'd abandoned me, I'd gone steadily downhill, a mother struggling both with the memories of her past and the alcoholism she'd fallen into to keep them at bay.

For now, my mind was focused mainly on drinking two, sometimes three litres of White Star a night – whenever the benefits money would stretch to it.

Christine, my social worker, would come to my flat to check on me. One day, in late March, she asked if I had any alcohol in the flat.

'No,' I said, but I think I must have looked a bit shifty. The next minute she was checking the fridge and finding a big bottle of cider. She went about as mad as a social worker can get. I went red.

As usual, it all went into a report about me.

Social Services called a conference on Chloe towards the end of April 2011. I went with my dad, and we had to sit around a table with fifteen professionals. The police were there, Sara and Jane too, and a couple of people from the housing unit. Christine sent her apologies.

They all agreed that I loved Chloe and was good at looking after her when I was sober. Not only that, they could see that I saw a future for myself. But it was the getting drunk all the time that ruined everything for me. Every night I was getting hammered because of both the new investigation and my memories of the abuse. Overall, it made me a disaster, and that's why they put Chloe on a protection plan for neglect.

The fifteen of them voted unanimously.

I wouldn't speak to Jane afterwards. I just brushed straight past her.

What I didn't know then was that she and Sara were furious with Social Services. Sara had actually written a letter complaining that they weren't liaising with her team, and that Crisis Intervention hadn't even been invited to one particular conference. Basically, I think, she wanted them to pull their finger out and help me, rather than seemingly get in the way of everything positive all the time.

Around that time, with Social Services looking for an interim care order, I was sent to see a psychiatrist. He found me really quiet and, I guess, unresponsive, but didn't think I had a personality disorder. It was just that my emotions had been messed up by the abuse.

According to him, the attacks had left me emotionally 'quite blunted'. *Let him try living my life*, I thought. It just all felt relentless, as if I didn't have any time to get over things. Everything that was going on was constantly there, all the time, reminding me.

There was only so much that Susan and her colleagues could do, and no matter how caring, even loving, they were, it didn't stop me from trying to kill myself for a second time.

I'd been asked to help with the identity parades, as I say, but I was worried that I had forgotten some of the people because it was so long since it had all happened. I don't mean the main ones, the ones who took me here and there, or the ones who were always at a particular flat or house. I mean the ones I'd seen only once or maybe a couple of times. I found it harder and harder to remember them, and that's what was worrying me.

There came the day I was asked to go to the police station to do one of those sessions. This particular VIPER took longer to get through than I'd been used to. We went into a little room with no windows and just a TV screen on which they played the disc. There was a chair in the middle for me, one for a policeman, and one behind for the suspect's solicitor, if one was present.

With some of the men I identified, a solicitor had been there. Whenever the solicitor couldn't be there, they'd record me on a separate video so my reactions could be sent to them later.

I really wasn't expecting to feel the way I did; in fact, I went in thinking everything would be all right, that I was over it now.

The pictures came up on screen, and for a while I wasn't recognising anyone. Then Aarif's face suddenly popped up and a wave of fear swept over me. Even though I could only see him on a TV screen, and in the middle of a police station,

I felt terrified, and I began to recall scene after scene of what he'd put me through, like in a horror film. I remember I identified seven or eight of them that day; it took two hours to go through them all.

Once the session was over, the police drove me back to my parents' house so I could collect Chloe. Mum made me a sandwich and afterwards we set off back to the flat in the housing unit. We got back at about 2 p.m. Later on, I put Chloe in her cot.

It was a spur-of-the-moment thing when it happened. I'd started drinking at around 6 o'clock: just a glass of wine, which became two, then three, then a second bottle. Chloe was asleep.

I don't know why I did it. Like the first time, I certainly didn't plan to. I think everything had got to me so much again – their faces, seen again in the VIPER line-ups, peering at me, taunting me, it seemed, after being out of my life for so long. I remember thinking about the evidence I'd given, and wondering whether the police and the CPS had not believed me because I hadn't cried enough for them in the interviews. They weren't to know I'd become so used to it all that tears felt cheap now. I just felt useless.

I'd no need to buy the pills; they were already there. It wasn't a cry for help, it wasn't – I just knew at that moment that I wanted to die, so I grabbed the pills. There were sixteen in a packet and I took four packets. I started gulping them down, washing them down with wine and then with just water once I ran out of wine.

Then I just lay on the sofa, waiting for the darkness to gather me up. I didn't write a note, I couldn't see the point in that.

By then I was so drunk I was half asleep and half throwing up – throwing up some of the pills I'd just swallowed. That's maybe what saved my life.

I woke up in hospital and, straight away, like before, was full of remorse. I'd left my daughter in her cot and hadn't even gone into the bedroom to say goodbye to her.

The staff at the housing unit had found me, apparently not long after I'd taken the pills. They said later that people had been knocking on my door and I wasn't answering, so they came up. Because I wasn't answering, they used their own key to get in. Just like before.

After the overdose Mum and Dad were looking after Chloe, so I had to go back to my flat in a taxi paid for by the hospital. It was the loneliest of journeys.

I felt as though I hadn't learned anything, and I was back to square one. Again.

* * *

A few weeks later, in mid May 2011, I was on anti-depressants and Christine was back at the flat. She knew I'd drunk loads on the night of that second overdose, but I didn't give her any reason, I just promised to change. I went down on her report once again as 'high risk' and 'spiralling out of control'.

Spiralling out of control I may have been but, somehow, for all that I doubted myself, there was something in me that wouldn't give in. I had a will to live, a will to survive, and a resolve, somehow, to do well.

When I got my college results, Mum and Dad couldn't believe it, and nor could I: a double distinction and enough to get to university. Maybe I wasn't the failure I'd convinced myself that I was!

Added to this, the new chief crown prosecutor for the north-west, Nazir Afzal, ordered the case against Daddy and Immy to be reinstated, which meant that, finally, I'd have the chance to put them away for what they'd done to me. It was a moment of pure joy. I celebrated with a bottle of white.

Later on, I heard the CPS had taken a lot of persuading because once they've made a decision, they hate to change it. Most of all, though, they have what they call thresholds – a way of deciding whether to go ahead with a case based on the chances of a conviction at the end of it.

Not what you or I would call justice; not what's right. Just statistics.

My dad says it's so that someone, somewhere, probably in London, can stand up in front of a Government minister and say the CPS has a 90 per cent success rate, or whatever, in the cases they prosecute. So they can look good.

According to the CPS lawyer who looked at my case, and one of his colleagues who approved it, the chances of getting Daddy convicted – in spite of all the evidence – fell below this threshold.

Mostly it came down to me being too flaky. The jury might not believe me, they thought. And if that happened, they'd lose the case and their 'success' rate would come down.

Dad reckons that in the days before the CPS made the decisions about whether to charge people, good detectives tended to go on their gut instincts. Did they think someone was a rapist? Yes? Then charge him.

And if the jury got it wrong, then at least they'd done their level best to do the right thing.

But the people making the decisions in my case were operating in a very different world.

Detectives from Operation Span made the strongest case they could to the CPS and then waited for them to react. For the lawyers at regional headquarters, and perhaps in London, too, it must have felt like sucking razor blades. They dug their heels in for a while, until Mr Afzal looked at the case afresh and decided it was time to bite the bullet. It was one of his first decisions in the job as chief prosecutor and I think he realised that by taking it he was giving me – and all the girls like me – a voice. I'll always be grateful to him for that.

At the time, though, my life was still messed up and, just as I could see myself finally getting justice, everything else in my life started to fall apart.

I moved out of the housing unit and into my mum and dad's house because Social Services were threatening to remove Chloe. The idea was that Mum and Dad would control me. If it didn't work out, they'd remove my little girl.

And of course, I buckled and the social workers suspected that Dad wouldn't level with them if I'd been drinking or whatever. In the middle of June 2011, Social Services made Chloe the subject of an interim care order, and the following week, Christine, my social worker, called at Mum and Dad's house.

Chloe was asleep, her head resting in my lap, when we heard the knock on the door.

Social Services had given the impression that if I went back to live with my mum and dad everything would be fine; that they, as responsible adults, would be a safety net even if I went off the rails.

So that's what I'd done. I'd gone back home for six weeks or so, and actually managed to give up drinking. But it wasn't enough, not for Rochdale Childcare Services.

They had held a gateway meeting and, suddenly, it wasn't suitable for Chloe to live at Mum and Dad's house any more. That was it: she would have to go into temporary foster care.

With a child under five, you only get nine months to prove yourself a fit parent again. At the end of that time, the authorities decide whether they're going to return your child to you, or else have it adopted.

The next few minutes shattered my heart into a million pieces.

There were forms to fill in – they always have forms – and a farewell to make that would tear me to shreds. Maybe Christine found it hard too, but it didn't show; at least, not to me. I tried to hold on to Chloe, but it was no good. The social worker knew why she'd come, and she knew she had to go through with it. So she scooped my little girl into her arms and headed towards her car. She had a car seat in the back, and Chloe went into that.

Back then, Chloe had only ever been around me and my family. We were all she knew. She was just beginning to wake up properly and looked up at me, bewildered, as I clicked her in. She could see the tears streaming down my face and started crying herself. My parents, leaning into the car, were distraught. I was beside myself.

When it was over, Dad wrapped me up in his arms and led me back to the house. I was sobbing, inconsolable, my daughter gone. Social Services had taken her.

As the car pulled away, heading over the speed bumps towards the motorway, I was swamped with guilt as I knew it was me who'd made it happen. I started to think how confused she must feel, being taken away in a stranger's car, soon to be finding herself being handed over to a couple just as alien.

I hung about the house for an hour or so, suffocated by my parents' sympathy and outrage, feeling all the time that, for all that the gang had damaged me, it was me, and me alone, who'd inflicted this upon my little girl. Chloe didn't deserve this. Not this. And I felt it was me who'd brought her to it.

I couldn't deal with it.

The thought gnawed away inside me until I reached the point where I couldn't bear it any longer: I couldn't cope with the thought of her crying her heart out in that car and then arriving at a stranger's house, frightened and alone in a new world. Suddenly, I stood up, threw on my coat and rushed out, brushing past Mum and heading out of the back door and on towards the shops up the hill.

At the off-licence, I bought two litres of White Star, then caught a bus to some local woods, thinking about Chloe all the way.

They're a bit minging, the woods, but everyone knows them around my way, and as a little kid I'd played there in the days before we moved to the seaside. I remember thinking about that as I looked for a bench to sit down on, and it reminded me of Chloe – that she should be there, playing, picking flowers, something she loved to do. But today, all I had was a bottle of cider to keep me company.

The more I drank the guiltier I felt, and the more hopeless and lonely and torn up inside. I wanted all the feelings to end because I just couldn't cope.

I was drunk by the time I staggered onto the bus heading back towards home. This time, though, I didn't get off at my normal stop; I carried on to the one by the shops so I could buy some paracetamol.

They only let you buy two packets at a time, so that's what I did, washing them down with the last of the cider. Then I walked on to the shop closest to home, and bought another two packets.

I took those once I'd sneaked in and gone upstairs. Then I lay on my bed, pretty much out of it, waiting, hoping to die, clutching a photograph of my little girl, the girl whose life I'd ruined.

But the pills and the cider just made me feel sick and I had to rush into the bathroom. My sister, Lizzie, heard me throwing up and ran in. She saw lots of the pills floating in the bath and screamed for Mum and Dad.

When Dad got there he grabbed me around the waist and started to squeeze my stomach so I'd throw the whole lot up. Mum ran downstairs to find her phone and dial 999. I was going in and out of consciousness by the time the ambulance arrived.

It was a pathetic attempt, I know, but, just like the other two times, I really did mean to go through with it. I really did want to die.

But I regretted it as soon as I came round in hospital. Susan came to see me that night. She was off duty, but she still felt close enough to me to come. She sat there, asking why I kept trying to kill myself. 'You've got so much to live for, Hannah,' she said. 'You really have.'

In the days that followed, I promised myself that I'd get back on my feet and try, finally, to grow up. I knew I had to, if there was any chance of me getting Chloe back. It wouldn't happen overnight, though, that much I knew.

* * *

With Chloe in care, it was left to the police, not Social Services, to press for me to be moved out of the immediate area; away from Rochdale. Susan and her colleagues knew that it wasn't just a question of guiding me through video interviews and VIPER parades. It was about helping me to cope with the day-to-day traumas of my life so that, come the trial, I could go to court and give the evidence that would put my abusers away.

They found a supported flat for me in a different area, and I moved there a couple of weeks later. That's where I met Richie, a lad I went out with for a few months through the summer. It wasn't a proper relationship, really: me damaged and pretty much a down-and-out; him homeless if he hadn't got a place there. He didn't really have anything going for him apart from being funny.

Richie didn't drink as much as me – I don't think many people did. We never really went out, we'd just spend our time together in the flats, his or mine, getting drunk all the time. Sex with him was OK, but it wasn't great. At least it wasn't abuse.

It ended in September after we'd gone to a christening and got hammered. I took a fiver out of his pocket to go to the chippy and he found out once I'd got back home. He got mad at me and retaliated by robbing my phone.

Because I was drunk I punched him in the face. A few times. The staff heard the row kicking off and called the police. They arrived just in time to see him head-butting me in the face, so they jumped on him and carted him away. I had blood pouring out of my nose, but I still laughed because it seemed so funny to me, for some reason.

They took me to hospital for treatment, but when they checked the CCTV and saw the earlier bit with me punching him, I got arrested too. I got a caution for it, and Richie and I split up.

Just after that, I got an email from UCAS – the Universities and Colleges Admissions Service – saying the university that had offered me a place was withdrawing it. I suspect Social Services had something to do with it. Maybe they'd said I'd be a liability.

* * *

It was another massive blow, but somehow I started to pick myself up. Maybe I was helped by the people around me trying to drag me back into some kind of normal life ahead of the trial that was expected to start in the following February.

Social Services decided they wanted to monitor me 24/7 so they moved me to a foster place, to live with a couple. That way they could keep an eye on me and get reports from the family I was staying with. I joined Alcoholics Anonymous and went to another parenting group.

Jane was still sticking up for me with Social Services. She said I was under a lot of pressure because of the new police investigation. I saw one report in which she'd written: 'Chloe is a delightful little girl. This has not happened by chance and shows that on the whole Hannah is doing a good job as her mother.'

In another she talked about the loving relationship I had with her. 'She is affectionate with her and whenever I have seen her with Chloe I have noted that she responds to her needs in an appropriate manner.'

I think it was 21 September 2011 that I stopped drinking: well, mostly. They'd put me on a drug called Campral to help me, and it seemed to work. They say it restores the chemical balance inside your brain, helps it work normally again. I moved into more supported lodgings the next month, still trying as hard as I could to get my life back.

I didn't have a drink on Christmas Day, nor on New Year's Eve. I was having contact with Chloe three times a week – even Social Services could see that I was finally coming back from the bad times, and they started talking about giving me a second chance with the little girl they'd taken from me.

Things were looking better than they had been for a long time.

Chapter Twenty-Three
The First Witness

The 'Girl A' trial – my trial – was supposed to start on 8 February 2012. The police put me on stand-by and I changed my contact times with Chloe to the weekend, to fit in around it. As usual with Social Services, who were still being obstructive, the police had to push for it for me.

Then I heard it had been delayed. These things often happen, the police told me. Don't worry. It was only later that I found out the reason for the delay – that two defence barristers, both of them Asian, had suddenly withdrawn from the case. They'd done so because of intimidation by far-right protestors: one of them had been punched by a protestor just outside the court complex, the other illegally filmed in one of the corridors.

They'd only been doing their jobs, just like all the other barristers, some Asian, some white, but they were both terrified that images of them would start appearing on the usual racist websites.

Those same websites had already been telling their followers that the trial was coming up, and newspapers and TV had carried reports of the arrests and charges. The difference between the two is that, at least on a good day, people in the media know about the law, and that everyone deserves a good trial; whereas the racists hiding behind their websites either have no idea, because they're stupid, or else don't care because all they're looking for is hatred and blood.

Mr Justice Gerald Clifton – the judge for the case, who'd be retiring as soon as the trial was over – was furious, not least with Merseyside Police who'd put extra officers in the square outside Liverpool Crown Court, but hadn't reacted quickly enough before the barrister got thumped. A high-ranking officer was called in to get what I heard was a real telling-off. From that point on, the square looked like a chessboard of coppers in yellow fluorescent jackets while, inside, security was even stricter than normal.

The thugs from the British National Party and English Defence League thought they'd struck a blow for justice, but I can't work that one out. You don't get justice by waving placards comparing white girls to halal meat, as they were doing outside the court. You get it by letting us get into court so we can give our evidence.

Anyway, the original jury was discharged and it took two weeks to get new barristers.

Once they'd been found, the judge sorted out a seating plan in the dock: he wanted the defendants to be directly in line with each of their legal teams, but every time a plan was supposedly finalised it had to be changed for one reason or another. By the time Rachel Smith, QC, finally rose to give her opening address, the eleven defendants had played a series of games of Musical Chairs, but the judge and all the lawyers had print-offs of the final seating plan – necessary, in a trial with so many defendants.

Susan went to the court with quite a few of the other detectives involved in Operation Span, but because she, too, was giving evidence, she had to stay away from the actual courtroom. For the same reason the two of us weren't allowed to even meet up, so instead she introduced me to some of her other colleagues.

The detectives in court would vary, because if any of them were giving evidence they weren't allowed to sit in until they'd gone into the witness box. Whichever one of them was free would sit in the public gallery, taking it all in. The policewoman in Court 3:1 on Day One was there to see the defendants, over to her left, the eleven of them sitting in the glass-panelled dock with two interpreters and an assortment of security guards.

Apparently, Daddy had been seated in the front row as the jurors filed in. His arms were folded and he had had a smirk on his face.

When I heard about that first day the bit that amazed me the most was that one of the jurors was young, a girl, and apparently Daddy had focused in on her and given her a huge smile as she sat down. She was so flustered she went red, but then looked away and concentrated on looking at Judge Clifton.

Miss Smith's laptop was open on the desk in front of her, its screensaver the image of a snow leopard. On the press benches reporters fidgeted, skimming the copies of the opening address they'd been given, pens poised over pads or fingers resting over their iPhones, ready to tweet the best early lines.

Miss Smith – who at first meeting had seemed almost as scary as the snow leopard on her screen – started by telling them how me and the other four girls all knew Emma. I was the eldest, while Roxanne, thirteen when she was attacked, was the youngest. All of us, she had said, were the sort of kids who were easy to identify, easy to target, and easy to exploit. And we'd all been procured for the gang by Emma.

She gave each of the jurors a piece of paper that gave the defendants' names, nicknames and addresses. It would help them get to know them as the case unfolded, she explained.

Daddy was the first to be mentioned, then Immy, Tariq, Cassie, Saj, Billy, Tiger, Car Zero, The Ugly One, Shah and Hammy.

Aarif wasn't there, of course, because he'd run off to Pakistan, but he still got a mention. In fact, I only found out on that first day of the trial why I'd first been taken to Aarif's flat in the first place: it was because he and Saj were bored with Emma and wanted a new girl.

Chef wasn't there either, but not because he'd done a runner. It turns out he was less than five miles away, at HM Prison Liverpool, serving fifteen years for rape and indecent assault. His real name was Anya Miah, and at the time he'd been molesting me he was on the run.

He should have gone on trial in 1998 but failed to turn up at court. The police finally caught up with him in 2011. He was fifty-two years old when the jury at Liverpool Crown Court put him away on 3 February. At the time I knew nothing of this.

Only a few days later, in the same court complex, Miss Smith was moving on to talk about the two conspiracies – the one that Daddy was involved in, and the later one with Tariq. The case involved chains of men, she said, and they all wanted one thing: under-age girls for sex.

'Some of you may find what you are about to hear distressing,' she went on. A female juror on the back row had looked nervy, like she wished the case could have been about a robbery or something. 'The events and circumstances described by the girls are at least saddening and at worst shocking. No child should be exploited as these girls say they were.'

She started with my story. At first, Miss Smith said, I'd liked the idea of living at Harry's house. I'd had no money but was given food by Harry and allowed to stay there.

But then I'd been exploited and raped – first by Daddy, then by the others he took me to. One thing she couldn't say was that eventually I'd been abused by Harry himself. She couldn't say it because the things he'd forced me to do to him would be the subject of a separate trial much later in the year. For now he could only sweat it out at home.

Miss Smith then got to the part where I'd kicked off in the Balti House. She knew how much I'd told the police at the time, and the detectives across the aisle from her – the ones from Operation Span – knew, too. But all she said about the failure to get the first Girl A case to court was this: 'Regrettably, the police officers who looked into the matter didn't take the investigation further at that stage.' She could have gone on to make the point that it took nearly a year for the file to reach the CPS, but of course she didn't: she knew the jury would have enough to think about. Not least that Roxanne, having been handed to the gang by Emma, became so brainwashed that she had actually fallen in love with Billy. And how I had been so brainwashed that I'd felt flattered at first; that I thought they saw me as pretty. But then how I got trapped and so scared that they were all able to rape me.

They hadn't always hit me, she said, and I hadn't always cried or protested. But they still forced me. Daddy had raped me when I was dead drunk, telling me he just wanted to talk. '"It's part of the deal,"' said the barrister, echoing Daddy's words. '"I bought you vodka, you have to give me something."'

At one point Miss Smith paused, then said, 'Hannah estimated that she was having sex with several men in a day, several times a week. There are many men she describes who have not yet been positively identified and who are not therefore on the indictment.'

And so it went on. Mulla, Immy's 'treat', all the others. Dozens of them.

The jury heard how Roxanne was different from me: very different. To her, according to her statements to the police, she was just going 'chilling' with the men. But she'd been thirteen, and she was lying. There was enough, though, for the jury to know how it actually was: that she was being raped and passed around just like me. Only she said she liked it.

'Roxanne described herself as having lots of friends,' said Miss Smith. 'She said her number would be passed around amongst the Pakistani men in her area. A situation developed where she would get calls from men she did not know who would ask her if she wanted to go 'chilling'. She'd go to the petrol station or Morrison's car park and the men would call her and describe their car so she could find them and get in.

'She said, "Most of the time, I didn't know who it was. They'd just ring me and say are you coming and I'd go 'Yeah.' I didn't care who they were. I didn't know them, didn't know where we were going, I just got in the car with people and then they took me to wherever."

'She said she was also taken to houses where men would either be waiting or would arrive afterwards and they would want to "chill with me". She said sometimes she was persuaded to kiss them and she pretended "to be with them".

'The police asked her how the men had got hold of her mobile number. She told them: "When you've got Asian friends, numbers get passed and they pass them on to their friends and they pass it on to their friends and you end up with a massive circle; everyone's got it."'

Miss Smith, already tall, seemed to rise even higher when she said, 'The prosecution says that what Roxanne was describing was the group activity of a number of adult men, including these defendants' – she gestured at the men in the dock – 'who had spotted the opportunity to sexually exploit children who were vulnerable to that sort of exploitation.'

To Roxanne, Miss Smith explained, the men were her 'good friends' who bought her vodka and other gifts because they were 'nice people'.

She'd drink a litre of vodka, but that was only so she could feel 'loud and good'. The men were so nice that they'd wait until she was sober before ever having sex with her. And she was the one that wanted it. She was the one who suggested it, not them. And, anyway, she had told the police, they all thought she was sixteen.

The prosecution blew that lie away by showing the jury a photograph of Roxanne when she was thirteen. Poor kid, she looked younger.

Miss Smith then told the court that somewhere in this drunken haze Roxanne had got pregnant by Billy. He denied it, but because she had had a teenage abortion, and certain procedures had had to be followed, the police were able to prove the baby was his. Apparently, Roxanne had started off by saying she'd had a six-month 'relationship' with him. Then she said she'd only had sex with him the once. Then that it was four or five times. And, finally, that she was the only one of the girls to have 'chilled' with him.

Miss Smith looked over to the jury and said: 'You will have to decide whether Roxanne was telling the truth at first and that she did have sex with him over several months. If so, you may feel that the accounts she gave later were an attempt to protect him.'

She brought me back into it then, telling the jury how I'd seen Roxanne being abused by the men, and also being hit by Emma if she resisted.

'Roxanne also told Hannah that she was having sex with Billy and that she was in love with him.'

Girl B, or Leah, had been in a children's home when the gang got to her. I never met her, but she'd heard of me from Emma. I'm guessing she was one of my replacements, and the thought made me shudder. The gang had kept asking for younger girls, and she was only fourteen when she came to Rochdale.

She used to walk out of the children's home and not come back for days. And where do you think she went? She went to Harry's house, and from there, just like me, she'd go out into Rochdale and beyond with Emma. The gang first got to her in the months after I'd escaped.

Again like me, she had lost count of the number of times she was forced to have sex. She'd try to blank it out the same way I'd done – by getting hammered on the vodka they gave her. Sometimes she was so drunk she'd wake up to find men having sex with her. It had got to the stage where she had to have a shot of vodka as soon as she woke up in the morning. The rest of the day, every day, she'd drink more vodka, along with Sambuca, Jack Daniel's and Lambrini.

In her video evidence that was played to the court, she told police how she and another girl from a care home had been picked up in Manchester by three men in a car, who'd taken them on to Oldham. She had got so drunk she had blanked out. But she knew she'd been raped.

Leah told the court how Tariq liked to slap her face a few times when she got into his taxi, just to make sure she knew not to mess with him.

She was finally rescued after scribbling a note and dropping it down the stairs of her care home for staff to find. It read: 'Asians pick me up, they get me drunk, they give me drugs, then have sex with me and pay me not to tell anyone. I want to move.'

After that, Social Services sent her off to another place, in the south of England. She'll be out of there by now.

Girl C was Roxanne, Girl D was Anna. Next, we heard about Girl E, Alicia. Saj, who, it turned out, came from the same village in Pakistan as Tariq, and, of course, his cousin, Aarif, was twenty-eight when he got to her, in 2005. She was thirteen, and they had sex in Nelson once he'd got her drunk on vodka and cola.

It was only a one-off with Alicia but, three years later, he was mauling me. Some time after that, it was Leah's turn to satisfy his craving for under-age girls.

The really clever thing about Rachel Smith's opening address was how she made it sound as though the abuse I went through was part of one, almost seamless case. That yes, there were two conspiracies, but that the five victims were all linked. Well, we were, to an extent, but it was only when you looked at her speech in detail, and took in the various dates on the indictment, that you realised my part of the case was historic, and that the suffering of the other girls had either been much more recent or else had come to light more recently.

And what the jury would never have fathomed was that some of those other girls might have been rescued had my case gone ahead when it should have done. In 2009.

Miss Smith was doing her best, quite properly, to convince the jury that the men in the dock were guilty.

And it would have made no sense for her to let on that the CPS had initially decided against prosecuting over my own abuse. But looking back, you can sense how relieved the senior people at the CPS must have been to hear the detail of that opening address because, rather conveniently, it glossed over their failure.

The police, too, were spared their blushes. There was a single, brief reference to the failed first investigation. 'Regrettably,' Miss Smith told the jury, 'the police officers who looked into the matter didn't take the investigation further at that stage.'

The trial would carry on for three harrowing months but, for that first day, Miss Smith was almost done. She turned to the jury and said, 'This is as much as we feel we can assist you at this stage. The first witness is Hannah...'

Chapter Twenty-Four
Daddy in the Dock

I was brought to give evidence that day – 21 February – in an unmarked police car. Social Services had let me stay with Mum and Dad for the five days I was needed at court, but after that I had to go back to the foster place they'd put me in. A detective who introduced herself as Liz knocked on the front door of Mum and Dad's house at 7.30 a.m., and Mum and I got into the back.

Mum spent the journey chatting to the police; I just sat pressed against the door, thinking about it all, wondering what they'd be asking me, wondering whether, having finally got to this point, I'd ruin it all by saying something to the lawyers that stopped it all and would let them all off.

We pulled into the car park at the side of Liverpool Crown Court just before 9 a.m.

Two more police officers met us, both of them in uniform, and they walked with us into the building to a witness waiting room. It was just a plain white room with a window looking out onto the Albert Dock across the road. It felt like being at the doctor's: sitting in a room, not speaking, while my mum flicked through the magazines on the table.

I didn't read any of them, either that day or the other four that I went to court. I just sat there, worrying.

Rachel Smith popped in to see me. She didn't have her gown on then, just a black suit. She was really nice, trying to get me to relax and saying well done for coming forward. As she left to go up to Court 3:1, she turned, smiled and said, 'Good luck, Hannah. You'll be fine.'

Mum and I continued to sit there until an usher came to collect me. She took me to the video suite they always use for kids, so you don't have to actually go into the courtroom. They base it on the age you were at the time things happened to you. So even though I was nineteen by now, I was protected as I would have been at fifteen. It was a relief to know I wouldn't have to see Daddy and the rest, but it also felt a bit lonely, sitting there with just the court usher and the cameras recording my every move.

The usher checked that the sound was working and that the people in court could see me when it was time. There was silence again for a few moments before I saw the judge, Mr Clifton, appear on the video-link monitor in front of me.

He introduced himself, then said he'd introduce me to Miss Smith. There was a few seconds' delay while the camera angle was changed in the court, and then I could see her. They're very careful about what exactly you see as a witness. You never get even a glimpse of the defendants or the press, or even the jurors; just whichever person is speaking to you.

Then it was back to Judge Clifton, who said we were all going to view the video interviews I'd done with the police, back as far as the very first one in August 2008.

This was now four years before, and it was weird to see the image of the fifteen-year-old me appear on the monitor, the date at the top of the screen and the timer reeling off the seconds.

I knew the men would all be watching, and the defence barristers, with their instructing solicitors behind, all taking notes, looking for ways they could try to defend people I knew had no defence. In my own head, I was trying to think beyond the actual words to the way I'd felt that first day, telling the police exactly why I'd blown up at the Balti House, when I'd been wondering all the time whether the detective believed me.

I'd given so much detail in all those interviews that it would take a couple of days to get through them all, and then it would be time for me to be questioned, first by Miss Smith and afterwards by the eleven defence barristers. That was going to be the hardest part. I shuddered at the thought of it, even then, because they were all slick, smart lawyers and I'd be trying to remember things from nearly four years ago. What if they somehow tripped me up? What if at the end of this whole process, Daddy and all the other rapists were set free?

But Mum had been right when she'd hugged me in the waiting room. 'Just tell the truth, Hannah,' she'd said. 'It will be enough, I promise.'

They were tough days. I was fine when Miss Smith took me through all the horrors I'd been through and how trapped I'd felt. But once she'd finished with me and there was a short delay, I started shaking at the thought of how the defence lawyers would try to twist everything I said.

They tried, of course, and there were times I must have looked a real idiot to them, because I just couldn't remember some of the things they were asking. Like what I'd been wearing on a particular day, what colour a car was, who'd said what. I didn't even know the men's proper names. For me, it had always been nicknames; either the names we girls had given them or the names they told us. It was only because Emma had kept so many names and numbers on her phone that the police had been able to link them all up.

I'd been through things so many times before that, actually, I managed to stay pretty calm. I got annoyed with some of their questions, mind, and with the way they'd ask them – all smooth voices, trying to make me feel I could trust them but all the time circling me with their clever words.

The police told me later that Daddy's barrister, Simon Nichol, is a really nice guy, but he got me to snap when he tried to make out that I'd tried to frame his client by swapping knickers with Emma. 'What, when she's about five sizes bigger than me?' I asked him, to laughter from the court.

On it went, barrister after barrister, all trying to make it look like I was lying or it was mistaken identity. But I wasn't, and it wasn't, and they knew it.

The worst part of the whole five days was seeing two of the men who'd raped me in the public areas of the court complex: Cassie stared at me from the end of a corridor, but when I looked back he turned his head, and I started walking away as quickly as I could; then, another day, I saw

Immy walking down the stairs. He didn't see me because Liz shoved me into a doorway so he couldn't catch sight of me.

Eventually, after all those days of watching tapes and being cross-examined, it was finally over and I was free to go.

The court usher that day was great. She said I'd done brilliantly and should be dead proud of myself. Liz smiled and just hugged me. 'You were really strong, Hannah – the best witness I've ever seen in a case like this. The jury have just got to believe you.'

Dad had come to court that final morning and so joined in all the hugging, before we headed home.

The trial would carry on until May, but for me it was over.

* * *

Daddy didn't do a lot to help himself in court.

At home, I kept hearing stories about him falling out with everyone: the jury, for being white; and the judge, the police and all the girls he'd abused for being racist.

His first tirade from the dock was to complain about the fact that there were no Asian, black or Chinese people on the jury, just twelve white people. There was indeed a conspiracy, he said, but it had nothing to do with him and the rest of the men in the dock. It was a white conspiracy intended to persecute the Asian minority. No white people had been brought to court because if they had, 'You would not get your all-Asian trial.'

The people in the public gallery loved it. Daddy would sit there for a while, arms folded, a smirk on his face, and everyone in court would know that any minute he was going to kick off.

He managed to put everyone's back up, and I'm guessing that reflected on the rest of the gang as they gave their own evidence. The media people would gather in little huddles, reflecting on how things were going and how the body language among some of the jury suggested he was going down and maybe taking a lot of the others down with him.

He also managed to fall out with another member of the gang within three weeks of the trial starting.

Cassie liked to pray while he was in the dock. Liz said that normally the sound of him muttering prayers to himself was drowned out by the two women interpreters – one of them specialising in Mirpuri, the other Pashto. But all the chanting eventually got on Daddy's nerves. He apparently kicked off during a lunch break, just as the defendants were being led away from the dock.

'Fucking shut up,' the man I'd once thought of as a jolly Father Christmas lookalike yelled at the taxi driver, 'or I'll sort you out later.' Then straight away he had punched him full in the face.

Cassie's barrister, Zarif Khan, was the one to make a statement when the court reconvened, telling the judge, 'My client was extremely shocked. He feels intimidated and threatened, and the interpreters are also worried because he made a comment to them about talking too loudly.'

Liz gave me chapter and verse that evening. Judge Clifton had glared at Daddy, she said, and warned him that if he did anything like it again, he'd spend the rest of the trial down in the cells.

'Daddy raised his hand to speak,' Liz chuckled, but the judge had stopped him and said, 'No, none of that. And don't say you haven't been warned.'

The police in court reckoned that for all his patience Mr Nichol must sometimes have wondered why he'd agreed to represent Daddy. Most defendants take the easy route of doing everything their legal team tell them, but not Daddy.

He started off OK by pleading not guilty when the court clerk put all the charges to him but, after that, he did everything to ruin any slight chance he might have had of getting away with it all. To use one of the phrases he'd once thrown at me, he was like 'a bone in a kebab': he'd snarl at the detectives in court, claiming they'd framed him because of his colour, and accused the judge of being 'more of a prosecutor than a judge'.

He was the first of the gang to give evidence, and it was apparently like watching stand-up – except that the 'comedian' in the box was actually a paedophile rapist. There was a bit of a delay though, before he started his testimony, and Liz told me about it later.

Mr Nichol said Daddy couldn't take an oath on the Koran as he hadn't bathed. A washbasin wouldn't be enough; he'd need either a bath or a shower – neither of which was available at the court. So in the end he had to affirm or promise to tell the truth rather than take an oath on a religious book. The judge was apologetic, telling him: 'I'm sorry, I've done my best, but short of bringing in a bath myself I can't see that there's anything else I can do.'

Daddy, who said he'd settled in Oldham after coming to Britain as a boy in 1967, denied everything, of course. Nor did it take long for people to realise that he hated Rachel Smith. Maybe it was because she was a woman, I don't know, but from what I've heard, he just kept trying to embarrass her with the things he'd say about sex – and even about her barrister's wig. 'If you didn't have that sheep on your head, you might be my equal,' he said once. She wasn't having any of it, though, and would usually wait till he'd run out of steam and then just say wearily, 'Just answer the question, please.'

Daddy's contempt for women wasn't confined to the prosecuting barrister. Vicky Crook, a CPS case worker, came to court one day wearing a trouser suit and a low-cut – but still perfectly respectable – white blouse.

He probably meant it as a distraction, but he suddenly burst out: 'This woman is sitting half-naked in front of me. How am I supposed to look at Miss Smith with her bloody tits coming into my eyeline?'

He made out the case against him was all white lies, of course, made up by me and the other girls he'd raped and trafficked. 'They were intelligent, they were clever, they knew what they were doing,' he told Miss Smith. 'If they'd gone on Lord Sugar's Apprentice programme, they would have won.'

It was the white community who'd 'trained' girls like me in sex and drinking, he said. 'When they come to us they're fully trained and they start their own business. They start their own business and then the police very conveniently in 2008 pick me up.'

In all my time as his victim, I'd never known Daddy to have sex with Emma, but in court that's what he claimed. It was the only way he could even try to explain his DNA being in my knickers – that it was actually Emma he'd slept with, and that I'd then come along and switched her knickers with mine.

To go with the alibi, he'd made up a story of how he and Emma would meet up in secret so people wouldn't think he'd 'infested' his own community by sleeping with a white girl. 'You see, we are racist too,' he beamed.

He said he'd always told Emma to wash before they had sex, and afterwards he would go home, shower, say two units of prayer, and ask Allah to forgive him for doing wrong.

He'd never raped me, and nor had he told me he'd get someone to kill me the night he'd got me into his car at Morrison's.

We were all prostitutes working for Emma, he said, and her 'business empire' stretched as far as Leeds, Nelson and Bradford. 'The police know,' he said. 'Whatever happened, it happened with the blessing of the police.'

His problem, though, was that the final forensic test proved beyond doubt that Emma hadn't been near the knickers I'd been wearing when he'd raped me.

And under cross-examination by Miss Smith, he started contradicting himself.

'Nobody did anything to anybody,' he said now. 'You should look in the mirror at your own community. Where's school? Where's Social Services? Where's everybody else?'

Things got really interesting when he was told about me describing his body as really hairy. Was that accurate?

He must have guessed the question was going to come up, because suddenly he started pulling his T-shirt over his head.

'She would have seen this,' he said, triumphantly, displaying his incredibly hairy torso. Then, to the court usher, sitting horrified a few feet in front of him: 'Don't be nervous. I lose hairs.' And to prove it, he tugged at the hair on his chest and threw a clump of it into the well of the court.

It landed on the carpet just in front of the witness box, where it remained for the rest of the session and presumably until the cleaners arrived to vacuum it up.

The public gallery got a matinee performance at court that day, as the two female interpreters also got told off for giggling at another part of Daddy's evidence. They were hauled up by the judge and told to behave. One of them apologised, but as soon as she'd turned away from the judge her face broke into a smile. Those who saw it cringed.

It wasn't just his hair that Daddy was having trouble with. He told another of the defence barristers, Ahmed Nadim: 'Sex didn't take place every day because of my age, you know.'

But that only confirmed the way he'd been with me sometimes; sometimes he couldn't physically do what he wanted to do.

As he left the witness box for the last time, Daddy flashed one more of his greasy smiles to a female juror and walked slowly, swaggeringly, back towards the dock.

By then, every scrap of detail about his attacks on me, and the way he'd trafficked me for sex, had been aired before the jury. But it wasn't everything, not by a long way. I had no idea at the time, but months later I learned something that underlined just how violent and disgusting he could be.

It turns out that shortly after Daddy's arrest, back in March 2011, another of his victims had come forward: a girl who had been abused two decades before he attacked me.

As a different jury, in a different city, would discover, she had been raped from the age of three.

This little girl, Lanika, was Pakistani and because Daddy was well known to her family, he would often come and stay.

The first time he raped her, she was so young and so small that afterwards she had had to push a chair towards the bathroom sink before climbing up and washing the blood from her knickers. She was only able to turn off the bathroom light because it had a cord that hung down.

When she had come back to her bedroom, she recalled him watching her in the darkness as she stuffed her knickers into a drawer.

She couldn't actually swear that the time with the chair was the first time, but it felt like it. Maybe it was earlier. Daddy raped her so many times that the memories of each attack just merged with the rest. And it was actually only when she opened a copy of Roald Dahl's *The BFG* that all those hideous memories came rushing back.

She was about seven at the time, still at primary school, and *The BFG* was that week's reading book. In the first few pages, she read about how the little girl in the story had tried to scream as a giant figure loomed over her bed, but no sound had come out.

It jogged the worst of memories.

The girl, now a woman, would scream again as she gave evidence against him – scream at him via a video-link, just as I would like to have done. And this time the sound did come out.

'He ruined my life,' she yelled at the camera above her, 'and I will never forgive him. Not ever. Nothing will ever make up for what he's done to me.'

She told the jury, the jury in her court case, how he liked to make her kneel on the floor in a pose called the *murgha*, 'chicken', with her arms threaded through her legs and touching her ears. He'd then beat her with a cricket bat.

Once, when older, she'd whispered, 'Sex maniac,' under her breath, and he'd giggled, saying: 'Yes, that's what I am!'

Like me, the girl had been too frightened to tell anyone. She got as far as telling a policewoman in 2005, but then had backtracked, refusing to give a full statement for fear that it would bring dishonour to her community.

But the officer's notes had stayed on police files, and they were still there three years later when I made my own complaint about Daddy.

The detectives involved in my case, or at least someone in Greater Manchester Police, should have known about those notes, or been able to access them. Maybe it was as simple as someone typing two words – his real name – into a police computer. But for whatever reason, it wasn't done, and so no one made the link between what he'd done over all those years before, and what he'd done to me in 2008.

If they had, they would surely have realised the first time around that I was telling the truth – or that it was highly likely that I was. Whatever they'd thought at first, the police could have gone back to the girl in Oldham who had told them he'd been abusing her but had then got scared; scared because of the pressures of her own community, the pressure not to tell.

She would have been interviewed – properly, I hope, and they might have thought, *This all fits together. He started off by attacking a girl in the Pakistani community, and then later turned to the only other kids he felt were available to him: white kids.* A kid like me.

Actually, I reckon the fact that I was white was pretty irrelevant, really. It was just that I was available. And once you're a rapist you're always a rapist, whatever the colour of your skin.

One Operation Span detective would sum up this part of the case against Daddy perfectly, in four words: 'A total cock-up.'

The girl Daddy had attacked wasn't lacking in courage, no way, and eventually she did something about it again. She came forward in 2011, after Daddy had been questioned and then released over his attacks on me.

When Lanika's case came to court, she said she couldn't ever imagine having a normal relationship, because every time a man came near her she thought of Daddy. But I think there is hope for her. Once she'd given evidence, she told the detective who'd guided her through it that maybe, just maybe, she'd be able to find a way to a happiness she deserved.

I hope so – if she can, then so can I.

Chapter Twenty-Five
Judgement Day

It was around the time of Daddy's cross-examination, as the trial stretched on into March and April, that the police rang to say they'd identified three more suspects and wanted me to do another VIPER parade.

There were three of them this time, though I could only identify one guy. Operation Span officers carried out a dawn raid on his last known address a few days later, but he'd already fled to Pakistan.

But I was oblivious to it all this time, because I finally had some brilliant news: Chloe was coming home!

Rochdale Social Services still had a care order in place, but from the day in late April that she came back to me, I was given joint responsibility for her.

The appointment with the social workers was set for dinner time and I got everything ready. I'd bought all sorts of new things for my little girl – clothes, toys, everything. And I was cooking corned beef hash for her tea because she loved it.

I was still living with the foster couple, and I was waiting in their living room, dead nervous, heart beating like a drum, when I heard the doorbell go.

It was the social workers who came in first, two of them, carrying the papers that I had to sign; then, two minutes later, there was another ring at the door and this time it was Chloe, standing there, holding the hand of her foster carer, but beaming up at me then flinging herself headlong into my arms.

'Mummy, Mummy,' she cried. I just dissolved. Finally, finally, she was back with me.

She sat on my knee, munching a chocolate biscuit and stroking my face, while I filled in all the forms, telling the social workers I'd make sure that this time she was home for good.

Chloe's foster carer was about fifty, and looked nice. Once she'd brought in the last of Chloe's things we went through the routine she'd got her into. It sounded so weird hearing about my own daughter's routines from a stranger, but I knew I had to listen and take it all in.

When it was time for her to go, I gave her a box of Thorntons chocolates I'd bought her. Well, it wasn't her fault, was it? She gave Chloe a kiss and a hug, then turned to me. I thanked her for everything she'd done, saying I felt like I was going to cry.

'Don't,' she said, her face beginning to crumple. 'You'll set me off.' And, of course, we both started crying.

Once they'd gone, I sat playing with Chloe for ages, overwhelmed, but happier than I'd ever been in my life, thinking to myself, *Everything is finally over. I've got her back!*

* * *

Just as the trial was nearing its end, and the day before Chloe was returned to me, Greater Manchester Police held a pre-verdict briefing at their new headquarters. People from the CPS were there, too, and from Rochdale Social Services. I heard about it later from journalists who were there.

The briefing began, they said, with an apology from Assistant Chief Constable Steve Heywood. 'We do understand that we could have dealt with the issues better than we did,' he told the thirty or so reporters who'd turned up.

'We apologise to any victims who have suffered because of any failings on our part, but at the time we did what we thought was best. We have learned a lot of lessons.'

The issue was genuinely about vulnerability, he insisted, and it 'just happened' that the men involved in the trial were all Asian.

'We did not sweep it under the carpet,' he continued. 'We didn't understand the problem. We do understand it a little bit more now and we have it at the top of our priority list. We are open to ideas about how we can do it.

'Hindsight being a wonderful tool, we will probably look back and say we could have done things better.

'This is cutting edge stuff and we are dealing with it legally, investigatively and technically. If there is a light at the end of the tunnel, it is that we are in a better place and in a wider partnership to deal with these issues.'

Never mind that they'd had 'partnerships' at the time girls were being abused many years earlier. Never mind that the 'hindsight' was actually there in front of so many people, so many officials, in scores of documents that had been left to gather dust.

Mary Doyle, the chief superintendent who ran the later, and ultimately successful Operation Span, said the sort of abuse I'd suffered was a 'hidden crime' and a 'hidden issue'.

John Dilworth, head of the CPS complex case unit in the north-west, said the original decision not to prosecute Daddy and Immy had been reviewed 'in the light of further information'.

The CPS had simply reconsidered the decision and taken a fresh view. 'Clearly we regret any decision that is perceived to be wrong, but it was made on the evidence available at that time,' he said.

The reality, of course, was that the evidence hadn't actually changed. It was all there: the interviews with me, the forensics, everything. All that had happened was that the CPS decided against taking it to court because they didn't think I'd make a credible witness, and the police hadn't bothered to appeal the decision.

So a trial that should have come to court in 2009 didn't actually make it there until three years later.

And now they just wanted to apologise!

Mr Dilworth was still trying to fight his corner. 'You cannot say the decision was wrong,' he blustered. 'We simply reconsidered the decision and took a fresh view. Clearly we regret any decision that is perceived to be wrong, but it was made on the evidence available at that time.'

Mr Dilworth was asked what was at the root of the decision not to prosecute. Floundering by now, he would only say: 'The lawyer said that there was not a realistic possibility of conviction.'

It was too much for his boss, Nazir Afzal. Mr Afzal, a British Pakistani and the region's chief crown prosecutor, rose from his seat away from the panel, beside the assembled media, and took charge.

Reporters craned their necks, surprised by this sudden intervention and sensing that an unexpected hero was about to write himself into their scripts.

He certainly seized the moment, telling his audience: 'The original decision was based on evidence from the victim in this case. Initially the lawyer formed the view that she would not be credible.

'I came here last year and I reversed that decision. I decided that she was entirely credible and that two suspects in relation to her should be charged.

'It is very rare for us to reinstate prosecutions and I exerted that power and the two men were charged.'

The original lawyer had made a judgement: 'I looked at it completely afresh without any prior knowledge and formed a different view.'

Mr Afzal was asked whether he thought I'd been betrayed. He paused, momentarily, before answering: 'I have no difficulty in apologising to her,' he said. 'She was let down by the whole system and we were part of that in some respects. But we reacted to that as soon as possible.'

As soon as possible, that is, after the Operation Span team had put pressure on the CPS to re-instate the Girl A case.

Because they'd known precisely how strong it was – that for all they'd clustered other cases, other girls, around it, mine was the one that would form the cornerstone of the entire trial. Mr Afzal realised that and I think, too, he saw the justice of it finally coming to court.

* * *

In Liverpool, the defence was in full swing. After Daddy had been in the witness box, next came Immy, then Tariq, then the rest, all of them denying the 'lies' of their accusers.

Then came closing speeches from Rachel Smith and all eleven main defence lawyers and, after that, the summing up of all the evidence by Judge Clifton.

Finally, on 1 May, the jury filed out of Court 3:1 to consider their verdicts, almost all of them looking away as they passed the glass-screened dock to their left.

I'd been told that after such a long case it would take them a while to make their minds up. I crossed my fingers that they would make the right decisions. I knew the men who'd attacked me were all guilty, but would they?

As it turned out, the process wasn't anywhere near as simple as it should have been.

The far-right protestors had tried to make trouble right from the start of the trial, and now, as it moved towards its conclusion, they were trying one more time.

At first it was just the usual, with seven of them getting arrested outside the court complex. But two and a half days into the jury's deliberations their idol, Nick Griffin, posted a notorious tweet that would cause legal carnage.

The press tend to have a nose for trouble, and that afternoon they started twitching when the lawyers were called back into court while the public and media were held back at the outer doors.

The media people protested, of course, but it was no use. The 'Court in Chambers' sign went up with a flourish from a court clerk and they were left outside to fume.

When the barristers finally came out, reporters sidled up to the ones they knew best, hoping to get a steer. For once, that didn't work – all they got were mutterings: 'It's a scandal,' said one barrister. 'We've been stitched up,' snapped another, as he headed towards the lifts.

On a bench, Andrew Norfolk, a reporter from *The Times*, was sitting with an A4 pad resting on his iPad, putting the final touches to a note to the judge, demanding that the press be allowed into the next session.

It all became clear – well, sort of clear – when the court reconvened, press included. The jury seats, though, were conspicuously empty.

The scandal, it turned out, was this: at 1.53 p.m. Nick Griffin, the leader of the BNP, had posted a comment on Twitter that read: 'News flash. Seven of the Muslim paedophile rapists found guilty in Liverpool.'

He later backtracked on Twitter after being told the jury hadn't officially returned any verdicts. But by then the damage had been done.

Judge Clifton was livid. He brought the jury back in, and behind closed doors, asked if any of them had passed on any information about their deliberations. They all said no.

The problem was, though, that Griffin's tweet about seven convictions was exactly what the jury had decided up to that point.

One by one, the defence barristers rose to say that any convictions now would be tainted. They argued that the jury's impartiality must have been compromised. The only solution, they said, was to discharge them all and start the whole trial again.

Mr Nichol led the charge. 'The most reasonable inference,' he said gravely, 'is that the confidentiality of the jury's deliberations has been breached and that someone outside the jury who has an improper interest in the outcome of the trial has been receiving communications from within the jury room.

'It seems at the very least that if such communication has taken place then it will be two-way traffic. If there has been such improper communication, the independence of the jury is compromised and there has been a breach of their obligation to reach an impartial verdict.'

Judge Clifton listened to all their submissions, but said he was satisfied that none of the jurors had been at fault, either deliberately or accidentally. The tweet had first appeared on the 'Infidels of Britain' website, at a time when the jury were in a room where all electronic equipment, including their mobiles, was banned. So he decided the jury should be left to carry on with the rest of their deliberations.

The barristers were furious. 'It's not right,' said one. 'These men may be guilty, but they're entitled to a fair trial – and this isn't fair. It leaves a bad taste in the mouth.'

Daddy must have worked out that he was one of the ones the jury thought was guilty. He wasn't stupid, after all. The next time the jurors came in, he seized the moment, shouting: 'I don't want this biased jury. You are a biased judge. You are a racist bastard. You bastard!'

The security guards grabbed him, pushed his arms to his sides and forced him out of the dock and towards the cells. Billy decided he'd had enough, too. He shouted something about a BNP jury and walked out of the dock without needing to be restrained.

* * *

The jury finally came back with all their verdicts – all of them unanimous – on 8 May.

But while Daddy and the others stood in the dock at Liverpool Crown Court, sweating, fidgeting, not knowing where to look, I was at the park with Chloe.

She was on the swings, giggling, the comfort blanket she'd once so desperately needed just resting on the buggy nearby – now back to being just an accessory, something more for warmth than for comfort.

When my phone rang, a sixth sense told me what the call would be about. I had to fumble in my pocket for it, nearly cutting the caller off, but just managing not to.

It was Susan. From the moment she said 'Hi', I could tell she was smiling. And then I could hear the excitement in her voice as she rushed on: 'They've all been found guilty, Hannah. All the ones involved with you have been convicted. Daddy, Tariq, Billy – all of them.'

She went on to say that a couple of the defendants had been cleared, but I wasn't taking it in.

Guilty!

I was shocked and elated at the same time. In some dark corner of my mind, I'd still been so worried that they'd get away with it. I just hadn't counted on this: that after nearly four years of doubt and betrayal, a jury of ordinary people had seen through the gang's lies and recognised that I was telling the truth. The heartache, the pain; the terrifying, degrading memories would never go away – they were branded onto my soul. But at least now I had justice. They'd thought they were above the law, unstoppable, free to pick up kids like me as if they were pieces of meat on a butcher's slab. And all the time they were doing it, in all those back streets and dark country lanes, the rest of the world had been looking away.

I'd never even caught a glimpse of them, but I knew that those twelve ordinary, wonderful people in the Liverpool jury had done what so many others hadn't done in the past: they'd believed me. And in doing that, they'd set me free.

At the age of nineteen, having been raped so many times I couldn't even begin to count them, I had my life back.

Daddy and Tariq, and Billy and Saj, all of them, were going to be sentenced the next day, and from then on they'd never be able to get to me again. I'd be free.

Until this perfect moment, I'd convinced myself that they'd somehow find a way to get out of it, or that the jury would decide that the other girls and I were lying.

I suppose I'd tried to steel myself for that. I'd imagined them all smiling as they were cleared, and then smirking as they walked out of the dock, slapping each other on the back, out into the lifts with their solicitors, and down to the revolving door and away past the lines of police officers.

But no, each and every one of the men who'd attacked me left the court complex that day in handcuffs, knowing their days as paedophile abusers and traffickers were over, and that they'd know in the morning just how many years they'd be spending behind bars.

* * *

All the men who'd attacked me had seen me distraught and in tears often enough, but even though a part of me would have liked to have seen them sentenced, I knew I couldn't have faced it. I'd seen enough of them in the months they'd controlled me, pawing at me on their cheap, dirty beds or on the floors of empty houses.

So, to keep myself busy the next day, I caught the bus into Heywood and went shopping in Morrison's, crossing the road by the Balti House with its angel clock and heading past the spot where Daddy had forced me into his car those four years ago.

My dad had said he'd pick me up after I had finished, and so I was outside, waiting for him, near where the taxis park, with Chloe sitting on the wall, eating chocolate. There was a line of cabs there that day and it was there that I heard one of the drivers say to the woman he was picking up: 'Have you heard about them from Heywood? One of them got nineteen years.'

Nineteen years.

That was all I heard before the driver shut the door on his fare, got behind the wheel and drove away past the petrol pumps.

Nineteen years.

I assumed it was Daddy, but I wasn't sure. Nineteen years. I'd never imagined any of them would get that long. I thought it would be five years max. I stood there in the car park, three bags of shopping in front of me, fighting back tears.

A few moments later my phone rang, and it was Susan. 'Hi, Hannah,' she said. I asked her if it was true, and if it was Daddy who'd got the nineteen years. 'Yes,' she said, and then she went through the session with me.

The judge had called my fifty-nine-year-old rapist by a name I'd never heard before – Shabir Ahmed – and told him he was 'an unpleasant and hypocritical bully'. He made a point of saying he'd given me to Immy as a birthday 'treat'.

Six of the gang became the first in Britain to be convicted of sex trafficking – Daddy, Tariq, Saj, Billy, Cassie and Hammy. All of them had their real names read out, but until I read them in the papers the next day I'd only ever known them by the nicknames they'd used to stay safe.

Daddy, or Shabir Ahmed, was given nineteen years for rape, trafficking and conspiracy to have sex with a child. The child, of course, was me.

The jury also convicted him of carrying out a sexual assault on the girl called Shauna at around the same time he was telling me how beautiful I was and how he'd given me a treat.

He didn't know it then, but by the end of the year he'd have another three years to serve – for all his attacks on Lanika.

Tariq, real name Abdul Aziz, aged forty-one and married with three children, was cleared of two counts of rape involving Leah but got nine years for both conspiracy and trafficking me and all the other girls in his empire.

Saj, or Mohammed Sajid, thirty-five, got twelve years for trafficking, conspiracy and having sex with Alicia when she was thirteen. Once he's served his sentence, it looks as though he'll be heading back to Pakistan – there's a deportation order waiting for him at the prison gates.

Billy, or Adil Khan, forty-two, married with a child, claimed he'd only ever met up with his mates to play cards or watch cricket. He denied even knowing Roxanne, let alone getting her pregnant when she was thirteen. 'How could I get her pregnant if I never saw her before?' he told the police. Forensic tests on her aborted foetus had proved otherwise. He got eight years.

Cassie, or Abdul Rauf, forty-three, who'd always wanted to kiss me, turned out to be something special. When he wasn't driving a taxi, often for the gang, he was giving up his spare time to teach religious studies at his local mosque. He liked to wave goodbye to his wife and five kids in the mornings, before collecting Emma and me and taking us to Ashworth Valley for perverted sex. I heard he'd be on the school run later on the same days. Despite this, he only affirmed in the witness box rather than swearing on the Koran. He got six years.

Hammy, or Hamid Safi, twenty-two, wasn't involved with me. But it turned out he'd only recently sneaked into Britain from Afghanistan when he'd started trafficking some of the other girls. He'll be deported, too, once he's served his four-year sentence.

Those were the traffickers, but there were others in the dock, all still waiting to be sent down.

Immy, or Kabeer Hassan, twenty-five, received nine years for slipping away from the Balti House counter for his 'treat' with me. He got that long a sentence because not only was it rape, but it was also what they call 'a joint enterprise' with Ahmed.

Car Zero, or Mohammed Amin, forty-five, loved to drink but had miraculously turned teetotal by the time he got to court. He was given five years for conspiracy and a sexual assault on Leah.

Tiger, or Abdul Qayyum, forty-four, a 'pillar of the Rochdale Pakistani community', got the same for his part in the conspiracy.

Oh, and Harry, my white 'father figure' abuser? He went on trial a few months later and got four years.

By the time Dad pulled up ten minutes later, my tears had dried and I had a huge smile on my face. Chloe was still eating her Galaxy bar as I strapped her in.

'Dad,' I said. 'He got nineteen years! Daddy got nineteen years!'

Then I was crying again, and Dad started punching the steering wheel like a man demented.

As we headed towards home, he held out his left hand towards me. I gripped it and he squeezed back.

I didn't need to look up to know he was crying, too.

Epilogue

On the estates I know the teenagers are so broke they'll save up a fiver over the week from their dinner money, then go out on Friday, buy a bottle of cider and ten fags, and walk the streets with them. They might buy a kebab or chips or whatever and then get a taxi home with their mates.

That's it. No cinema, no Caffè Neros, no Nando's afterwards. Just a walk around the streets and a few cigarettes on a park bench. Then another week of poverty to get through.

If there's a breakdown in white communities, it's on estates like mine – and the hundreds and hundreds of others just like it up and down the country – where most people are on benefits and parents don't have any spare money to give their kids.

My dad says now that Daddy and his kind are predators, hunters, and if you're hunting for lion you'll go to Africa, where you know they are. And so these people don't go hunting in Cheltenham or Guildford or Bath. They go hunting on council estates and all the rough areas, where kids are poor. Society's changed, and it's made their hunting ground wider. Poverty doesn't help, nor the recession, and with the youth clubs either closed or closing, these people are giving young girls some of the things they don't get otherwise: food, 'friendship', gifts.

They've watched girls like me coming out of school in the daytime or walking the streets with alcohol in our Lucozade bottles at night, getting drunk, using the local taxis, going into the kebab shops. And they've seen that we're vulnerable. We just happen to be white, or mostly.

They'll talk to us at first and they'll sound like fun. We'll act like idiots and have a laugh and they'll laugh with us, or so we'll think. Then it's, 'Have some more of this, have some more of that.' At the time you think it's you taking advantage of them, but it's not. That's how they do it. That's how they get you. That's how they hunt you down.

After the trial, all hell broke loose, pretty much. Some people saw it as a group of white girls being used and abused by a gang – maybe two gangs – of mostly middle-aged Pakistani men. And they could see that, despite some people trying to sweep it under any carpet they could find, it had been going on for years.

Others couldn't, or wouldn't, see it. They could only see the sort of political correctness that said, 'No, that can't be happening. It would be awful, wouldn't it? And how could we explain it? And wouldn't it all be ammunition for the far-right?'

It was the kind of thinking that had left me, and the generations before me, to the 'lifestyle decisions' we'd supposedly made. In doing that they'd condemned us.

Rochdale Council claimed not to have known, or at least not to have understood, what was going on. They've been on a 'journey', they said, as if they'd signed up for some kind of fancy self-awareness course and everyone was supposed to say, 'Well done, that's nice. We hope you've learned a few things.'

But they did know, or they should have done.

I was still safely by the sea, with my bike and my Barbie dolls, at the time Shannon started to be abused in 2002.

She had walked along some of the same streets that I'd come to know, and been driven along them as well, just like me, terrified, sometimes drunk, sometimes drugged by men who were just the same as Daddy, Tariq and the rest of my abusers.

It was all documented, sitting in files that had done nothing more than gather dust by the time I came onto the scene six years later – the latest girl to find herself on the conveyor belt of grooming and abuse.

When things eventually got tough for both the police and Social Services, they'd claim that grooming like this wasn't fully understood then. They knew about it, of course, but just dismissed it as girls like me going off the rails and making what became their new buzz word: 'lifestyle choices'. No, they said, they didn't understand it. Even though they had files full of evidence that told them exactly what sort of behaviour was going on in their town and how they could have moved in to stop it, and rescue at least some of the girls like me.

Shannon had lived in Rochdale and was regularly picked up by taxis on streets within sight of the town hall. So were other girls she knew. They were all the same sorts of ages:

thirteen, fourteen, fifteen. All of them vulnerable; all chaotic and somehow going off the rails. Just like me, a few years down the line, they would end up some nights in sordid flats and houses where the men, almost all of them Asian, would use them for easy sex.

The police call it a *modus operandi* – an established way of doing something – and it was always exactly the same. It hadn't changed over the years, not even down to the vodka they'd use to get us all drunk. It was just that in 2008 we were the new intake; we just had different names.

Crisis Intervention knew about it, and they'd been telling both the police and Rochdale Social Services for years.

They all knew that in August 2005 Shannon had been kidnapped, raped and left on the moors above her home town. Police did investigate, and they got as far as arresting two men, both of them Asian. But it never came to court because she withdrew her complaint.

It's no wonder Jane and her boss, Sara, were frustrated and, no doubt, angry. Two and a half years before Daddy started raping me, Crisis Intervention had sent out another letter, another referral, marked 'To Whom It May Concern'.

In it, Sara had written:

'On 15th Feb '06 Shannon presented to the Crisis team office at 8.30 a.m. in a distressed state stating that she had been taken to a hotel the previous evening by a nineteen-year-old man and his friends.

'She had been given a substantial amount of alcohol and couldn't remember who or how many people had had sex with her.

'Shannon had lovebites on her neck and back, was dressed in a sari and was complaining of lower abdominal pain. Her outfit was soiled, she smelt and was very hungry. She said she had left the hotel in the early hours and walked back to Rochdale.'

In the same letter – copies of which went to both Greater Manchester Police and Rochdale Social Services – she said:

'I believe from discussion and on-going involvement with Shannon that she is being sexually exploited by a significant number of adult men.

'I also believe that much of Shannon's sexual activity is non-consenting and done under duress and threat of violence. I also believe that Shannon is being given substantial amounts of drugs and alcohol in order to further impair her judgement.'

Not even this letter told the whole story. An official document Sara had received earlier the same day – something they call an 'outline of concern' – talked about Shannon having sex with specifically 'Asian men'.

It said the abdominal pain had been so bad she'd had to go to the local accident and emergency department. But she was never given any treatment.

'She was escorted away by three Asian men before she was seen,' said the report. 'She is now missing.' Police had been informed and were 'concerned'.

The document moved on to an incident two days earlier, 14 February. Valentine's Day, of all days. Again it said she'd been wearing a sari, but this time referred specifically to her being 'carried across the road by three Asian men'.

She was 'obviously under the influence of some substance' and 'had no memory of what had happened at the hotel'.

It turned out that Shannon's mum had asked Social Services to put her under a child protection order because she couldn't cope. It didn't happen. Eventually, Shannon became pregnant by one of her abusers. She lost the baby. Given what she'd been through, I'm guessing that was a good thing.

If Social Services had been on a 'journey', it wasn't the same one I'd been on. Nor Leah, Roxanne, Alicia, Paige, Courtney, Nadine, and all the others they're still either investigating or who never came forward.

What we went through was real. Not packaged, not dressed up, not made to fit someone's politics or agenda. We didn't care about things like that. We just wanted to be rescued.

It's only very recently, while I've been at home with Chloe, that I've learned just how badly I was let down by the police. Maybe I mean betrayed.

Because it turns out they actually knew about one of my attackers in the very early days of my abuse.

They knew because three weeks before I was bundled into a police van and questioned about smashing the Balti House counter, this particular round, thickset man had been seen in a takeaway in Rusholme, home to Manchester's so-called Curry Mile.

He wasn't alone. He was with two girls aged twelve and thirteen. One was actually a friend of Paige, called Kirsten, two years below me at school. The other was Grace – another victim, I guess, but a girl I'd never heard of.

You know how the police always ask people to keep an eye out for anything suspicious, and to report it? Not to be stupid; just to use their common sense?

Well, that night there was a 23-year-old student from Manchester Met waiting in the queue for some chips, and she noticed this odd grouping ahead of her. An Asian guy, pretty old-looking, with two very young girls. And the guy, she said, had the sort of look on his face that reminded her of a kid at a sweet counter.

'Have anything you want,' she heard him telling them. 'Anything.' He was all smiles and happy. Behind him in the queue, the student looked uncomfortable. Like, she knew instinctively something was wrong.

The takeaway had a couple of booths for people to use if they were eating in, and the guy collected the food and led the girls to one of them: him facing away from the counter, the older girl at his side, the younger one opposite him.

To the student it all looked weird. Too weird. She made eye contact with Kirsten a couple of times and felt a connection; sensed an unspoken desperation. She just knew she had to intervene.

By this time she'd been handed her chips, but instead of heading for the door she leaned over towards the girls and said: 'Hey you two, who's the guy you're with?'

She glanced at the man. His eyes darted away. Grace did likewise, momentarily, but she recovered enough to say: 'Our uncle.'

'Your *uncle*?' said the student. Given the man's colour, it still felt wrong. Grace realised too. 'He's my dad's friend,' she explained.

The student, out with her boyfriend, wasn't giving up. She asked the girl for her dad's number. Then, as she began to dial, she noticed the man reaching for his phone under the table. She had a sixth sense he was turning it off so it wouldn't ring. Her call went straight to voicemail. She knew, she just knew.

And then she looked at Kirsten, knowing, instinctively, that this man was looking at her too, and asked: 'So what's this guy's name?'

Kirsten wouldn't answer at first, but then she said: 'He tells me to call him Daddy.'

The student's boyfriend had had enough. 'He tells you to call him *Daddy?*' he asked, a menace in his voice.

By now a real scene was developing, and others were starting to get involved, crowding in on the melamine table with a middle-aged guy and two kids sat at it. The student tried to calm her boyfriend, but by now he was a liability. She decided it would be best to take him outside.

A few moments later, out of the corner of her eye, she noticed Shabir Ahmed and the girls – their food abandoned – scurrying away from the takeaway and on towards a pharmacy a little further down on Wilmslow Road.

My rapist was in a silver Honda that night, but just before he headed away the student scribbled the registration number onto a piece of paper and immediately rang the police.

The last image she remembers was of Kirsten looking back at her, seemingly bewildered, from the back of the car.

It turned out that both Kirsten and Grace had been reported missing that night and to their credit the police took the student's call seriously.

Detectives were knocking on her door just after midnight, and a little while later Ahmed was being arrested at his home in Oldham. He claimed everything had been completely innocent; that the girls had asked for a lift and he'd just been happy to help out.

Kirsten and Grace were spoken to, as well, and neither would make any disclosures. Maybe they, too, had been told he owned them; that they were his bitches. Or maybe they managed to break free before he'd fully groomed them.

The end result was that Ahmed was set free, without charge and without so much as the abduction warning that police might have thrown at him.

The big thing, though, was that his involvement with two young girls at a time he was already raping me had triggered what police call a Force Wide Incident Number. It's an automatic procedure. An officer logs a FWIN on a computer and there it is, a permanent record. For ever.

So the night I was driven into Rochdale police station for questioning about a smashed counter – the same night I told them Ahmed had raped me – the FWIN from three weeks earlier should have rung massive alarm bells.

It was there for the whole of Greater Manchester Police to see.

And, it gets worse.

The night before I threw that jar of mayonnaise at Chef, Paige had plucked up the courage to come forward and tell police how a guy called Taz had forced her to give him oral sex. And where had this taken place? The Balti House.

So, within twenty-four hours, two of us had told police about separate attacks at a single takeaway in Heywood. And yet it had taken three-and-a-half years to get some kind of justice.

In Paige's case, the man was charged, it seems, but the investigation fell by the wayside and it never came to trial.

I know now that there had been other mistakes, other oversights, in the days before Operation Span.

The jury never got to hear, for example, about some extra DNA evidence against Kabeer Hassan because the police hadn't sent my jeans away to be tested.

This, despite me having talked about them being pulled down just before he raped me. By the time the forensic results came back, years later, the trial was about to start and they were ruled inadmissible. The people in Operation Span were gutted, but there was nothing they could do.

* * *

At the end of my trial, the Girl A trial, Steve Heywood, the assistant chief constable of Greater Manchester Police, took a lift down from the third floor of the Queen Elizabeth Law Courts in Liverpool and stood in front of the TV cameras to make the sort of glib statement senior officers usually make at the end of big trials.

As soon as he'd finished, he brushed away questions, turned on his heel and went back through the revolving doors. 'I wasn't hanging around,' he was overheard to say as he pressed the lift button to head back to the third floor. 'If I had, all they'd have done was keep banging on about the race issue.'

His force is now at the forefront of the war against the grooming gangs, Asian or otherwise, but it's also come under investigation by the Independent Police Complaints Commission for its handling of the Rochdale case.

Things have changed massively among British police forces, not least the one in Greater Manchester, and there's certainly a greater awareness of what always was, and remains, a comparatively small pocket of crime.

But in the future they will have to remain vigilant, and they'll have to be prepared to investigate what they see in front of them: not hide from it because it might make for some uneasy issues to be dealt with.

Mr Afzal justifiably took the plaudits in the aftermath of the Girl A trial and since then he's gone on to become a passionate campaigner on the issue of child sexual exploitation. But it shouldn't be forgotten that the CPS did not bring my case to court all those years earlier.

Rochdale Social Services, though, are the people I blame the most. The top brass at Rochdale Council remain so scared of what might still come out of the woodwork that they keep sending a girl from their legal department scurrying from hearing to hearing, trial to trial, so they can be ready to deal with the issues they suspect are heading their way.

Whatever the issues, I'm guessing they'll be expensive. Steve Garner, the man in charge of children's social care, left the council 'with fond memories'. And both he and two former chief executives were hauled up before the Home Affairs Select Committee of the House of Commons.

However, heroines have emerged, namely Miss Crabtree, who tried so hard to help me at school, and Sara from Crisis Intervention. Sara gave evidence to the Home Affairs Committee and, bless her, she told it as it was.

'It was about attitudes towards teenagers,' she said. 'Vulnerable young people did not have a voice. They were overlooked. They were discriminated against. They were treated appallingly by protective services.'

She had tried her best, she said. 'I told everybody these children were being abused.'

And then Jane. Jane who has seen so many girls like me that she must have spotted straight away just how vulnerable I was; how at risk.

For all that I tried to throw her off the scent, she battled through even the worst of times to reach out to me: in her office, at school, at the Asda café in Pilsworth, and on all those harrowing journeys to and from the VIPER parades.

Mum and Dad, for so long bewildered and out of their depth, came through for me and are even now fighting desperately hard to help save kids like the one they almost lost.

Sometimes I think about the other girls too. The other victims. About Shannon who'd gone before me; about Roxanne who never stood a chance; about Leah, who might have been saved if only people had acted sooner; and about all the other girls who have over so many years just slipped, unnoticed, between the gaps in the care that was supposed to protect them.

Courtney wouldn't even admit to me what had happened to her, let alone open up to the police. She's moved away now and we've lost touch. I've no idea what happened to Paige, but I fear for her because she's another of the girls who wouldn't tell her story to the police.

Nadine's still out there, still believing herself to be 'in love' with the Asian men who see her as easy meat, still refusing to talk to the police about them so they can go on trial for what they did to her when she was twelve and thirteen. Maybe, just maybe, she'll come forward.

I even think about Emma. Emma the recruiter, who once, a long time ago, was also one of us. I hope that even she has found some sort of peace.

In darker moments I recall that some of the men who abused me are still out there, perhaps because I'd not recognised them in the VIPER parades, sometimes because the police never managed to trace them, or else because they've fled to Pakistan. Men like Mulla and Megamuncher, like Boss and Juicy, like the 'gangster', Lateef, like Gulshan, and like Ali and the others from Leeds and Bradford.

They and all the others can all go to hell as far as I'm concerned and, in Daddy's case, I think Lanika would back me on that one. It's not Christian, I know, and it's not Muslim either, but I imagine it's the way we both feel.

Jane is still in Heywood, still doing the same job she's done for years. She rang me the other day to see how I was.

'Yeah, I'm fine,' I said. 'I'm in my own place now with Chloe. She's thriving and I'm finding that, yes, I actually do have a future. I really do.'

Acknowledgements

I would like to thank my mum and dad and all of my family and friends for their love and support. Thanks to the support services that gave me their time and guided me through this experience. And, a special thank you to Nigel Bunyan for his hard work and passion while helping me to tell my story.